Praise for *I Feel Great and You Will Too!*

"The owner of the Philadelphia 76ers is a go-getter par excellence, and in telling the story of his life, he works in a lot of the get-ahead philosophy that has served him well both personally and professionally and, he hopes, will help his readers in maintaining their drive to achieve their goals."

—Brad Hooper, *Booklist*

"This book will lead you down a path of inspiration and encouragement, offering many practical tools for capitalizing on all of your life experiences."

—Michael Jordan

"A great read from a fascinating man. Pat Croce tells his life story with the humor, honesty, and good sense that has long won him so many friends and admirers—a group I am lucky and proud to belong to."

—John McCain, U.S. Senator

"Before I met Pat Croce, I was a ten-dollar crack whore, but then I read his book . . . and look at me now!"

—Chris Rock

"I thoroughly enjoyed Pat Croce's book, *I Feel Great and You Will Too!* It's a fast, funny, candid, and intelligent read. It's great to read a story that reminds us that the American Dream lives on!"

—Bruce Willis

"Pat Croce has written a book that can be easily applied to everyday life experiences. He is an inspiration to everyone."

—Will Smith

"Pat Croce's amazing success story is about motivation, inspiration, and a fair dose of chutzpah! Pat's advice, liberally sprinkled throughout the book, will cause you to nod in agreement—and smile."

—David Stern, NBA comissioner

"The best Hollywood sports story to come out of Philadelphia since *Rocky*."

—Scott Greenstein, chairman USA Films

"Pat Croce is the model and mentor for the next generation of sports and business entrepreneurs. He leads . . . we follow."

—Ted Leonsis, president of America Online's Interactive Properties Group; owner of the Washington Capitals and Washington Wizards

"Pat Croce's the poster child for passion. In *I Feel Great and You Will Too!*, he spotlights his remarkable climb from everyman to owner of the Philadelphia 76ers and the architect of one of the NBA's greatest turn-around stories. Sports needs more owners like Pat Croce; you need to buy this book!"

—Dick Ebersol, chairman NBC Sports & Olympics

"For someone like me who needs an inspiring, motivating, get-my-spirits-up-out-of-my-shoes shot in the arm, Pat Croce's book comes straight from heaven! He's Saint Croce, as far as I'm concerned!"

—Chuck Barris, creator of *The Dating Game, The Newlywed Game,* and *The Gong Show*

"Pat Croce's life story is truly inspirational and I consider myself blessed to have been a small part of it. I'll never forget our friendship and what it means to my career and life."

—Mike Schmidt, member of the Baseball Hall of Fame

"Pat Croce's life is packed with amazing, humorous, and inspirational incidents. He obviously is someone who has prevailed through dedication, honest effort, and a unique aptitude for dealing successfully with challenges. Croce's precepts of customer service are must reading for anyone who deals with the public."

—Joe Paterno, head coach, Penn State football

"Pat Croce is a true inspiration to anyone who has ever had a dream."

—Brian L. Roberts, president of Comcast Corporation

I Feel Great

and you will too!

•••

An Inspiring Journey of Success

With Practical Tips

on How to Score Big

in Life

by Pat Croce
with Bill Lyon
Foreword by Bill Cosby

A Fireside Book
Published by Simon & Schuster
New York   London   Toronto   Sydney   Singapore

To my Queen of Diamonds,

my Princess, and my Hero...

May our "Croce Holidays" last forever.

FIRESIDE
Rockefeller Center
1230 Avenue of the Americas
New York, NY 10020

FIRESIDE and colophon are registered trademarks
of Simon & Schuster, Inc.
For information about special discounts for bulk purchases,
please contact Simon & Schuster Special Sales:
1-800-456-6798 or business@simonandschuster.com

Designed by Bill Jones

Manufactured in the United States of America

Library of Congress Cataloging-in-Publication Data
Croce, Pat.
I feel great and you will too! : an inspiring journey of success
with practical tips on how to score big in life /
by Pat Croce, with Bill Lyons ; foreword by Bill Cosby.
p. cm.
"A Fireside Book"
Originally published: Philadelphia, PA : Running Press, c2000.
1. Success—Psychological aspects. 2. Success in business. 3. Croce, Pat.
I. Title: I feel great. II. Lyon, Bill III. Title.
BF637.S8C76 2001
158—dc21   2001034226

ISBN 0-7432-2213-X

Acknowledgments

●●●

I would love to hug and high-five

all of my friends

who have made this book a reality,

either by their participation

within the pages

or by their assistance

in creating the pages,

with special thanks

to my co-author Bill Lyon,

editors Greg Jones and Jennifer Worick,

and most importantly,

my personal assistant

Sue (Susie) Barbacane.

Contents

●●●

Foreword

❦ ❦ ❦

*T*o me, Pat Croce paints a wonderful picture. He breaks the mold of the white-shirted, stiff, business-suit, sports-team owner. This is a man driven by his passion. He gives a bright and wonderful new feeling to team ownership. You never get the impression that this is a man who will be demanding a new arena every 24 months—or that he is simply interested in selling or moving ballplayers.

More important, he is a true hands-on kind of person. He's the type of businessman who opens the store with pride—by himself. And if you listen very carefully, you can actually hear him rolling up the storefront gates every morning. He's ready to personally welcome everyone into his store. And he continues to grow this business every day. Then without warning, something terrible happens to him.

One day, while he is working at this business, greeting everyone with his trademark smile, it happens. It is something so horrible, so blood-chilling, that only Stephen King or Robert Louis Stevenson could have first visualized it, and then written it.

Amazingly, despite this terrible situation, the man still smiled. And, he still kept his positive attitude.

I won't tell you anymore. You just need to understand that this book illustrates how Pat Croce is a man who accepts the unexpected with a smile. He faces the most difficult situations and says, "I'm not going to take the worst. I'm going to work for the best. Because I love life."

—Bill Cosby

Chapter 1

The View from
the Top of the Rainbow

❧ ❧ ❧

Michael Jordan is beating my brains in.

The best basketball player there has ever been is putting the torch to my team and I'm sitting here not knowing which I want to do most—applaud him or strangle him. I'm in awe of his skills, but the competitor in me wants to rush out there and reach my hand inside his chest, rip out his heart, and stuff it in his face.

And then something else hits me. I look around here in the owner's suite of the CoreStates Center*—one of those plush Nero boxes appointed in leather and chrome, and lavishly stocked with food and drink—and I see all my friends and my family shouting their lungs out, and suddenly this thought whooshes at me like a freight train:

When are the guards gonna come and throw me out?

You see, part of me feels like a man sitting on top of the rainbow, and part of me feels like an imposter. I own a professional basketball team. Me! And not only that, but I own the Philadelphia 76ers—my home team—the team I grew up with and eventually worked for. It's like the janitor suddenly owns Disney World!

How can this be? I'm the guy who used to tape the players' ankles. Now I sign their paychecks. I'm the guy who used to sneak into stadiums and outrun ballpark security. Now I get in through the front door, with the red carpet and the primo parking. It's an evolution that Darwin himself might not have imagined. So no wonder I'm expecting that tap on the shoulder, that stern look, that familiar jerk of the thumb, and that uniquely warm and cordial Philadelphia salutation: "Yo, pal, you're outta here."

But no…there is no tap, there is no ejection. Just more noise from the owner's suite. They're all here this night, all the skeletons from my closet. My biker buddies, karate sparring partners, college cronies, guys from

* "The CoreStates Center" was renamed the "First Union Center" in 1998.

1

the street corner, dudes from down-the-shore, business associates, my wife, our two children, my mom, and my Aunt Corinne, the nun.

And I know someone else is watching too, from a seat even higher up than the top of the rainbow: my Pop. He's the one wearing the T-shirt that says: "*I'M THE REAL PAT CROCE.*"

Pasquale Croce gave me my name and my drive. He'd box my ears one minute and crush me with a hug the next. Like all sons, all I ever wanted to do was make my father proud. So here I sit, humbled and grateful and more than a little overwhelmed, and wish he were here. And, oh yes, still wondering when that tap on the shoulder is coming . . . .

Instead, Michael Jordan taps my arousal button again. He goes slashing toward the basket, and you know this is going to be special because his tongue is lolling down around his knees. He elevates and levitates and detonates one of those dunks that makes the rim quiver like a tuning fork. The crowd is in a frenzy. I hear someone screaming, "Are you shitting me?" Then I recognize the voice. It's *mine.*

Now Jordan is at the free throw line. My gaze drifts from him to the baseline. The 76ers fans in the seats behind the basket are especially rabid. They're on their feet, yelling and waving their arms and doing everything they can to distract Jordan. He's used to this, of course. (That's another thing I admire about him—his composure in the midst of chaos, the way he can focus. He would probably be very good at the martial arts.)

Right in the middle of the clamoring crowd that's testing Jordan, right there in front, grinning at all the excitement, is one of my oldest and best friends, Jerry McElhenney. He works game nights helping with the crowd and game operations. His full-time job is as a roofer, so he knows what it's like to work without a net. We go way back, and for as long as I've known him I've called him Jakester. The "Jake" comes from Jerry, and the "ster" comes from gangster. He's got the walk and the talk straight out of an old James Cagney movie—that cock-in-the-walk strut and that side-of-the-mouth delivery—mixed with the DeNiro *are-you-talkin'-to-me?* attitude. Also, if you tried to cross him or me, Jakester would probably have you rubbed out. He'd prefer to do it himself.

Jordan makes the free throw, of course. And then he looks directly at the Jakester, and right into that howling mob that's taunting him, and he gives them this huge smile and holds up his right hand and spreads his fingers apart to show them, ever so lovingly, where it is that he wears each of his world championship rings. But it's not an act of arrogance; it's just a man who knows he's good at interacting with the people who have paid to see him perform. When you're Michael Jordan, you're never allowed to take a night off because somebody may be in the audience who's never seen you before and never will get to see you again. That's a philosophy worth imitating.

Jordan starts back down the court and the baseline fans continue to scream at him and at each other, slapping high-fives and trading forearm smashes. They're having fun, and that, after all, is the whole point of being here. Jakester is still smiling as he exchanges slaps and forearms with some of the customers and then walks over behind the Sixers bench. On his way past Allen Iverson, he taps the eventual rookie-of-the-year on the shoulder for luck, and then turns toward the tunnel through which the players enter and exit. Here he does a belly-bump and a high-five with Joe Masters, our director of fan relations.

PAT CROCE POINTER
When you're Michael Jordan, you're never allowed to take a night off because somebody may be in the audience who's never seen you before and never will get to see you again. That's a philosophy worth imitating.

Joe is a Saint Bernard in human form—big and shambling and very friendly. He has just the right personality and temperament for this job, which basically consists of listening to the moans and complaints of disgruntled customers, and then turning their frowns upside down. (Well, at least sideways.) Unfortunately, the satisfaction of fans at a professional sports event is usually in direct proportion to how the team is doing. And here, in 1997, my first year as the president and part-owner, we were struggling. The losses were running ahead of the wins by about 3 to 1, so Joe needed to muster a mountain of charm and charisma. And I knew he was good for it.

Joe's been watching my back since the ninth grade. We went to college together. He was best man at my wedding. And my nickname for him—"Bator"—goes all the way back to our adolescence. As you'll see, I have a habit of giving everyone nicknames. In Joe Masters' case, his nickname was inevitable. Put it all together and you get: Joe Masters-*Bator*.

It's a rather crude shorthand for the act of male stimulation. But the only thing Bator likes better than having a good time is making sure that everyone else has a good time.

As I watch Bator in the tunnel behind the Sixers' bench, still kind of expecting the security guards to come and throw me out (and half expecting to see guards walk up and throw out Bator and Jakester, too), it crosses my mind that I might not be sitting here now, on top of the rainbow, if I hadn't first found myself in the seat next to Bator in our high school English class. That was twenty-five years ago. Oh, not that Bator was of any particular help in improving my writing skills. No, his impact on my life was due mainly to his powers of persuasion. Bator can not only talk you into something you don't think you want to do, but he can make you think it was all your idea in the first place.

❦ ❦ ❦

So there we are in the spring term of our senior year at Lansdowne-Aldan High School, just outside of Philadelphia. Nineteen-seventy-two. We're supposed to be writing a composition. Bator is instead writing me a note inviting me to join him in applying to West Chester State College. (It is now West Chester University.) The invitation puzzles me because Bator knows I have already applied—and have been accepted—to Drexel University, in Philadelphia. I plan on being an accountant. So I write Bator a reply that, in effect, questions his mental capacity. He writes back: "But you'll love it there." And I write back to him: "Why?"

His answer is too important to waste time writing down. Instead, he breaks the silence of the classroom by shouting: "There's three girls to every guy! We'll play on the freshman football team! And you get to live away from home!" In all honesty, he could have stopped after the first reason. I was convinced. Bator always has had a knack for knowing exactly which buttons to push.

The next day we were on our way to West Chester. It was spring; the bees were buzzing and so was the testosterone. I was revved in anticipation. This was going to be my first visit to an out-of-town college campus, and it was shaping up as a grand adventure. Then again, every trip when Bator drove was an adventure.

The registration papers in the glove compartment identified the thing we were in as, indeed, a moving vehicle. And technically, it did move, though it felt like it had an incurable case of the hiccups. It was a Ford station wagon, built like a tank and just about as responsive as one. Ah, but it was transportation. And when you're a teenager, wheels represent freedom, and nothing else matters quite so much, not even the color—in our case a bilious seaweed-green mottled with polka-dot rust spots. The tires were rumored to be whitewalls, though there was no white visible anywhere. Then again, there was no tread visible, either. And only one headlight worked, so at night we looked and sounded like a bedraggled Cyclops.

What really gave this vehicle its personality, however, were the floor-boards. They didn't exist in the back. So at a stop you could rest your feet on the pavement, and then when Bator would—you'll pardon the expression—*accelerate*, you could run in place like Fred Flintstone and Barney Rubble. To Bator, though, the clincher was how much time you could save because you never had to make that annoying stop to take a leak. We irrigated as we went.

Bator's Flintstonemobile had replaced a Rambler that looked like the first contestant eliminated in a demolition derby. The Rambler had started out white, and then Bator decided to paint it black. This was his own personal homage to the Rolling Stones and their hit song, "Midnight Rambler." Remember, when you're a teenager, that kind of allegiance and loyalty seem important. Bator painted that car with unbridled gusto. He painted everything—door handles, bumpers, and even parts of the windows. The end product was the color of midnight in a graveyard. But it moved.

Right after he finished his paint job, Bator drove to the high school to show it off. The corner hangout was crowded with teenagers. You know how teenagers feel more comfortable in groups; there's nothing more important than that sense of belonging. We called this "Hangin' at the High," where the main order of business was to generate laughter.

And the laughs were big that day when Bator pulled up and, with his customary disregard for conventional parking techniques, banged the bumper of Jakester's blue Chevy. Bator was notorious for "nudging" while parking, and he was so adept at mugging that you were never certain whether the nudge was intentional or the brakes really had failed. We all figured he had gotten his driver's license on the bumper car ride on the Wildwood Boardwalk at the Jersey shore. Whenever you were sitting in a car and found yourself suddenly being propelled forward against your will, you knew when you turned around you'd see Bator . . .

Saying "Ooops!"

It became his signature line. To this day, if I look up and find Bator in my rear-view mirror, I instinctively flinch.

The minor dent that Bator had put in Jakester's car was no more meaningful than one more pimple when you're fourteen. But of course at that age you take everything as a challenge. So Jakester needed to retaliate. He jumped in his Chevy, backed up a couple of car lengths, shot forward, and jolted Bator's Rambler with enough force to put it over the curb and into a telephone pole. Jakester leaned out the window and, with just the right Cheshire cat grin, perfectly mimicked Bator: "Oooops!"

Everyone whooped, and immediately began instigating. It's what guys at that age do best. Egg 'em on! Anything to get the juices stirred. All it took was two minutes of everyone challenging everyone else's developing manhood, and we had a motorized joust going. A bunch of guys piled into Jakester's Chevy, and others got into Bator's Rambler, where I had the shotgun seat. The two cars faced each other, a block apart, like a couple of bull moose ready to duel over a female. They gunned their engines. About this time, it dawned on us that this was not going to be another casual game of "Ooops." It also dawned on me that where I was sitting is known in the insurance trade as the "death seat," so I dove into the back. Fortunately, there were enough bodies back there to cushion my fall.

The cars started toward each other. It was a classic game of "chicken." Not especially smart. And definitely incredibly dangerous. But by now everyone had an adrenalin buzz and no one wanted to be the first to wimp out, especially not Bator or Jakester. The cars growled toward each other, picking up speed, and neither driver showed any signs of flinching. We braced ourselves against the back of the front seat, and screamed!

Just as they were about to collide, Bator dodged in, swerved out, and clipped the left rear bumper of Jakester's Chevy. It spun 90 degrees, screeched, and skidded to a stop at the corner. Bator stuck a fist of triumph out the window and tried to get Jakester in his cross hairs for another go. Meanwhile the rest of us had a sudden attack of sanity. The back doors of both cars flew open and we bailed out so frantically that it looked like a mass parachute jump. Such outbreaks of common sense were rare, but they were what kept us all alive.

But Bator and Jakester weren't done. Neither one wanted to be the one who quit. If you quit, you couldn't live with all the razzing and verbal abuse, and for sure you couldn't live with yourself. So they lined up to do it again, and no one could stop them. No one even tried, because it would have been pointless.

Neither one feinted the next time. Neither one faked. Neither one chickened out. Jakester came in like a pile driver square into the Midnight Rambler's left front fender, collapsing the tire and leaving Bator tilting to one side, like the Titanic going under. Jakester pulled away, parked in the middle of the street, got out and climbed on the hood and struck a Rocky pose in triumph. We all cheered him. And then we remembered the vanquished. What had happened to Bator? Was he just a grease spot?

Bator emerged dramatically then, climbing out the driver's side window. He surveyed what was left of his car, turned to us with that grin, and said: "Ooops!"

All these years later and I can still see that. That's what's so nice about making memories. You have fun at the time, and then you get to have the fun all over again reliving them. There's only one thing I like more than laughing. That's sharing it.

❧ ❧ ❧

Bator and I arrived at West Chester with four items on our to-do list: (1) apply for admission, and get accepted; (2) introduce ourselves to the head football coach; (3) eat; and (4) find a place to live. Not necessarily in that order.

We found the office of the head football coach, John Furlow. The door was open. He was talking with one of his players. At first we thought he was using a bullhorn but we would come to learn that this was just his usual decibel level when he was chewing out a sinner. Conversation over, the player left; he looked to be about eight axe handles wide at the shoulders. We swallowed and introduced ourselves.

Coach Furlow recognized Bator's name from his reputation. Fortunately for us, it was Bator's football reputation the coach recognized.

He didn't recognize me from my reputation, probably because I didn't have one to speak of. But I had brass. And I was blessed with confidence and a positive attitude. I have never doubted that things would get done, that dreams would be realized. And why not expect good things? There's a lot of truth to that saying, "If you expect the worst, you'll never be disappointed." But I think you can reverse that, too. I think our efforts tend to match our expectations. So I try to go through life like the little kid who comes down the stairs on Christmas morning, sees a steaming pile of manure, and instantly thinks: "Oh boy, oh boy, there's just got to be a pony around here somewhere!"

 PAT CROCE POINTER
 It never hurts to ask. The worst thing they can do is say
"no." And as my Pop said, "If you don't ask, then the
answer is always 'no'."

I told Coach Furlow there were no lengths I would not go to in order to play for the Golden Rams. And then I asked if, by the way, could I use him as a reference when I applied for admission to West Chester?

Now the application was a little matter that should have been taken care of, oh, a year or so ago. But Coach Furlow just laughed at my boldness. He must have thought (and I wanted him to think this) that if I had the nerve to ask to use him as a reference after just meeting him, then I must be crazy enough to catch flaming spears for his football team, too.

Sure, he'd be my reference.

See? It never hurts to ask. The worst thing they can do is say "no." And as my Pop said, "If you don't ask, then the answer is always 'no'."

Bator and I left the coach's office giddy. Hungry, too—as usual. We jumped into Bator's bomb, filled out our applications, and went looking for grub.

The cafeteria wasn't hard to find. Neither were the two old women standing guard at each of the entrances. They recognized only two forms of eligibility for eating: cash or a meal card. We had neither. What we did have were appetites and a talent for improvisation. So we passed ourselves off as recruits, a couple of football studs whom Coach Furlow was lusting after. It sounded convincing to us. Not to them. They had invisible antennae that seemed to pick up on scams. (After all, they dealt with college kids every day.)

We went around to the back of the building. A produce truck was being unloaded. We identified ourselves as students who worked part time in the cafeteria, and, *by the way, where would you like us to take those heavy-looking produce boxes while you catch your breath?*

It worked. We made four convincing trips from the truck to the cooler, then detoured through the kitchen, past the serving line and into the main seating area. There was food everywhere. And at just the right price—free. In the middle of the room was a large round table occupied by a salad bowl the size and shape of a Jacuzzi. Bator and I looked at each other like a couple of hogs called to the trough.

(A couple of years later, we would be forced to quit eating from that salad bowl. That was about the time, during a Saturday evening food raid, that a 300-pound lineman named Bomber shed his clothes, climbed into the bowl, and rolled around in the greens while we rained condiments on him, giving a horrible new meaning to the term "tossed salad.")

Well-fed, we set out looking for lodging. We had heard of an off-campus rooming house that had quite a reputation. It was called the Yoder House, and was named after Dick Yoder, the owner of the house and an assistant football coach. A more accurate name would have been the "Odor House."

The place was in no danger of being seen in *Better Homes & Gardens*. Eight bedrooms. Two bathrooms. No kitchen. Capacity: twenty. Most of them football players. There was stuff growing in that house that they wouldn't have been able to identify in the chem lab. The basement turned into a beer-soaked party room every single weekend. What went on there was the stuff of legend. Naturally, Bator and I thought it was the Taj Mahal.

Guys were lifting weights, playing cards, watching TV, and girl-watching from the front porch. The occasional textbook could be found—some of them actually open, too. The place reminded me of Hangin' at the High with a roof. Mostly, there was laughter, my favorite sound. It felt like home to me.

Bator knew two of the occupants, both senior physical education majors. We talked with these guys for a while, and by the time we were on our way home, the compulsive list-maker and obsessive goal-setter in me had my immediate future planned:

(1) Attend West Chester, (2) play football, (3) major in physical education, (4) room with Bator, (5) buy a meal card, and (6) live in the Yoder House.

I wrote down all those goals. I'm a fanatic about that because there's something about setting down on paper your hopes and aspirations that make them attainable. You write them and study them, and then they don't seem so overwhelming, so daunting.

Plus, when they're on paper staring back at you, it's harder to ignore them.

Chapter 2

By the Light
of the Neon Moon

❦ ❦ ❦

I got accepted to West Chester as a Physical Education major. I started on the freshman football team. I got a meal card. And I got a place to stay . . . but it wasn't the Yoder House (that would come later).

My housing was a dorm, Killinger Hall. (As you will see, the "Kill" part of the name was appropriate.) I had been assigned a complete stranger for a roommate. I preferred to have Bator rooming with me, so I asked my roommate if he'd be willing to relocate. He declined. I decided to persuade him. So while he was relaxing on his bed one day, I moved my desk chair to the foot of his bed and invited him to participate in a game of darts.

He wasn't required to do anything, I told him, except lie there and be still. Very, very still. The bed's headboard would serve as the dart board, and the goal of the game was for me to form an outline of darts around his head without actually piercing him. If he got hit, I lost. So to speak.

My roommate got a little bit anxious. But, I said, there was nothing to worry about. It was just like being at a carnival—I was the knife thrower who blindfolds himself and then outlines the girl on the spinning wheel with knives. Except I didn't blindfold myself, and I wasn't using heavy knives. This didn't seem to be of much comfort to my roomie, though.

Thunk . . . Thunk . . . Thunk! I had a dozen darts ready to go, but after only three he decided he didn't want to play any more. Nor did he want to share a room with some wild-eyed lunatic dart-thrower. Can't say that I blamed him. Bator moved in the next day.

Word of that spread, and this brand of darts became *the* game for the dorm, and our room was the headquarters. Bator kept score. He also refereed. And as always, he instigated.

Among those living on our floor who got hooked on darts were two crazy guys from Long Island and another guy who became a good friend—Adrian Sinko, (alias "Age.") These guys were always game for a game. Our inventiveness in the realm of darts grew in proportion to the amount of beer we consumed. "Chicken" became a personal favorite. It was very important to select an experienced dart thrower as an opponent. You could always beat one who had a bad aim, but the price of victory was too dear.

 PAT CROCE POINTER
An intriguing thing about human nature is that as soon as we suffer something painful, we can't wait to share it with our friends.

Chicken went like this: You'd sit in the wooden desk chairs, facing each other, about eight feet apart. You'd spread your legs as wide as you could, exposing as much wood as possible, and as little of yourself as possible. It helped to be flexible. If you could do gymnastic splits, you had a good chance to walk away without a permanent limp. The winner was the dartist whose lobs landed closest to his opponent's groin. If you impaled any portion of your opponent, you lost. Of course, as far as the competitors were concerned, it was the *Wide World of Sports'* trademark line in reverse—"the agony of victory and the thrill of defeat."

Usually as the night got later and the participants became drunker, the distance between the chairs grew and the darts' arc got higher. On really special nights it sounded like we were holding auditions for the Vienna Boys Choir. The "winners," of course, would take the part of soprano.

One dart game became especially popular. It was our version of Pin the Tail on the Donkey. The "donkeys" in this case were any newcomers. They didn't even know they were playing until the game had already begun, and by then it was too late. They were in the dark, literally.

This game was born on a Monday night during the football season. Guys would pile into our room to watch Monday Night Football on the little black-and-white TV set Bator and I had. Everyone got fired up—most of us were football players, remember. And there may have been some beer involved.

One night Bator leaned over and planted in my ear the seed of a fiendish idea. The seed didn't need fertilizer to take root. Just as the game reached halftime, Bator turned off the lights, yanked the TV cord out of the wall, and hid in the closet. The first scream came about four seconds into the darkness. More followed. I was flinging darts at shadows and outlines. There were so many people in the room I was bound to hit something with every throw. There was a shrieking stampede for the door!

Of course, Bator had locked it.

An intriguing thing about human nature is that as soon as we suffer something painful, we can't wait to share it with our friends. So instead of guys who had been darted staying away from our room on Monday nights, they kept coming back. And they'd bring fresh meat with them. Of course, the veterans knew to seek cover as soon as the lights went out. But the fresh meat, well, they had an experience they'd never forget.

It became a sort of badge of honor on campus to show exactly where you'd been darted.

❦ ❦ ❦

One night I was at my desk doing homework. Really. For all the time and energy I spent in the pursuit of laughter and adrenalin, I've always tried to keep my priorities straight. My studies mattered most. I wanted to make the dean's list. So it was books first, darts second. It's possible to be a lunatic and also an earnest laborer.

While I was studying and Bator was lying on his bed listening to music, an upperclassman with a bad attitude walked in. He announced with great self-importance that he was taking a dorm inventory survey. Participation was, he said ominously, mandatory. Bator said no, but thanks anyway. I asked, politely, if he could come back when I was finished with my homework. First he was persistent, then belligerent. I admire persistence. But belligerence triggers something in me—a need to retaliate and eradicate. Same with arrogance.

The surveyor persisted and I resisted. As he got nastier I began to feel like everything was turning the color of the sun just before it sets. Bator recognized the warning signs. He tried to tell the surveyor that, really, he should come back. Too late. I opened my top desk drawer and pulled out a handful of darts, and even before Bator could get out his trademark "Ooops," I had buried one in the guy's right thigh. He squealed and threw the sheaf of survey papers straight up. It looked like there was a parade in our room. The surveyor got one step out the door when I nailed him in his posterior. He squealed again and, limping, ran down the hall.

Unfortunately for him, he ran directly into the room occupied by my two lunatic buddies from Long Island.

"Some madman's throwing darts at me!" the surveyor yelped, his arrogance clearly replaced by fear.

"Do they look like these?" And they each speared him with one of their darts.

It may help to have friends in high places and it may be of some comfort to have friends in low places, but there is nothing quite equal to having friends in strange places. Check that. Better just to have strange friends. You're never at a loss for something to do.

And I took two of my stranger friends—Bator and Ed Skalamera (alias "Skal")—with me when I was summoned by a resident assistant to defend myself against charges of dormitory mischief. No, it wasn't the darted surveyor—this was *another* incident.

 PAT CROCE POINTER
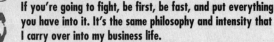
If you're going to fight, be first, be fast, and put everything you have into it. It's the same philosophy and intensity that I carry over into my business life.

It had been alleged by some faceless coward that I had come down from my third floor room to the first floor and created turmoil. As it turned out, someone had busted up all the ceiling lights on that floor. And while this may have sounded like me, this time I was actually innocent. I had never even been in that part of the dorm. But that didn't keep the resident assistant from presuming my guilt.

Worse, he laid a hand on me. Well, technically, it was only his forefinger, jabbed into my chest. But push, poke, or punch, they're all the same to me. I take them as equal in intent. My father taught me to fight when I was very young. He taught me not to pick fights, but he also taught me to be the one who finished them, and that the best strategy was to get them over with in a hurry. If you're going to fight, be first, be fast, and put everything you have into it. It's the same philosophy and intensity that I carry over into my business life. So as soon as that finger jabbed my chest I was throwing a long, looping right hand.

You know the sound a crisp stalk of celery makes when you bite off a chunk? That's the sound his nose made. He crashed against the hallway wall and started to slide down to the floor. I popped him again. I didn't want him getting up. To hell with the Marquess of Queensberry!

Upperclassmen poured out of the surrounding rooms and piled on me. Bator and Skal waded in. Skal was a South Philly kid, tough as cheap cheesesteak, with a walk that oozed cockiness. He favored Italian shoes with the toes pointed to tips like stilettoes. He called them roach-killer shoes because you could stab a cockroach when it had scurried into a corner and thought it was safe. Like me, Skal believed in getting a fight over with as soon as possible, so when he aimed his shoes, he always went for the groin.

The resident assistant I cold-cocked had been carrying a pot of chicken soup. Now it was all over the floor. So there was this pile of humanity cursing, bleeding, punching, kicking, and trying to stand up on a floor slick with the grease from chicken soup. Actually, it was pretty funny. (Well, at least it got funnier in the retelling and reliving.)

What wasn't so funny was the letter that followed, from the dean of the college, stating that I had been found to be "a detriment to dormitory living." I was labeled an outcast, and was forbidden to live on campus. Effective immediately. Of course, my parents were upset. And Bator and the boys mourned my exile.

But the varsity football players were properly impressed, so much so that the two captains allowed me to rent a room—actually a walk-in closet with a mattress—where they were residing. It was called the "Railroad House" because it had been abandoned by the railroad, though the freight trains still ran right through the front yard. You never had to set your alarm. There would be the sound of far-off thunder and then the whole house would commence to shake. It was like living in a room with a vibrating bed, only cheaper—you didn't have to feed it quarters.

But the Railroad House was a long way from campus, so I hitchhiked to class. And most evenings I would go to the J&R bar (it is now simply Jake's Bar; R died) to wait for a ride home, which would usually happen when my senior roommates ran out of beer and money. It was your basic no-frills, shot-and-beer joint. I'd use the shuffleboard table for a desk and do my homework by the light of a neon moon.

You have to understand that a desk is as important to me as a womb is to a baby. It's my sanctuary. There I can seal myself off from the outside world, even in a bar. I made the dean's list, by the way, and as it turned out I got a pretty good second education in that bar. I learned the value of negotiation over retaliation. I learned that if you just sat and observed and listened, you could learn a lot about human nature.

It's fascinating to watch people get drunk. I had to scuffle for my money, so I learned how to throw parties in the Railroad House that would make a profit, and I learned a few bar games that kept me fed through college. People are generally gullible to begin with, and the more they drink the easier they are duped. My favorite barroom wager was this one where the pigeon was convinced that he absolutely, positively, couldn't lose. You'd tell him to take a quarter from his own pocket and place it face down in the palm of your hand. Then you bet him that just by looking at the tails side of the coin, you could tell him the date.

All you do is say the date of that particular day.

The pigeon will splutter and protest, but you did exactly what you promised you would. The key is to get them hooked, and the key to getting them hooked is being a good salesman. That was a valuable part of my education: learning about salesmanship.

Salesmanship is convincing someone who is scared to death of flying to go skydiving with you. Not only to go up in an airplane, but also to jump out of it.

❦ ❦ ❦

My sophomore year arrived, and with it reinstatement. Of sorts. I was found to be fit for residing in the Yoder House, my original dream lodging. And half a dozen of my friends from the third floor of Killinger Hall moved into the "Odor," too. Age roomed with me and Bator roomed with Skal. We were in adjacent rooms on the first floor. No one got in, or out, without us knowing about it. The furnishings were antiques. An antique is something no one would want if there were two of them. We had bunk beds. I started out on the top but, unfortunately, I had a habit of walking in my sleep. It's difficult to get much rest when you keep falling off a cliff.

Age eventually agreed to switch. I helped him arrive at that decision the night that he brought a female companion home and entertained her in the lower bunk. Age was proficient with darts, but he was even more adept with coeds.

This particular night, I was fast asleep when the bed began to rock, slowly at first and then with increasing urgency. The first thing I checked when I awoke was to see if I was on the floor. No, still in bed, so I hadn't been sleepwalking again. So far, so good. Earthquake? No, only the beds were moving. Then I heard the noises, the unmistakable heavy breathing. I leaned over the edge of the top bunk and sneaked a peek. Their eyes were closed in rapture. I grabbed the hair on the back of Age's head and gave a stout yank. In the midst of his panting he gave out this shrill yelp. I muffled my laughter as best I could but I still made the bed shake. They didn't notice, though, because they were so absorbed in creating tremors of their own. So I leaned back over and this time got Age's right ear lobe and pulled on it like you'd start a lawn mower. He strangled a scream and I muffled a laugh.

Now knowing he was completely helpless, I leaned over, timed his rhythm, and just before the climatic moment pulled, *hard*, on the hairs of his buttocks. He let out an unearthly sound, the kind that shatters glass and sets dogs to baying miles away. It turned out I had actually done him a huge favor—the girl thought it was her extraordinary prowess in bed that had triggered such maniacal sounds from Age. So she left feeling quite proud. As he escorted her out the door, Age turned and hissed through the dark at me: "You're dead meat!"

I survived, of course. So did Age. We survived in spite of the monthly parties we hosted at the Odor. The parties we threw had a reputation that spread far and wide. They made Animal House seem like a sedate lawn party. We used that reputation to our advantage, and our profit. My training from the Railroad House days paid off. Rules were few but without exceptions: Everyone paid to get in, girls got in for half-price, we never ran out of booze or food, and partying was like fighting—you didn't ever hold back. The parties were limited to once a month because the rest of the time was required to recover, recuperate, and nurse the Odor back to life. How that house remained standing, I'll never know. *None* of us ever did.

❦ ❦ ❦

During my sophomore year, I decided not to play football. Instead, I joined the college karate club. I was six feet tall and weighed the most I ever would in my life—175 pounds. I had played football ever since the sixth grade. I didn't start a single game in high school but I never stopped believing I could play. You see, when I looked in the mirror I didn't see what my high school coach saw when he looked at me. Eventually my body grew, matured, and finally caught up with my enthusiasm and optimism. I had become a starter on the freshman team at West Chester, as a defensive safety. But now I realized I had to face up to the fact that no matter how fanatical I was with running, weight lifting, and gorging myself with food and supplements, I was never going to be big enough, strong enough, and fast enough to play football at the professional level.

So I looked around for something else. I'm a dreamer, but I'm not interested in dwelling on the past. If you look long enough, and hard enough, you will find something you're good at. I'd always been able to fight. It's just something inside me. It started with my father. He taught me how to box—not wild flailing, but scientific combinations—at a very early age. When most boys were getting their first baseball glove, I got Popeye boxing gloves.

We'd shadow box together, my father and I. He'd hold the palms of his hands up for me to use as punching targets, and he'd shout out instructions, and I just fell naturally into the right rhythms. Of course, I wanted to impress him, too. It set a pattern that would follow me my whole life—I did a lot of things just to show him I could.

My father was a self-made man. I've heard it said that life is like playing the violin in public and learning the instrument as you go along. Well, he escaped from an orphanage and pretty much grew up on the streets. He joined the Navy and learned to box. He got out and got married and had four sons, and he was holding down three jobs at once to make it work. He ushered at Connie Mack Stadium (where the Phillies used to play), he delivered milk, and when he finished his route he'd go to his job in a factory. Later he became an insurance agent. From him I learned an unrelenting work ethic.

He was very loud, very vocal. If you and I have ever talked, then you know that he passed those traits on, too. What I consider whispering makes other people cover their ears. My father also believed that no matter how old you were, you were never too big to give him a hug and a kiss, and to get them back. That's probably why I'm such a demonstrative person. My father was also the embodiment of tough love. He could wallop me—and he did—and I'd just stand there and take it. Or *lie* there and take it. He smacked me countless times and I never lifted a hand against him, even though my instinct always was, and is, to punch back.

My father was Italian and my mother is Irish. My father gave me the Italian passion and the love of laughter; my mother gave me the Irish love of the underdog and the sense of humor. For both those nationalities, of course, family is everything. From my dad, I got drive and determination and discipline. From my mom, I got my dream genes. "Paddy, you can do it," Dolores Croce would tell me, no matter what I was dreaming and scheming. And I believed her. To this day, she sends me letters and motivational cards. I've kept them all. She's very creative and she has her own single-minded focus, too. Right in the middle of raising four sons, she went to school and became a registered nurse. Now that I think about it, with parents like that, no wonder I was a fighter.

PAT CROCE POINTER
If you look long enough, and hard enough, you will find something you're good at.

So in the fall of 1973, I decided to switch from football to the martial arts, but not for the reason you're probably thinking, which is: The little punk isn't happy enough darting people and breaking noses, now he wants to *kill* someone. This is the irony: I didn't take up karate to learn how to fight. In fact, exactly the opposite is true. Karate not only gave me an outlet for my energy, but it also gave me a channel for focusing. That power has a carryover effect into everything you do in life. It increases your self-confidence and your self-esteem. It gives you an entirely new attitude.

Instead of procrastinating, instead of hoping a problem will go away by itself (and of course all it will do is get worse), you develop an attitude for attacking. You want to face up to it. *Now!* I know that to the skeptic this sounds like so much bullshit. But it really does work. What some people see as a problem, others see as an opportunity. Those things you don't want to do are the very things you should force yourself to do. You find out, in the doing and the repetition, that they're not nearly as intimidating as you thought. I guess it's a combination of two axioms:

"Familiarity breeds contempt" mixed with "that which doesn't kill me only makes me stronger."

From the martial arts, I learned to appreciate self-discipline and control. That's why I continued to work at it, to fight in tournaments, to strive for higher-degree belts. And here is another irony: I still have my report cards from when I was 10 and 11 years old, which include almost consistent "D" grades in self-control. While I could be rightly proud of most of the grades, my conduct was so bad that sometimes it was a *red* "D." First the nuns would hit me, then I'd get home and Pop would see the "D's" and he'd hit me, too.

Now here I am, thirty-some years later, feeling like a man on top of the rainbow, and everything I've accomplished has come about because of my self-control. The nuns who gave me the D's and then smacked me for them, they'd never recognize me as the Pasquale Croce they remember—that dead-end kid who never could sit still. I try to remember that even the wildest raging river, when it's harnessed, can convert all that untapped power into something really productive. I don't mean to suggest that I've got the force of a hydroelectric dam by any means, but I have my moments when I can light up a few things.

As you've deduced by now, I have the devil in me. We all do, to varying degrees, but, geez-oh-man, I've really got him inside me, and every day of my life I'm stomping on his head, trying to keep him from getting out. So every day, first thing when I get up, I work out. Keepin' the devil down . . . Some days he wins, some days I win, and some days we draw. I guess we'll keep at this 'til one of us dies.

PAT CROCE POINTER
Everything I've accomplished has come about because of my self-control.

This realization of what I had in me, and how it might be turned into an advantage, began to dawn on me the farther I progressed in karate, first at West Chester in '73, then at the University of Pittsburgh after that. During my college days I earned concurrent black belts in two different Korean-style disciplines—Tae Kwon Do and Tang Soo Do.

Karate, like football, is great for bonding. Anything you do with others that requires sweat and hardship and practice and dedication brings you together in a unique way. But even more than that, I always seemed to gravitate to authority figures who dished out discomfort, tough love, and discipline. Deep down, I knew how badly I needed to be instilled with discipline—to keep the devil down. First there were the nuns and my father, and then football coaches, and then . . .

Master Kwon.

❧ ❧ ❧

Young Hyuk Kwon was about 5 feet, 10 inches tall and cut like a diamond. He looked remarkably like the late Bruce Lee. You could scratch a match on any part of him and start a fire. His head was a massive square, like the business end of a battering ram. He had an exceptionally long torso which, coupled with his incredible flexibility, enabled him to sit down, stretch his legs straight out in front of him, and then bend at the waist and actually touch his nose to his toes! Try it. Unless you're a rubber band, you can't come close.

He didn't smile much.

When I met him, at the end of my sophomore year in college, he had just immigrated to America from Korea. He became my first karate master in the art of Tang Soo Do, and I became his fighter. Well, his favorite sparring partner anyway, probably because even though he would regularly kick the snot out of me, he knew I'd be back for the next class. It was an accomplishment simply to continue to subject myself to his instruction.

The techniques and training dished out by Master Kwon made my previous training at the college Karate Club seem like a day at the beach.

He was not only fanatically demanding, but he was also short-tempered, intolerant, and bordering on the psychotically sadistic. Where he came from, punishment was permitted, and expected, for any sort of failure. The dropout rate in his classes routinely ran up to 90 percent. His favorite punishment was the push-up. But not like any push-up you've ever tried. All your weight has to rest on the first two knuckles of both closed fists. This helps condition your knuckles for karate punching; it turns them into callous-layered razor blades. And as you strained through each push-up, at the top of each repetition you braced yourself for what was coming—a bamboo sword across your ass, delivered with gusto and relish by the muscular Master Kwon. Each smack sounded like a rifle shot. Believe me, a couple of those and your attention perked right up.

The best thing that happened to me during this intense training period was meeting Fred Scott—"Scotty." Scotty was Master Kwon's highest-ranking student when I joined the school. Even now, almost thirty years later, I continue to train and spar with him. And learn from him. In class I call him Sahbumnim (SA-BA-NIM), which is the term of reverence used to address a master instructor. Scotty was far ahead of me in karate knowledge and experience when we met, but I think my willingness to endure Master Kwon's torturous regimens with him earned his respect, and we became very close friends. Scotty probably knows me too well—he describes me as "an exposed nerve." That's an uncomfortably accurate assessment. Sometimes the truth can feel like the sting of Master Kwon's bamboo sword across your butt.

To look at Scotty, you'd never suspect what a lethal machine he really is. He's got gray hair, wears glasses that make him look scholarly, and is mild-mannered and unassuming. But he is supple and ferociously single-minded, and he can reduce you to kindling in about two-point-five seconds. Fighting him is like trying to throw a lamb chop past a starving wolf.

Scotty and I were partners in pain under Master Kwon, who always seemed to select the two of us to relieve his boredom or to hone his techniques. Once we were in a class concentrating on kicking, and Master Kwon asked me to go buy him a pack of cigarettes. I obeyed, of course, but found it curious because I knew he didn't smoke. Neither did Scotty or I. But shortly there we were, facing each other while standing on folding chairs about four feet apart, still as slaves, each with a cigarette protruding from his mouth. Master Kwon blindfolded himself. At that point, I'd have preferred that he blindfold me. I really didn't want to see what was coming. He emitted a piercing war cry so frightening that I'm pretty sure the other students wet themselves. And then he performed an astonishing athletic feat, a jumping double front kick in which he sliced the cigarettes dangling from our lips in half. It was an incredible act of agility and focus. (I adapted that move and have perfected my own little barroom act—I can take a beer bottle off your head with a roundhouse kick. Just to show off a little. Or win a bet.)

One time Master Kwon sent my brother Vince—whom I had lured into karate class—for apples. That seemed as strange a request as the cigarettes. It turned out Master Kwon wanted to sharpen his skills with the nunchakus, the weapon made of two sticks connected by a couple of metal links or cord that you see in martial arts movies. Master Kwon put an apple on top of Vince's head and one on mine, and then sliced them so deftly with the nunchakus that I think he made applesauce right there on top of our skulls. I almost made applesauce in my pants.

I came to love the discipline of Tang Soo Do. It's all about Yin and Yang. Passive and aggressive. Ballet and ballistics. The Yin part is the melodic, the flowing stream, the slow, precise, elegant movements. The Yang part is the fighting, all fury and passion, thunder and lightning. I'd do the Yin forms but only because they were compulsory; it was the Yang I yearned for and lived for.

As you've gathered by now, I had—and still have—enough Yang for a battalion of Green Berets. I've spent my whole life searching for the Yin to balance my oversupply of Yang, and probably will continue that quest right up to the grave. But Tang Soo Do has been of incalculable help to me in life. It helps serve as a governor on my emotions. Usually I can summon enough Yin to keep me out of trouble. Even now when I'm driving, if someone tailgates me I'll slow almost to a stop. And then when they get the chance to go around me, if they flip me the bird, I'll want to pull them through the window. While it's closed.

But no. Deep breath. Hold it. Exhale. Yin. Remember Yin. Calm. Serene. Unruffled. Yin . . . Yin . . . Yin . . .

All the while, the devil is whispering in my other ear: "Yang, Pat, Yang! Punch the motherfucker's eyeballs out! Go on, you know you want to . . . ."

Chapter 3
In Search of Yin

❦ ❦ ❦

*P*ersistance is biting off more than you can chew, and then chewing it.
Very early, I learned all about rejection. I learned that it's not fatal. I learned you should not take it personally. And I learned that it need not be a permanent condition.

I've heard *"No"* all my life.

The first major "No" that I still remember is the one that I heard from my father when I asked for $9.95 to buy a new pair of Converse All Star Chuck Taylor sneakers. "No," he said. "Too expensive." He was the one person I didn't press.

And Harold Katz told me "No" the first time I asked if I could buy the 76ers from him for a lot more than $9.95. And he told me "No" the tenth time I asked, too. And the twentieth. But I kept asking because I had come to realize that the one time you decide you'll quit asking is liable to be the one time you might get a "Yes." And wouldn't it be a shame to have squandered all that effort and energy because you stopped just short of your goal?

 PAT CROCE POINTER
Persistence is biting off more than you can chew, and then chewing it.

The first big chorus of "No" that was sung to me came at the conclusion of my sophomore year at West Chester. I had become intrigued with physical therapy and decided to pursue a degree in that field. But West Chester didn't offer a degree in PT. In fact, there weren't a lot of schools that did at the time. I would end up applying for admission to every school in a 6-hour driving radius that did, though. And I would be turned down by every single one. It would take a year before even one school would change its mind, and even then . . .well, you'll see.

My mother was a registered nurse at nearby Fitzgerald–Mercy Hospital, and she suggested I become a volunteer in the physical therapy department there to find out if my interest would hold up under actual hospital conditions. It did. I was smitten from the start. The appeal of healing was—still is—powerful. Healing and teaching are the most noble causes mankind can pursue, I think. I have always liked magic and puzzles (Rubik's Cube, stuff like that), and diagnosing a patient—trying to find out what's wrong and what will set it right—is kind of the ultimate puzzle.

I watched the physical therapists at Fitzgerald–Mercy and I was mesmerized. It was magic! They made people better. They made people smile and say "Thanks!" And there, right in front of them, was tangible evidence of the good they were doing. I thought briefly about a career as an orthopedic surgeon, but I realized I didn't have the patience. I needed to see results *right now!* And the notion of blending physical therapy with fitness really sounded enticing. I was ready.

 PAT CROCE POINTER

 Maybe friends are so important to me because you can't ever have enough of them. They're your allies in life, and you can't get very far without them. And even if you do go far on your own—without friends to share your success with, what's the point?

As a volunteer at the hospital, I was the Rickshaw Man.

On speed.

My primary duty was transporting patients to and from the physical therapy department within the hospital. Early on I realized that the faster I got the patients to their destinations, the more time I'd have to observe the PTs (physical therapists) at work. So I scouted out that hospital and became familiar with every little crevice. I mapped out every shortcut and determined which were the swiftest wheelchairs and which were the fastest elevators. Every hallway became a drag strip. I'd leave a vapor trail behind us, and the great thing was, the patients loved it. Oh, some of them asked for seat belts, but they genuinely got a kick out of riding the jet stream to therapy.

That's when I first realized the importance of personalizing treatment. People who are hurting physically are also hurting emotionally. They're depressed and they feel like they don't matter, they're just another piece of meat, just another number. I saw how they perked up when I asked for their names, and began to call them on a first-name basis. I then resolved that when I had patients to treat, they would all be welcomed and they would all be sent on their way, every visit, no exception, with their first names ringing in their ears. Personalized service in any area of life is the key to success.

The patients that I jetted around the hospital expressed their gratitude in a way that a college student could appreciate most:

They gave me food. Tons of it.

Which I promptly shared with the orderlies and the janitors. Very soon, I had a gang of friends. You see, I'm not a loner. In fact, I'll do almost anything to avoid being alone. And when I am alone, I'm either reading or writing or watching a movie so I'll feel as though I have company in some form. I have a need to feel that I belong. And yet at the same time I'm not a follower. I'll drift in and drift out with a group.

I was voted "most congenial" in high school. It's just that friends are important to me—so important that when I get them I latch onto them and don't let go. I collect friends. I keep them for life. I'm always gathering new ones, and I never lose the old ones. I've never, ever, had a fight with a friend. I'll just walk away instead. It's a little schizo, I know. I'll fight a stranger in a heartbeat—and try to pull his gizzard out through his windpipe while we're going at it—but I won't even argue with a friend.

Maybe friends are so important to me because you can't ever have enough of them. They're your allies in life, and you can't get very far without them. And even if you do go far on your own—without friends to share your success with, what's the point?

I remember a great line from the old TV show *Barney Miller*. Barney had just gotten Wojo out of a big jam, as he often had to do, and Wojo clapped him on the shoulder and said: "You 'n' me against the world, right Barn?" And Barney looked at him and said: "Wojo, those are truly frightening odds."

So they are. But those odds get a little better with each friend you have.

❧ ❧ ❧

Friends, I had. What I didn't have was acceptance by a school that offered a physical therapy degree. My interviews all went well. My grades were just fine. And even though I was a lunatic around campus, my reputation at West Chester wasn't ruinous. No, the reason I couldn't get in was that I needed a couple of physics courses to qualify. So I went to summer school and got that taken care of, but by the time I did, the deadline for application was past (and there was no Coach Furlow to bail me out this time). That meant I'd have to wait until the following school year to re-apply to the few schools that offered a PT program.

Which meant a whole year of . . . what?

Work.

I needed money. And labor, even the dirtiest and most demeaning of jobs, never has bothered me. I'd shined golfers' shoes at Chester Valley Country Club, and I'd hefted bundles of newspapers off the presses during the weekend late-night shift at the *Philadelphia Inquirer*. Work like that, mule work, is as good for the soul as it is the wallet. It teaches you a little humility and an appreciation of the real world, and it sure does reinforce the value of a college degree.

So my first job during my one-year educational hiatus was as a roofer. And to make things interesting, I got Bator a job with our crew. He, too, was taking a sabbatical of sorts, though rather than resting his brain, I think he was hoping to allow his liver to recuperate from all that partying. Now Bator as a roofer was like a one-armed paper hanger in a high wind. And he was afraid of heights. Of course you can guess how much compassion and understanding he got from me. Thirty feet up, and a friendly little brush up against him as I strolled by would have him defecating bricks.

We were just finishing up a particularly extensive and expensive job when the bosses decided to bail out early to get in on the start of deer-hunting season. We had refaced an addition to an old home in yellow siding and had installed new white windows and storm gutters. The refurbished house looked so bright you had to squint when you looked at it. All that was left to do was tarring the roof. Bator and I drew that short straw. It would consume most of the afternoon.

But after lunch, instead of getting right to it, Bator suggested we make a slight detour and check in with our friends at West Chester. We were, after all, in the vicinity. Once we were back on our old stomping grounds, it became a toss-up which was going down first: the sun or us.

I finally convinced Bator that if we didn't kick into gear we'd be black-topping that roof in the dead of night, which is roughly comparable to taking an eye exam in the deepest shaft of a coal mine.

We used push brooms to slosh on the tar. Sure enough, it got dark and we had to finish up using flashlights. But we did finish and we started to drive away feeling quite pleased with ourselves. And then I took one last glance back and saw long, dark streaks crawling down the newly sided house. Uh-huh. That black goo had oozed over the edge of the roof and was decorating the brand new, bright yellow siding like a kindergarten finger painter who couldn't care less about staying inside the lines.

We used paint thinner and the adrenalin of desperation. That combination turned out to be an effective cleanser. We scrubbed madly and at last had the house restored to its original sparkling state.

Except for the trim just under the roof line. It was supposed to be pearly; it looked more like old dishwater. I swear I saw a light bulb come on over Bator's head. He went to the truck and returned with a can of white paint.

To this day, he thinks he's the guy who invented "white-out" for houses.

❀ ❀ ❀

Winter arrived and the roofing jobs disappeared. So I became a detective, working undercover for Gimbel's department store. In all humility, I must say I was perfect for the part. I could fight. I could run. I could sweet-talk or street-talk, and I was adept at sniffing out a con, having pulled a few myself. My hair was long and my uniform consisted of jeans, a T-shirt, and a worn leather jacket, inside which I kept handcuffs and mace. I looked more like a law-breaker than a law-enforcer, which was the whole idea, of course. (Those handcuffs would become more famous for the inventive uses we found for them at friends' bachelor parties than for cuffing shoplifters.)

Frankly, the job was depressing. I'm a positive person by nature and prefer to give other people the benefit of the doubt. But the people I had to deal with, the shoplifters and the blatant thieves, they could destroy your faith in human nature. They would look you dead in the eye and lie until you thought surely their tongues would burst into flame. You'd catch them red-handed and they'd be spraying your face with outraged spittle as they proclaimed their innocence. They were dead-bang guilty—you knew it and they knew it—and yet they were the ones who claimed you were persecuting them. It got to where I could assess degrees of guilt just from listening to their routines. A steady diet of that, though, will leave you sour, cynical, and perpetually suspicious, and that's a ruinous way to go through life.

Nothing was sacred. Women would claim to be pregnant when, in fact, their swollen bellies were nothing but clothes they had stolen and wrapped around themselves. Others would stash their booty in baby carriages, right in with their real children. Men would stroll around with gift-wrapped boxes to deceive you into thinking they had paid for what they were carrying, except the boxes would have false bottoms through which they'd hide whatever they could scoop up. And the most brazen thieves of all never bothered with deception—they'd head straight for the storerooms and come out wheeling a whole rack of suits, or TV sets, or stereos, or any other big-ticket item you can imagine. They'd move with exaggerated confidence and nonchalance, trying to make you think they were employed by the store.

You had to have someone you could entrust with your back in these situations, and my foxhole buddy in Gimbel's was Charles Knapp (alias "Corky"). Another one of my guys from the corner. Like I said, once I get a friend I don't let him go. To me, friends are forever.

The previous spring, 1974, Corky and I and three other buddies had gone to Myrtle Beach, South Carolina, during Easter vacation. There was Mutzi (Steve Palis) and Navajo (Jim Noveral) and Herms (Dave Herman). On our first night there we were in a bar, a redneck kind of joint, and Mutzi played James Brown on the jukebox. Apparently it wasn't a popular choice. Some of the regulars made some remarks, things escalated (as they tend to do in those situations), and the next thing I knew we were out in the parking lot. I tried to talk us out of it. Really. And then one of them touched me. That lit the fuse. One punch and he was down. He got to his hands and knees and I punted him so hard that his hunter's hat flew up in the air. I was disappointed that his head wasn't still in it. I picked up the hat and flung it at his friends. And then I heard them say, "Get the guns." Holy shit! We scrambled to our van. There was this incredibly loud noise, and instantly the back window was blown out. We got away, but the state police pulled us over in no time and actually escorted us to the state line, where they told us not to cross back over. *Great,* I thought. *Oh, swell.* First I couldn't live on campus at West Chester, and now I've been thrown out of South Carolina. At this rate, I was going to end up a man without a country . . . .

PAT CROCE POINTER
You had to have someone you could entrust with your back in these situations . . . . Like I said, once I get a friend I don't let him go. To me, friends are forever.

Corky and I didn't last long as store detectives, though we did go back and visit the rest of the detectives one night at Gimbels. It turned into a party—a dangerous party. All those guys had grown up with guns and were forever debating firepower and trying to impress each other with tales of marksmanship. So after the alcohol kicked in, it was inevitable someone would draw. One of them finally did, and fired his revolver at a male mannequin, which was dressed only in its skivvies.

Blam! Blam! Blam!

The first shot obliterated the dummy's right hand.

The second blew open a new belly button.

The third was a kill shot to the head.

The noise was fearsome, maybe even louder than that shotgun blast in Myrtle Beach. Corky and I covered our ears and scurried for cover, as did most of the guys. After a time, we all began to emerge, one cautious inch at a time. You'd think they would have sobered right up after the thunderous noise and the realization of what had happened—firing live rounds in a department store in the dead of night. Instead, they (okay, *we*) lined up mannequins in various shooting gallery poses and blazed away. When they were done shooting, they thought they had cleaned away all evidence. But a stray bullet had actually found its way through a storeroom wall and ventilated an entire rack of suit jackets.

Very soon after this incident there were several undercover detectives looking for employment.

Corky claimed—and still does maintain—that the extra button holes in all the suits were a direct result of his famous (if unproven) ricochet shot.

And now for the handcuffs story.

I mentioned how those detective handcuffs I used to carry served a fiendishly useful purpose at some of our more riotous social gatherings. Well, never were they more handy than at the bachelor party we served up years later for my youngest brother, Johnny.

One of the key performers at these functions was my brother Joey (Croce boy #3). When people first meet him, they are always astonished to learn that Joey has a mischievous side. They sometimes even have a hard time believing that we are related because Joey is a big, sweet soul, always so placid, always so interested in what you have to say, whereas I'm Mr. Yang. That's what makes Joey a dynamite salesman. He'll listen to you, and listen, and listen, and listen. He'll listen until he knows more about what you want than even you do. He cut his teeth in the casino industry in Atlantic City, ran my company's national sales team, and now he's our vice president in charge of advertising sales and premium seating sales for the 76ers and Flyers. He's still that sweet and placid soul, but when it's time to throw back your head and howl at the moon, you can hear Joey baying from a mile away.

It was a week before Johnny's wedding and all the gang was at our favorite watering hole to celebrate his swan song as a single. He had no idea what was about to hit him, except for maybe a few shots. Joey, Bator, and Mutzi, three great guys to have watching your back (but not in back of you), were in charge of cuffing and trussing up and subduing Johnny, and escorting him into the men's room.

It was one of those "Call of the Wild" evenings where everyone is ready to howl and snort and let it all hang out. As best man, I felt it incumbent on me to provide my youngest brother with a night not soon to be erased from the memory banks. While Bator and Joey held him, I lathered him up with a generous dousing of black hair dye. (Johnny is normally a sandy blonde.) Then I taped a shower cap over his head. Being a trainer, I loved tape. I used about five miles worth on poor Johnny. Then Bator gave him a spritzing of that sulfuric acid we all remember from school—that really putrid stuff that smells like a cross between rotten eggs and fresh skunk.

Johnny made quite the picture when we were done with him. In fact, we took a picture of the finished product—eyes bugged out and blood-shot, inebriated to the brink of being anesthetized, leaking various bodily fluids, dyed jet-black hair, and a hapless pretzel box taped to his head as a crown. At the wedding reception, the high point of my toast was the unveiling of a poster-sized portrait of Johnny in that condition.

Thoughtfully, we had also placed a beautiful 5 x 8 copy of the photo at each setting—a delightful souvenir for all who attended. As I recall, that was Joey's idea. Sounds like something a salesman would dream up, doesn't it?

☙ ☙ ☙

You can imagine my father's surprise the day the mail brought him a letter from the University of Pittsburgh congratulating him on being accepted as an "alternate" in the School of Physical Therapy. In all official records, I went by Pasquale Croce; hence the name confusion. He was almost as pleased as I was to get the acceptance, even though there was a catch to it . . . .

One of the other applicants who had been accepted was going to have to change his mind. Had I known any of them, I might have paid one a visit with my trusty darts to help along the decision. That wasn't needed, though. A slot eventually opened up, and so after a year of scuffling as roofer, painter, bouncer, store detective, and physical therapy volunteer, I was able to resume my education.

And my pursuit of a black belt.

My goal was to wed a physical therapy degree with an athletic training certification. This meant I had to find a way to co-exist with cattle ranchers and sheep herders, so to speak. See, there was a bitter feud between therapists, who worked in hospitals and in home health care, and trainers, who specialized in the care and treatment of college and professional athletes. Each had a deep dislike for the other, mostly based on prejudices fostered in their respective environments.

To get the athletic training experience, I had to volunteer again. Jay Irrgang, a PT classmate, helped me land an evenings and weekends assignment as a student trainer for the Pitt football team. The timing couldn't have been better. Pitt football was in the midst of a titanic resurgence. My senior year, 1976, the Panthers won the national championship, tailback Tony Dorsett won the Heisman Trophy, and a dozen of those players went on to careers in the National Football League. So there was plenty of reflected glory to bask in. There were other perks as well—I gorged on training table leftovers and thus saved on meal money, I could restock part of my wardrobe (T-shirts, shorts, and socks) for free, and I had a view of the games that was almost as good as being in the huddle.

The job was not without drawbacks, however. Most of the work was menial, and frequently required waiting on athletes whose egos equaled their enormous size. The hours were long and, of course, there was no financial remuneration. But I was a sponge, observing and absorbing, and I could put up with any degradation in exchange for all the experience and knowledge I was accumulating. This is what it takes to succeed. But what I had increasing trouble taking was the verbal and physical abuse that was dished out to some of the other student volunteers. Most of them were about half the size of the athletes they were taping and treating, and some of the players were downright sadistic.

The Irish in me has always rebelled against oppression in any form. To me, bullying is an act of cowardice—it's indefensible and inexcusable. And when one of my co-workers, who was skinny and frail-looking and passive, complained that he had become the favorite target of a particular linebacker, I had to step in.

The player had an injured left knee and would stand on a training table while the volunteer taped him. The player would lower his jock strap, pull it down over the student trainee's head, and then force him, face first, into his groin.

PAT CROCE POINTER
I was a sponge, observing and absorbing, and I could put up with any degradation in exchange for all the experience and knowledge I was accumulating. This is what it takes to succeed.

Locker room humor is usually crude, usually involves pranks and practical jokes, and sometimes gets way out of hand. But this was more than a prank; this was abuse. The next afternoon, I noticed that the linebacker again had hopped up on the table assigned to the volunteer he had been tormenting. I changed tables with the other volunteer and commenced to tape the linebacker. I have to admit I was hoping the pig would try me. ("Yang, Pat, Yang!") I wasn't disappointed.

"Well lookee here, I got me a rookie," he announced to the room.

Some of the other players laughed. You could smell the anticipation.

"You been initiated yet?" he asked.

"No," I said evenly, still taping, "and I don't plan to be, either."

Now the players guffawed and egged him on. He taunted me. Some of the players and volunteer trainers smiled—not at him, but at what they knew was coming. My karate skills were known to them.

As soon as he moved to lower his jock, I dropped the tape, grabbed his strap with my right hand and pulled it violently down to my right side. At the same time, I shot my left hand behind his injured left knee and caved him in. He tumbled sideways and flopped to the floor. I was astride him, loaded and cocked and hoping he would give me an excuse. I wanted to drive his nose up through his brainpan and out the top of his skull.

"No more initiations," I gritted.

There weren't.

❧ ❧ ❧

The rest of my internship passed uneventfully. I enjoyed it and I stuffed myself with learning. The hands-on experience was of great benefit. I went to class every morning and afternoon, interned in the late afternoons, practiced at Master Kang's Karate School (a referral from Master Kwon) in the evening, studied whenever I could, and didn't leave myself any time for getting into trouble.

Well, almost none.

One weekend there was a rock concert scheduled for Three Rivers Stadium—Aerosmith followed by ZZ Top. They needed bodyguards, especially for around the stage. They needed beef. Large, imposing people. Logically they sought volunteers from the football team. Some of the players, knowing my karate skills, recommended me. I could tell that the guy doing the hiring was dubious when he sized me up. Here were all these behemoths endorsing this wiry little lunatic; the guy had to be thinking that all I'd be good for was giving transfusions.

"No, really, you gotta take this guy," they're telling him. "He can kick a building in!"

I got the gig. Guarding the front stage. Free food, free music, and twenty bucks, cash. Actually, I made forty bucks because I put on a cap and sunglasses and got back in line and got paid a second time.

We were stationed on a platform just above the crowd and just below Steven Tyler, the lead singer for Aerosmith. It was bedlam. The noise was shattering. It would come at you in waves and all but knock you down. So would the fans. They didn't seem to be interested in hearing the music, just storming the stage. It looked like a jail break.

The hardcore fans knew of Tyler's preference in liquids, so they'd lob bottles of Jack Daniels at us, and we'd catch them and place them on the stage. And Tyler, not wanting to offend any of his zealots, sampled every bottle. He'd take a swig and then toss the bottle back to his adoring fans. Of course that just made them crazier and louder. I remember being in awe of his capacity for bourbon and thinking: *Wow, I'd love to do the autopsy on his liver.*

It was a great workout, that evening. You'd tackle an exuberant fan, catch a bottle, duck fists and fireworks, then make another tackle.

As soon as Aerosmith vacated the stage, we left, too. ZZ Top was on their own. I did make a detour backstage and snared a pair of drumsticks, which I gave to Corky—who was a huge Aerosmith fan—for his birthday present.

❧ ❧ ❧

When I wasn't in school, I was busy being schooled—in karate tournaments. I competed in dozens of them, and amassed an impressive collection of trophies. I also collected at least two broken noses, several fractured toes, a couple of broken fingers, and spaces previously occupied by teeth. During the championship round of a national tournament, which I won, I sustained what the doctor termed a "displaced nose."

"Displaced" is a deceptive word. It sounded tame enough. What it really meant was that my nose was no longer between my eyes, in the center of my face, where it belonged. It had been moved, with my opponent's help, over to the side. Little things I had come to take for granted—breathing, for example—became a new adventure in pain. With every inhale and every exhale, a hundred strobe lights exploded.

To get my nose relocated in the approximate vicinity of the middle of my face, the doctor on duty in the emergency room took what appeared to be the stem of a spoon and inserted it into one of my nostrils. He dug around in there for a whole day, then pulled it out and stuck it up the other nostril and probed around in *it* for a couple of days. He described the procedure as "realigning my nasal bones."

It sounded like he was cracking walnuts. I dearly desired to hit him.

He packed my busted beak with gauze and then taped my entire face until I looked like something between a hockey goalie and *The Return of the Mummy*.

By the next morning, the pain was gone. It had been replaced by an excruciating itching sensation. I looked in the mirror and my face was a hideous, swollen mess, a grotesque combination of lumping and bruises. The whites of my eyeballs had turned crimson. And the itching! It was unbearable. I wanted to take a screwdriver and jab it up my nose and scrape and poke, anything to relieve that awful, awful itching. It turned out that I had an allergic reaction to the tape. I ripped it off. Half my face came with it. Which, of course, only added to my attractiveness. The next day I was in the dormitory lobby waiting for my brother Vince, who had come to Pittsburgh to visit. He walked right past me.

"Yo, V!"

He stopped, turned. "Pat? Pat, is that you?"

He came closer, squinted. And then he recognized me and he grinned. I started to croak out some wisecrack, but he beat me to it.

"Yeah, Yeah, I know. You ought to see the other guy . . . ."

◈ ◈ ◈

On the Pitt campus, I was on my best behavior. And I thought I'd make it through my two years without incident. I almost did.

One night I had just finished an intense study session in a buddy's dorm room and I was standing in the hall, saying my goodbyes, when a large figure at the other end of the hall said something that was apparently directed at me. I didn't understand what he said; in fact, I wasn't even sure at first if he was talking to me. He stood with his arms crossed, in the defiant, intimidating pose of a sentry or a bouncer.

"Are you talking to me?" I asked, but not in that belligerent *Taxi Driver* tone. I was polite.

He turned his head and said something into the room which he seemed to be guarding, and then he began walking toward me, purposefully.

Uh-oh. I recognized that stride. I'd seen trouble coming at me enough times before.

Behind him, the room emptied, and as they spilled out they formed ranks and fell into step. The hallway was narrow and I couldn't get a quick count, but they sure seemed to fill it. They were carrying long red poles. The poles were shaped like walking sticks, only they were at least six feet long. They looked like they would very effectively serve their purpose, assuming their purpose was to break bones. I could also smell the booze. These guys were armed, they were drunk, and they were about to have an ass-kicking party. And it became apparent that I had been randomly selected as the guest of honor.

Here I was, a short-timer, almost done with my formal education, proud of my unblemished deportment record, and a drunked-up fraternity hazing party was going to undo all my best intentions.

I retreated until there was no more room to retreat. I was cornered at the end of the hall, up against double doors that opened inward. No way out. I tried to talk my way out. But it was a mob by now. They wanted a head on a stick. The lead guy punched me in my left eye. I retaliated the way I had been taught—do everything in three's. Overhand right to his face, uppercut dug into his belly, and then while he was bent over, I seized him in a headlock and tried to ram his head through the doors. But there was no room to get a running start.

Then they started working on me with the poles.

Because of the close quarters they weren't able to wind up and take full swings. But they whacked my back, my left shoulder, and my head. And I knew that if I went down, I probably wasn't ever going to get back up. I needed to do something to get them off me, and all I had as leverage was the guy I held clamped in that desperate headlock. So I took my right index finger and jammed it as hard and as far as I could into his right eye.

I thought, *Maybe if I can rip out this eyeball and show it to the rest of them, that might scare the shit out of them and they'll leave me alone.*

He began to scream.

I dug my finger in even farther, and I could feel his eyeball squishing. His blood ran down my hand. I twisted him around so that he was facing the mob and I buried my finger in his eye until it felt like I was in him up to my elbow.

He screamed in agony now.

The mob stopped beating on me. But I knew they'd start again if they were given the slightest opening. So I used the man and his eyeball as a shield, and with the wall against my back, inched my way past one room until I found an open door. One of the occupants of the room was in there, studying. I can only imagine what he must have thought seeing me stagger into his room holding a screaming man by the eyeball. Fortunately for the innocent bystander, however, he was somehow swept outside to safety in the melee that followed.

I let go of the eyeball and its owner. He crumpled to the floor, still screaming.

I began to back my way toward the window. I grabbed a lamp off the desk. The mob came in the room. I smashed the lamp over the head of the first one in, hoping to decapitate him. There was a radiator in front of the window and I jumped up on it. The lamp had jagged edges now and I swung it as though it were a Samurai sword. I was howling and cursing and yelling gibberish. No one was anxious to have his jugular sawed in half, so they stayed just out of range. By now it had probably occurred to some of them that I was a madman. I might have been drooling.

The cops came then, but they made no arrests—just reprimands and warnings. It was such a relief. I hadn't jeopardized my graduation. The cost had been high, though. Lumps were rising all over my head. From the waist up my body was mottled with lacerations and welts. But then, on the other hand, a few select members of that mob weren't going to be available for beauty commercials any time soon, either.

One campus cop was escorting me out and we had almost made it to the double doors when some of the mob members began to yell at me: "We're gonna get you. Every time we see you, we're gonna work you over. You can't hide from us."

I lost it.

I sprinted up the hallway, hurtled past the cops and waded right into the middle of them. I wasn't about to spend the rest of my time on campus dodging shadows. I got off one good "nose-displacer" of a punch before a condominium fell on me.

This time the cops had to draw their guns to get it stopped.

The next day I went to Montifiore Hospital to continue my physical therapy affiliation. In retrospect, I probably should have admitted myself as a patient. I was spiffy looking in my white lab jacket and rainbow-colored left eye. It was a strange day. There I was, tending to patients, ministering to their hurts, easing their discomfort, healing them—and all the while I couldn't get out of my mind the man who had started it all, the sentry whose eye I had almost ripped from his head. I wanted to blind him. I still wanted to.

It really disturbed me that I wanted to put him in a wheelchair, or worse. The intensity of my anger frightened me. I said a prayer, asking to lose that horrible need for retaliation. It took me about a week, but the craving for vengeance gradually subsided. I resolved never to succumb to such intense anger again. That was my first step on the journey toward self-control.

Naturally that resolve was tested.

One night a couple of weeks later I was on the basement floor of a dorm with two of my friends, waiting for the elevator. The door opened. There was one occupant.

The Eyeball Man.

He had on sunglasses and an attitude. My friends tensed, worried they might get caught in the crossfire. I stepped into the elevator and looked directly at The Eyeball Man. He swallowed. And then I turned away and looked straight ahead.

PAT CROCE POINTER
I resolved never to succumb to such intense anger again.
That was my first step on the journey toward self-control.

I remembered an old Chinese proverb: The person who pursues revenge should dig two graves.

It was a shining moment for me.

It was maybe the best thing I did during my two years at Pitt.

Well, second best.

Getting engaged was the best . . . .

Chapter 4
Soul Mate

❦ ❦ ❦

I've heard it said that a friend is someone who dislikes the same people you do.

Well, there are friends and then there are true friends. A *true* friend is someone who knows all about you and loves you anyway. If you're very, very lucky, you'll find one true friend to last you your whole life through. I did.

Her name is Diane.

She's my ticket to heaven. We have been married since January 14, 1978. That alone qualifies her for a free pass through the pearly gates.

This will tell you all you need to know about her temperament: I had to teach her how to make a fist. And the only time she ever uses it is on me. The irony is, she's a redhead. A match has a red head, too, and you know what a match can do. But Diane's hair is a muted red, a deep auburn, and her temperament is muted, too. Most times, she is as serene as a Key West sunset.

She needs to be. Being made out of jalapeño peppers and napalm, I desperately need antacid, a counter-balance, a source of moderation. So Diane is the perfect Yin to my rampaging Yang.

I was asked one time: "Would you say your wife has sandpapered away some of your rough edges?"

And I replied: "No, she didn't use sandpaper—she used a hammer and a chisel, and several sticks of dynamite."

I spotted Diane McClaren when we were both attending Lansdowne-Aldan High School. But at the time, she was dating a guy who was a close friend of her brother, Willie. So I did the honorable thing: I exercised rare restraint and stayed away. I swallowed my natural inclinations, which would have been to rip the guy's legs off and use them to dig his grave, so to speak.

Truth be told, I regret that decision even today—not that I didn't displace some of the guy's body parts—but that I didn't pursue Diane right then and there. It did have a profound influence on my life, though. It shaped how I've approached things. Which boils down to this: I don't wait.

My idea of patience is to count to *one*.

We began to date when I was a freshman in college and Diane was a junior in high school. She was mature for her age and I was immature for my age, so that evened things out. We just seemed to click. I thought she was gorgeous, of course, but the attraction was more than physical. She was smart, she had common sense, and she was street-smart. She took no shit at all from my corner guys—she liked them and she fit right in, but she didn't back down an inch—and that sent her stock soaring in my eyes. Plus, I never felt like I had to pretend with her. I never felt like I had to be anybody other than who I was. She understood who I was and what I was, and she accepted me. Of course, I didn't know it at the time, but she had plans for changing me. Or at least trying to. I'm not sure what it was exactly, but she saw something there that she figured was worth committing herself to.

Our first date was on November 10, 1972. We still celebrate the anniversary of that date. Every year. It gives us a reason to celebrate. We went to the movies: Woody Allen's *Everything You Always Wanted to Know About Sex (But Were Afraid to Ask)*. Funny flick.

Our dating period lasted five years and sputtered along as fitfully as one of those old heaps that Bator and Jakester used to drive during our high school days. We were apart much more than we were together. First, I was away at West Chester State College for two years. Then, after Diane graduated from high school, she went away to Millersville State College, which was during my one-year wait between West Chester and Pitt. Then I went away again, to the University of Pittsburgh for two years.

In retrospect, it was probably just as well that we were separated for such long periods and saw each other so sporadically. Because as I look back on it now, I was so wild during that period that even her incredible tolerance might have wilted. Had she been exposed to me on a regular basis back then . . .well, there are limits to even the most angelic patience.

It's not that I was insensitive or purposely inconsiderate in the ways of romance as much as it was that I was oblivious, mostly clueless, and frequently thoughtless. I just didn't know any better. To cite one of my favorite sayings, "I didn't know what I didn't know."

For example: I hitchhiked home from Pitt one Friday night, full of good intentions about seeing Diane. It took six hours and three different rides to get back near home, and even then I got dropped off one exit earlier than I'd hoped. Ah, but that exit was temptingly close to the campus of West Chester. And Bator and the boys had recently relocated to an apartment there that I'd heard was awesome. So what could a quick detour hurt? Besides, Diane would understand. It was, after all, what she did better than anyone I'd ever known.

Like I said, I suffered in those days from occasional attacks of the *What-in-the-world-was-he-thinking?* syndrome. And the answer was, as always, *He wasn't.* (Thinking, that is.)

There was a party in progress. Of course. Bator and the boys were prepping for a concert scheduled for later that evening, on campus, at Hollinger Field House. Some new young rocker and his band, from New Jersey. They had everybody talking. Age was the only one without a ticket. I became the second. He intended to sneak in, and he knew how irresistible that would sound to me. There was something so challenging, so intriguing to me about finagling my way into a concert, a game, any event that required what I didn't have—a ticket. Maybe I liked the thought of matching wits. For sure I loved the adrenalin rush. And of course we shouldn't entirely discount the idiot factor.

While Bator and the boys lined up at the front door, Age and I skulked our way around the field house until we happened upon an open window on the side of the building. Once we had shimmied our way up the wall and through the window, we found we had dropped into the men's locker room. We walked with that brisk, purposeful pace of people who belonged, who knew exactly where they were going and what they were doing, so we would be undetected, unchallenged. We were convincing enough that the men who were changing clothes in the locker room—they looked like hippies and their leader was especially scruffy and disreputable—returned our nods and greetings. They looked vaguely familiar, but we didn't have time for a closer look. Mostly, we were immensely relieved that they weren't cops.

The door leading to the gym was unlocked, so we crept through and scurried under the empty bleachers. We only had to wait ten minutes until the doors would open and the crowd would rush in, but of course it felt like a minute short of forever. We expected to be discovered by security at any moment. Our hearts jackhammered. Naturally, we were incredibly juiced by the danger. And then the doors were open and the first rush of fans tidal waved in. Age and I merged into the crest and happily found ourselves washed up at the very front of the stage. First row, at the best possible price. The band began to play and the noise was one continuous thunderclap of sound, and then here came the lead singer, ripping at his guitar with the sort of passion I'd only seen at karate tournaments. He was the same scruffy dude we'd seen in the locker room earlier, changing clothes.

He had the ear of a poet and the soul of a balladeer.

We all agreed afterward that Bruce Springsteen and the E Street Band were going to have themselves quite a future. And back at Bator's house, at a riotous post-concert party, Age and I became instant legends—not only for our front-row-for-free achievement but for strolling past Bruce while he was in the almost-altogether. Everyone toasted us well into the next day and I was reveling in the celebrityhood. I remember feeling quite pleased with our daring and our improvisation. Yes sir, quite a night's work. And who couldn't be properly impressed by what we had done?

And then I thought of one person who might not. Someone who had been waiting for me, expecting me.

Diane . . .

One day later, and one inexcusable day late, I arrived at her house. I had gotten there just in time to have to leave. So she sent me back to Pitt, just as she had every right to.

But not without the feel of her embrace warm around me and the taste of her sweet kiss upon my mouth.

I was right. I really was dating a saint.

❧ ❧ ❧

The first week of January, 1977, during the holiday break before my last semester of college, I proposed. In my usual suave way:

Late night. Her parents' house. Couch.

Me, with the throbbing heartbeat of a hummingbird mainlining caffeine: "Do you want to get married?"

Diane, with surprise in her voice, almost as though she couldn't believe what she was finding herself saying: "Yes."

We sealed the deal with a kiss.

And then I uttered what has to be—at least from a guy's point of view—one of the most truly inspired and amorous lines in romantic history:

"Well, how about you buy yourself a ring and then let me know how much I owe you?"

I don't know why she didn't hit me. Or have Master Kwon bamboo my ass.

Instead, she said that would be fine. I've always suspected that she put up with my backward ways because she knew that I was lacking background and experience in some of the social graces. I just didn't know how these things were done. It wasn't that I didn't adore her, or that I didn't want us to have a partnership for life. It was that I had spent my time on the corner, not in the drawing room. I was a rough-cut diamond in the roughest sort of rough. To my everlasting gratitude, Diane recognized that. She was willing to look past the flaws and imagine the possibilities.

So a couple of weeks after the proposal, she called me at Pitt and lovingly described her glittering new star-crested engagement ring, with the tiniest of diamond chips on each point. From a distance, in just the right light, held at just the proper angle, and viewed through the eyes of the hopelessly lovestruck, it looked like a diamond star . . . .

Of course, I didn't have the slightest idea what she was talking about. But she sounded so excited and so delighted that it didn't matter. She was happy, so I was happy.

"And by the way," she added, "you owe me a hundred and twenty-five bucks."

I paid her back, by the way. And I am still paying. Now she wears an engagement ring that she designed herself and that gives off more lights than the Aurora Borealis.

Not that material things matter to her. She's always been content wherever we landed and with whatever we had. Every time we've moved on to a bigger place, I've been the itchy one and she's been the one saying, "this place is fine." I'm always looking for castles and she's looking for nests. She is a settler, and likes stability and permanence. I've got the buccaneer in me—always wanting to go see what's over the horizon.

Our first home was in Secane, a suburb of Philadelphia. It was a two-bedroom Sugar Shack that cost $33,000. I barely had 33 cents. My dad helped out with the down payment. We furnished it with whatever we could scavenge. I guess you could describe the decor as Early Poverty. A picnic table from my dad's backyard served as our kitchen table. Then for fancy entertaining, we'd move it into the dining room and stick a candle on it. If there were guests, however, we had to stand in the living room—we only had two chairs at the start, dug out from Diane's parents' basement. Our TV set was that battered old black and white from the dart days at West Chester. In the winter, there was more frost on the inside of the windows than the outside.

And you know what? We couldn't have been happier. Love, especially newlywed love, has this wonderfully limitless capacity for making everything seem all right. You don't think about what you don't have because you have each other, and everything else seems irrelevant. We were lost in each other . . . .

Until four in the morning.

That's when the guy-next-door's alarm would go off. Whenever he had too much to drink, he could sleep through an air raid. There I'd be, before dawn, an old bathrobe thrown around me, karate-chopping his door, shouting at his blissfully comatose fat ass: "Turn off your damn alarm!"

I'm sure the neighbors appreciated my early morning serenades.

"Is that a rooster we hear?"

"No, that's just Pat. Waking up the neighborhood so he can go to sleep."

Every house we've lived in after the Sugar Shack has been larger and more ornate, but most important of all, each has been set back from the road, away from neighbors. I was born in a row home, and lived in dormitories and dilapidated college housing, and I've always felt closed in, claustrophobic. I need my space and my privacy—and those who live around me surely need theirs. So with each new place—from Secane to Springfield to the Main Line (an exclusive suburban region of Philadelphia)—I've put more and more distance between us and our neighbors. If I had my way, I'd live on an island.

Matter of fact, I do.

We have an island home, we have our Main Line home, and we have a beach home. Every place we've lived, we've fixed up as though we were going to live there forever. Diane is a first-rate nester and I'm a neat freak. I mean obsessive, compulsive, anal-retentive neat. I make Felix Unger look like an unregenerate slob. That trait came from my father, who would go ballistic at the sight of a dust bunny. To this day you can catch me walking through the First Union Center, stopping to bend over to pick up a piece of litter.

"Is that guy one of the custodians?"

"Nah, he owns the team. We call him Mr. Clean."

❧ ❧ ❧

Diane worked at Sears when we were first married. I called her The Bag Lady. Every night she'd come home from work with something in a shopping bag.

"Got a great deal on it with my employee discount," she'd say.

We'd never have made it without her instinct for bargains. She could stretch a budget like it was Spandex. And she could stretch *herself*, literally. She was a student of ballet. Now she plays tennis, avidly and well. She worked right up to the day Kelly was born.

Our daughter is a college student now. She has her mother's distinctive hair and her beauty and creativity, and her father's balls-to-the-walls approach to life. Two and a half years after Kelly was born, we had Michael. He's just entering college and seems to have his father's exuberance, but tempered, thankfully, by his mother's sensibility.

Along the way, Diane and I have had some great fights. And every argument we've had has been my fault. I say this with no prompting, no threats, and no ulterior motives. I know they say it takes two to make a fight but, as you have seen, I need absolutely no assistance at all in that area.

The roughest going for our marriage was in the 1980s. I was running in a hundred different directions at once, so absorbed in my work—in expanding my business and accumulating a fortune for her, for *us*—that I was rarely ever home. And when I was, I really wasn't, because my mind was always on another project.

I was pretty raw and very intense then, wired all the time. Diane told me later I looked like a wild animal caught in a trap, trying to gnaw its leg off so it could get away. My work ethic was great for business, but ruinous for any sort of family life. I'd come home and forget to turn off the engine, and after a while even Diane's patience gave out. But she knew exactly how to get my attention.

She'd write me a letter.

That yanked my leash so hard I thought my head was coming off. She'd bring me up to date on what was happening to *my* wife, *our* daughter, *our* son, by writing me letters? Like I was half a world away? Which I was, of course. That was even more upsetting than if she'd called my secretary and asked for an appointment. It was more than I could bear. I got the message.

"Please, please, no more letters," I begged her.

❧ ❧ ❧

My brain was always churning out new ideas for business. It was like a sausage grinder, all these inventions and games and projects oozing out and spilling all over the floor. I've had some ideas that worked, and even a few that worked really well. And I've had a thousand cockamamie ideas that were flaming failures and deserved to be. But I never gave up. You can't ever give up.

Diane supported every one of them.

But not just blindly. She never threw cold water, but she never pretended to agree that any of my dubious schemes was a sure-fire, dead-bang success, either. She was honest. Well, she was honest up to a point. Love tells you where that point is.

 PAT CROCE POINTER
I've had some ideas that worked, and even a few that worked really well. And I've had a thousand cockamamie ideas that were flaming failures and deserved to be. But I never gave up. You can't ever give up.

She's really good at giving me a perspective when I get too involved, and at reminding me of some of the simple rules of civility. I'll be sitting there like a whistling tea kettle, all angry over some business deal, steam hissing out of my ears, and my head bobbing up and down, and I'll be planning such unorthodox corporate strategy as this: "What I oughta do at our next meeting is just rip the guy's head off and shit down his neck."

And Diane will look at me and say, in that calm way: "Pat, what you might want to consider doing instead is . . ."

"Yes, yes. You're right, of course. I wouldn't really take a guy's head off . . . ."

And then she'll give me that sideways look, the one that says: "Oh yes you would."

I'm not a total dirt ball, but I've got some of the elements. I am a corn ball. I love parades and pep rallies and bands and balloons. Diane never was intimidated or turned off by the dirt ball and she loved the corn ball. I guess more than anything, what she has done is help me get grounded. She helped me harness all that passion, all that energy.

That clueless street guy she first went to the movies with didn't even go to his own college graduation. No, the University of Pittsburgh mailed me my diploma. I couldn't wait for the ceremony, I was already back in Philadelphia, busy working, making a living for myself and my fiancée.

But I've been back on the Pitt campus. The first time back, fifteen years after graduating, I gave the "Distinguished Alumni" speech. And then I was back again on September 30, 1997, when the Pat Croce Anatomy Lab was unveiled. I've also financed a physical therapy scholarship at Pitt and an athletic training scholarship at West Chester University. I tell you this not to impress you, but to impress *upon* you the fact that you should never forget from whom and from where you received help. And we all need help.

(One of the winners of the West Chester scholarship was a coed who lived in Killinger Hall, my old dorm, from which I was exiled. She even lived on the third floor! I didn't ask her if there were still dart scars on the furniture. The building is reserved for honor students now. There's a strict code of silence. When it's real quiet, I wonder if they can hear the echoes of the bedlam we created . . . .)

You can get so caught up in chasing down life, in running toward goals, that you forget to look back. When you take the time to do so, you're surprised, and pleased, with just how far you've really come. And if you're really fortunate, you have someone to share the view with, someone who's run the whole way with you.

Have I changed that radically? Has Diane accomplished a complete makeover? You'd certainly think so, but I don't think you ever really change. Not the core of you. Not the essence of you. I think you adapt and adopt and you learn to make modifications and compromises and allowances, and you learn to turn what might be a self-destructive element into something productive, and you learn when the prudent thing is to back off, just a little. But what you absolutely, positively need is someone to help you do all that.

All of this was way too big a job for me all by my lonesome.

But not for me and my soul mate.

Chapter 5
In Praise of the Sponge

❦ ❦ ❦

I realized something about myself early on: I wasn't especially smart. But at least I was smart enough to recognize that.

Oh, I got a college degree. I made the dean's list. And I earned an additional certification in athletic training. But none of that came without fierce, unrelenting effort. I wasn't a natural scholar by any means. And in retrospect, that probably was a blessing because it made me understand the value of listening, of asking, of making myself a sponge.

There is an important distinction between hearing and listening. If you simply hear something, it can pass unimpeded through one ear and out the other—bits of information fluttering through your head like confetti. But if you actively listen—actually concentrate—you will be on your way to understanding. It's amazing how much you can learn just by listening. And asking questions. It really is true that the only stupid question is the one you don't ask. It is when you try to conceal your ignorance that you reveal it.

So for five years I had listened and asked and absorbed and volunteered, and then, in April of 1977, there I was, a newly minted college graduate, physical therapy degree in hand, ready to take on the world, ready to reform the world.

  PAT CROCE POINTER
It really is true that the only stupid question is the one you don't ask. It is when you try to conceal your ignorance that you reveal it.

The world, of course, yawned.

My first PT job was at an osteopathic institution, TriCounty Hospital, in Springfield, a suburb of Philadelphia. My starting salary was $11,900. Not per month. Per year. But there wasn't anything in my pockets then except lint, and not much in my wallet other than a driver's license, so that eleven-nine looked like a royal ransom to me. Especially when I tried to calculate how many roofs I'd have to tar or how many shoplifters I'd have to collar or how many noses I'd have to break to make eleven-nine.

So I did what most of us do when presented with what seems like immense wealth—I spent. I treated myself to a set of wheels—a black and silver Chevy Caprice. And to a new set of barbells and free weights. And I started scouting out Sugar Shacks for me and my new fiancée.

That PT job at TriCounty was only going to be a stepping stone. The job I really wanted was with the Philadelphia Eagles. If I wasn't big enough or fast enough to play in the National Football League, then I'd do the next best thing—I'd train and rehabilitate those who did play.

So on the first day of training camp, in early July, I walked across the football field at Widener University (the Eagles' pre-season home), resplendent in my white shirt and cool tie topped off with my crisp, starched PT lab jacket, which was as white and bright as a polar ice cap, in search of a job.

I looked, I was certain, every bit the dashing "Great Healer." There was pride in my stride. I brimmed with confidence and knowledge and honorable intentions. I was resolved to make the Eagles the healthiest, fittest aggregation of professional athletes in captivity. How could anyone possibly turn me down?

Without much trouble at all, as it turned out.

At the training room door, I inhaled a bracing gulp of courage and, after much deliberation on what the proper knock should sound like, rapped a knock that was supposed to sound assertive but not overbearing, confident but not cocky, eager but not desperate. A formidable man opened the door. From his attitude and bearing, I gathered he was the one in charge, the head trainer. There was a step between us that forced me to look up, which put me at an instant psychological disadvantage as well as a physical one. As it was, I already felt like I was coming to him with my hat in my hand.

"Can I help you?"

"Yes," I replied, brightly. "I'd like to apply to become the team's physical therapist."

From his reaction, you'd have thought that I had offered to administer an enema with a fire hose. He looked down at me, in more ways than one, rolled his eyes in tired disinterest, but managed to remain civil. Barely.

"No thank you. We don't have a job opening."

And he closed the door. Forcefully. To this day I can still hear that sound.

I stood there, rooted to the lower step, feeling like my Adam's apple had been crushed by a spinning back kick. I stared at that closed door and tried to will it open. Five years preparing, and it was over this fast? The dream of a lifetime shattered in two sentences?

No way! I knocked again.

Same man. Different attitude.

"I told you," he said curtly, "we don't have any openings."

And the door was closing again.

"Wait, wait, wait!" I begged. "Sir, do you have a physical therapist on staff?"

"No."

"That's the very job I want to apply for. And I'll even volunteer my time. You don't even have to pay me!"

What more could I do? Offer to wash his car? Shine his shoes?

He smiled. I felt a prick of encouragement. A smile! Maybe I had won him over with my persistence, my exuberance, my willingness to work for free. Maybe he was remembering what it was like to be young and eager and hopeful, and maybe those warm and fuzzy recollections were making him smile in fond remembrance.

No, this smile said something else entirely. It said: "What a pathetic wretch you are. Here's a dime, go buy yourself some pride."

Slam!

First I wanted to scream. And then I wanted to kick the door in. And then I wanted to body slam his arrogant ass right into the whirlpool. The Yang in me roared to be released. That sound of the slamming door was an ice pick in my ear drums.

I turned and trudged away. Dead man walking.

Is there any bile more bitter to choke down than that of rejection? I headed toward my shiny new car, which seemed to mock me, gleaming there in the hot summer sun, bright as my dreams that had just been shattered. At the end of the football field, I stopped and leaned on the wire fence and watched the Eagles begin practice. And I resolved then and there not to give up, not to give in. I had always believed that I was lucky and that somehow things would work out. No, wait. They wouldn't work out by themselves, they would work out only if I made them work, if I persisted and persevered with a positive attitude.

And attitude is vital. Your mental approach in anything is key. I've seen what a difference it can make in a million rehab patients over the years. Those who came in with an aggressive can't-wait-to-get-started attitude, anxious to begin making themselves better, invariably were the ones who mended fastest. And the ones who came in wallowing in self-pity, already curled up into the emotional fetal position, not expecting to get better any time soon . . . they usually became a self-fulfilling prophecy.

You know that old saying about people being in a foul mood, how we say they must have gotten up on the wrong side of the bed? Well, I don't think it's a result of how they got up in the morning as much as it is their frame of mind when they went to bed the night before. For some reason, I've always looked forward to the new day. I find something in each new day that I can focus on—something to look forward to.

  PAT CROCE POINTER
I resolved then and there not to give up, not to give in.
I had always believed that I was lucky and that somehow
things would work out . . . if I persisted and persevered
with a positive attitude.

I have this thing I do each morning—this quick routine. I rub my hands together (like you do when you're anticipating something good) and I say to myself, "I Feel Great! It's going to be a great day."

Try it yourself. Rub your hands together and think of the magic moments in your life. Maybe it's your wedding day. The birth of a child. Christmas morning. Those very special times that put a smile on your face. Rub your hands together, trigger a good memory, think of a happy thought, feel that happy feeling, and start your day with a positive, energetic attitude.

It's funny how it happens, but when you are excited about your day, your day becomes exciting.

Now I know some of you are thinking, *Right, sure. Here's Pollyana Pat throwing another shovel of crap on our bed of mushrooms. Listen, Pat, life is a shit sandwich and every day you take another bite. You got that, Sunshine?*

Yes, I got that. I understand. And I have also come to understand that things have a way of turning out exactly like you expect them to, so if you always expect the worse then you're probably never going to be disappointed. So why not vice versa?

I'll take a naive cockeyed optimist over a sour pessimist every time. I think it's possible to be an optimist and a realist. An optimist smells the flowers and sees only blossoms. A realist smells the flowers, too, but is careful to look around for bees first. When pessimists smell flowers, they automatically look around for coffins.

❧ ❧ ❧

Near the end of my Summer of Rejection, I did get a new job. No, the Eagles hadn't changed their minds. That door remained slammed shut. So I left TriCounty to take a staff position at Taylor Hospital in Ridley Park, also located in suburban Philadelphia. It was more modern than TriCounty, and was equipped with the latest PT technology. But most important, I had the opportunity to do volunteer work in the orthopedic clinic on Friday mornings.

This was the chance to get at fresh meat. I could observe—be a sponge, remember?—orthopedic surgeons evaluating injuries while they were still new. In physical therapy, the injuries you see were sustained long before treatment is scheduled. Sometimes weeks would have passed. Ah, but with the orthopods you had to start the injury evaluation from scratch—sometimes mere minutes after an injury occurs. And for me, doing the diagnosis and prognosis were the most intriguing aspects of the entire process. I wanted to be the one figuring out the magical puzzle, not have it given to me already solved.

And it was at Taylor Hospital that I was first able to do some teaching. While at the University of Pittsburgh I had taken graduate-level courses in spinal evaluation and mobilization. So during off-hours at Taylor, I offered seminars to physical therapists based on that knowledge. Instead of asking questions, I was answering them! It was good therapy for my own ego. It helped mute the haunting sound of that

Eagles door that had closed on me with the apparent finality of a jail cell clanging shut for eternity.

One of the attending physical therapists at my seminars was Matt DiPaolo. He had been my mentor during my earlier volunteer time at Fitzgerald–Mercy Hospital. Now I was mentoring my mentor. We became close friends and later co-authored a book on stretching and flexibility titled *Stretch Your Life*, published in 1979. We were before our time. In the 1980s, stretching exercises would become a permanent and emphasized part of physical fitness routines. Matt at that time had become the physical therapist for the Philadelphia Flyers (of the National Hockey League), and later, through him, I would become involved with them.

(So it would eventually be hockey, instead of football . . . but it was still a professional sports franchise, in Philadelphia. It reinforced my conviction that when one door is slammed in your face, you look around for another one to knock on. I believe in the adage that God works in mysterious ways. I couldn't get one team to take my services, even for free, but I kept working and believing, and eventually landed with another team. Then, twenty years later, after the second-most dev-astating summer of my life, I would *own* a team. I'm telling you, there really is something to rubbing your hands together and looking forward to each new day.)

At Taylor Hospital I met another person who would have a profound influence on my life. Her name is Lynny Ravitz; she was the staff occu-pational therapist. Lynny was petite, blond, brainy, bubbly, and bouncy. She was like a freshly uncorked magnum of champagne. She spoke her mind, which immediately endeared her to me. She also gave me my first exposure to a whole other world—the world of big money.

Lynny's family owned Penn Maid Dairies, a fact that was really under-scored one day when we were walking to a deli for lunch and she strode smack into the middle of the street, flagged down one of the company trucks, and procured free food for us on the spot. It gave a new meaning to the term "take-out." This truly was a woman after my own heart. (Lynny and Diane would become good friends and, years later, Lynny, to my finan-cial distress, gleefully would help Diane master the art of power shopping.)

At Taylor, there were three of us who lunched together regularly, and an odder, more curious threesome you will not find. There was Lynny, who hadn't let her social position keep her from following her noble instincts to heal. There was me, always revving my impatient motor. And there was Johnny "O."

John O'Connor had been a member of the Warlocks, the motorcycle gang of whispered legend and ill repute. Johnny O., however, had been reborn, and now was a member of Taylor's maintenance department. He wanted to rebuild his body as well as his soul, and so we worked out together during our lunch break. Using the various exercise equipment that we had on hand, I created a fiendish and demanding fitness circuit. We spiced it up with wagers on all sorts of physical challenges. Lynny was our impartial judge. You had to have a strong streak of masochism in you to survive my circuit. In fact, most of my patients used to joke that PT wasn't shorthand for "physical therapy," but rather for "pain and torture."

It was an interesting mix of cultures and backgrounds—the reformed Warlock, the heiress healer, and the street corner kid with big dreams. Johnny O. and I taught Lynny some things about our world, including some killer self-defense maneuvers (which would make a would-be assailant walk funny for the rest of his life), some parlor magic tricks, some sucker bar bets, and some colorful additions to her vocabulary. From her I got my first introduction to another social strata. Among other things, Diane and I went to our first catered party. What an eye-opener *that* was; up until then my idea of cultured snacking had consisted of Cheez-Its, pretzels, and a six-pack on ice. And while Johnny O. and I had never thought of ourselves as shy, we were awe-struck listening to Lynny voice her opinions and convictions.

"Girl's got a set of *go-rill-a* balls, man," said Johnny O., admiringly.

"No, she's got a set of brass ovaries," I said, equally admiringly.

She once refused a glass of Coke because the glass was not quite full. She said she was being charged for a full glass, so she not only expected a full one, she *deserved* a full one. From that I learned two perspectives that would shape how I conducted my own business in the future. First, as a customer, be assertive. Don't be afraid to speak up. You don't have to be obnoxious, you don't have to make a scene, but if you don't ask, then most likely you won't receive. Second, as a provider, treat everyone as though they are assertive customers. It will save you time and it will make you money. One of the first instructions my employees get is this:

"Exceed customers' expectations consistently." It ensures repeat business and encourages word-of-mouth advertising, which is the most effective kind.

❧ ❧ ❧

After a year split between TriCounty and Taylor, I had an itch I badly needed to scratch. I wanted to head up my own physical therapy department. I wanted to be the one in charge, enacting my ideas about treatment and service. I heard that there might be such an opportunity at Haverford Community Hospital in Havertown, Pennsylvania, just a few miles southwest of center city Philadelphia.

I led myself on a covert tour of the relatively small hospital before I approached the administration about opportunities there. My research revealed some interesting facts: the hospital had no PT equipment, no PT staff, no PT space, and no PT philosophy. In other words, the PT department didn't exist.

Perfect!

Rather than being disappointed that there wasn't an existing PT department to join, I was exhilarated because it meant I could create my own opportunity. If I could convince the hospital it had a need that it wasn't even aware of, and that *I* was the one who could satisfy that need, then I'd be able to start the department based on my plans and techniques. I wouldn't have to subject anyone to the trauma of sudden change. And more importantly, I wouldn't have to yield to another's philosophy.

So I did my research and drew up a detailed plan. I devised schematics to illustrate the physical needs of the department—including space and equipment requirements. I made projections of the patient participation we could expect. And knowing that hospitals (like other businesses) have to make money to survive, I emphasized the revenues that this new PT department—*my* PT department—would produce. Most importantly, I gathered plenty of data and evidence to back up every one of my claims. I was ready.

In the fall of 1978, I scheduled an appointment with the hospital administrator, Bob Bristol, and came at him with my best full-court press. When you're trying to sell someone, you want to make them believe that to exist without your product or service would be cruel deprivation. I wanted Bob to wonder why Haverford hadn't had a PT department long before now, and how could he make up for all this lost time . . . .

I sold him.

Director of Physical Therapy, Haverford Community Hospital. That was my new title. And the title was slightly longer than the space occupied by the new PT department itself! We have walk-in closets in our house today that are larger than my first PT department. Ah, but that didn't matter. It was a beginning. It was that proverbial first step that is required in the journey of a thousand miles.

The staff numbered two (including myself). Joe Murphy was my aid. Joe was naturally friendly and he liked people, and that was crucial because we were, after all, in the people business. We did the work of half a dozen. One moment you were a secretary scheduling a patient's appointment, and the next you were zipping another patient around in a wheelchair, and then you were rushing back to scrub out a whirlpool.

 PAT CROCE POINTER
When you're trying to sell someone, you want to make them believe that to exist without your product or service would be cruel deprivation.

I could have been shoveling five tons of manure and it wouldn't have mattered. Those were heady times. I felt that I was in control of my own destiny—at least as much as that's possible. I had always resisted being told what to do; now I didn't mind at all because I was telling myself. The best thing about being the boss is that if you've got a beef, you can go to the boss any time, anywhere.

Our place became the gathering spot for the hospital. Word quickly spread that there was this maniac in the new PT department who was leading crazed exercise competitions—tearing phone books in two and doing all manner of contorted handstands—so people would come by, curious, and then they'd want to stay and be part of the lunacy. Because while there was sweating and grunting and banging and moaning, the noise you heard above it all was laughter.

Workers began to congregate there on their lunch breaks. Some of them began to request personalized workout programs. We made it a fun place to be. And we made it the same way for patients, too. We made it fun to get better. And soon hospital patients were asking their physicians to approve increased physical therapy sessions to twice a day instead of only once. Naturally the physicians were pleased. And certainly hospital officials were pleased, because revenues from the PT department were steadily rising. And I was pleased because I had exceeded my projections and proved that I could run a PT department. That should have been enough to make me content.

It wasn't.

Within a year I could feel boredom creeping in again. That itch was back. I wanted to establish a brand-new enterprise—a sports medicine clinic.

The 1980s, which would be a decade of acquisitiveness and self-absorption, were almost upon us, and the fitness craze was sweeping the country. Aerobics became the buzzword. Nautilus machines sprouted like dandelions in spring. Ten-K runs and marathons and triathalons became staples of the weekend activity rosters in cities and towns around the country. Whether the reason was vanity, health fears, or fun, the country was chasing after physical fitness like at no other time in history. All this sweating and pumping and running and reciting the "no pain, no gain" mantra guaranteed one thing:

Injury.

You could open your window and hear the *twang* of hamstrings pulling and the *snap* of ligaments tearing as the Baby Boomers and the Yuppies relentlessly hurt themselves. But while fitness programs had been streamlined and made sophisticated, the methods of treating sports-related injuries hadn't improved a bit. Recovery was s-l-o-w and depressing, and probably as ruinous to the patient's psyche and emotional state as the injury was to his or her twisted knee, sprained ankle, or strained back. And I couldn't wait to test my theories on speeding up rehabilitation on the injured public—to give all those limping weekend warriors the same sort of treatment that enabled professional athletes to return to action so quickly.

I ran another full-court press at Bob Bristol. I provided demographics to reveal that there were thousands of adult and high school athletes within easy driving distance of Haverford Hospital who needed a specialized facility to cater to their injuries. In the absence of such service, many of them were forced to drive into Philadelphia for treatment. So we would not only be filling a need for thousands of customers, but we would be saving them travel time and expense. And the hospital would reap not only financial rewards, but would garner national attention for pioneering a new concept.

Sold him again.

So in 1979, the nation's very first hospital-based sports-medicine center was opened. We converted two operating rooms and their adjoining recovery rooms into a facility that was, for its time, state-of-the-art. Service was provided by a medical team, and the approach was similar to that taken in training rooms of professional and college athletic teams. It was a combination of physical therapy, athletic training, podiatrics, and orthopedics, with a few of my own wrinkles stirred in. Traditional doctors had never seen anything like it and, of course, many of them were leery.

PAT CROCE POINTER
The will is an incredible resource of power that exists inside everyone—if you apply it, you can change your life. I've seen it work too many times not to believe.

They thought we were mixing up a witch's brew, with our ice packs and contrast baths, our aggressive exercising instead of the conventional atrophy-encouraging immobilization. But we won over many of them with the rapid recovery rates of our patients. My theory was to go after any injury like you'd go after your opponent in a karate match—and, whenever possible, to coax the patient into that same aggressive attitude. I don't know that you can actually *will* an injury to heal, but I am sure that with a positive frame of mind you can hasten the healing process. The will is an incredible resource of power that exists inside everyone— if you apply it, you can change your life. I've seen it work too many times not to believe.

I became an evangelist, spreading the gospel of our new sports medicine approach. For five years, I hit every high school locker room, every weekend race, every tennis and racquetball facility. I was a traveling salesman who stuck his foot in every cracked door. If there was an audience of one, I still gave my complete dog-and-pony show. I may not have convinced everyone who heard my spiel, but I certainly entertained every one of them.

It was during this time that I determined that there was something else I definitely wanted to be:

Rich.

❧ ❧ ❧

One of the people who had read *Stretch Your Life* was Jay Snider. He was so intrigued by our concepts of flexibility and karate that he asked me to tutor him in the martial arts. I did, twice a week, for the next five years. We developed a warm relationship (nothing, remember, bonds like pain), and I got an up-close-and-personal look at life on the other side of the tracks.

Did I mention that Jay's father was loaded? Among other things, Ed Snider owned the Flyers and the Spectrum, the arena in which they and the 76ers played.

Our initial training sessions in Tang Soo Do were conducted in the basement of Ed Snider's Main Line estate. Of course, there is *basement* in the conventional sense, which is to say the underground room where you throw all your crap and hope it doesn't float away when the floods come. And then there was Ed Snider's basement, which was a pretty close approximation to what Donald Trump charges his hotel guests $500 a night for.

The Snider manse was immaculate; the surroundings impeccably manicured. There was a tennis court and a swimming pool. The four-car garage housed a blue limo and a variety of Mercedes Benzes. Everything in the house was either covered with leather or gilded with gold. And the carpeting . . . it felt like you had sunk in it up to your knees. I walked in trepidation and on tip-toe, certain that my next step would send a price-less Ming vase into irreplaceable disintegration.

The first time I set fearful foot in that house was on Memorial Day weekend of 1979. I remember the date because our first child was one week old, and as I gawked and gaped on my tour of Ed Snider's palace, I thought: *This is the life I want for my baby.*

As I said before, I wasn't smart, but I was smart enough to know that if I listened, if I made myself a sponge, there weren't any limits to what

I could accomplish. So most Saturdays, when our workouts were done, Jay would invite me to stay for lunch. He and his father invariably talked about things that were apt to produce a profit. I absorbed every word. I was starving, but not for a meal. The food was exquisite, but I concentrated more on digesting what they were saying and how they approached things.

And how they lived.

 PAT CROCE POINTER
Once a goal is set, it's just a matter of time—not to mention a lot of hard work and dedication—before that goal becomes a reality.

Ed and the rest of the Snider family was openly skeptical and concerned about Jay's interest in the martial arts. They were cordial enough to me, but I knew they wondered why he would want to endure the torturous training. Their fears certainly weren't allayed every time we showed up at the dining table with Jay dabbing at another bloody nose or icing down a new lump—the fruits of our vigorous sparring sessions. But Jay stayed with it no matter how often I pounded him, no matter what part of him I broke or bloodied, and he began to compete successfully in karate tournaments, capping it all off by attaining his first-degree black belt in four years. The rest of the family swelled with pride then.

Jay was a student at the prestigious University of Pennsylvania Wharton School of Business when we first began, and one time as we were stretching out and cooling down after one of our spirited sessions, I asked him, "What do you want to do when you graduate?"

"I want to become an entrepreneur," he said.

It was a new word for me. The sponge in me was curious.

"What's an entrepreneur?"

Neither one of us knew it at the time, but the street corner kid stretched out next to Jay Snider was going to become one himself.

❧ ❧ ❧

P.S. All the time I was tutoring Jay, I would tell Ed: "You're my idol. One day . . . one day, I'm going to stand where you're standing now."

And he was unfailingly polite. He'd smile indulgently, but I'm sure that inside he was thinking: *This is like the kid who cleans the pool fantasizing about owning my house.*

Maybe it *was* a fantasy at the time, but it quickly became a goal. And once a goal is set, it's just a matter of time—not to mention a lot of hard work and dedication—before that goal becomes a reality.

And then, sixteen years later, on the night before the press conference that would introduce me as the new president of the 76ers, Ed Snider came to *my* Main Line mansion. I showed him around, and once we got inside my office he looked around and said: "I really love this office. And the cherry woodwork, it's marvelous. There's something about it that just feels so familiar."

And I looked at him and said, in barely a whisper: "You should recognize it, Ed."

It hit him then. My office was a dead-on exact replica of the one in his mansion.

Chapter 6

The Unscratchable Itch

◈ ◈ ◈

*H*omer was beating the crap out of The Rat.

They were in my backyard. Homer would knock The Rat down and then belt him again just as he was trying to get up. The Rat would squeal and scurry for cover but Homer would track him down. Homer was always exuberant anyway, but when he fought he tended to get especially carried away.

Reminded me of, ahem, someone I knew.

Homer was, is, Paul Holmgren. The Rat was, is, Ken Linseman. They were professional hockey players—members of the Philadelphia Flyers. The Flyers' physical therapist, Matt DiPaolo, my mentor from my days as a hospital volunteer, had engaged me to work with Homer, much as I had with Jay Snider, imparting the skills and philosophy of the martial arts. Our primary aims were to increase Homer's flexibility (so that he would be a more efficient skater), to refine his fighting skills (as he was one of the fiercest fighters in the NHL), and to stuff a cork in that volcanic temper of his (which, I might add, rivaled my own).

I had to smile at that last directive. Me teaching self-restraint? It was a classic case of "do as I say, and not as I do."

Homer was 6 feet, 3 inches tall, 225 sculpted pounds, and had muscles in places where most people don't even have places. He came from Viking stock and looked like it. In fact, he probably was born about eleven centuries too late. He should have been off pillaging Europe. But playing professional hockey was about as close to that as you could come in the 20th century.

Homer and I would work out on a little porch that I had built on the back of our first house, the Sugar Shack. It was sweltering in summer, freezing in winter. But Diane, wanting to keep what furniture we did have from being turned into kindling, wouldn't let us indoors. Smart lady.

One day, The Rat came over to watch us work out, and when we were done I got out my dad's old 16-ounce boxing gloves to show them. Homer's eyes lit up. I might as well have placed a fresh zebra carcass in front of a lion. Homer invited The Rat to spar. The Rat was a feisty little yapper, a real irritant and instigator, on and off the ice. He was just full of himself enough to think he could last with Homer.

Paul Holmgren was one of the true tough guys in hockey. Part of his job on the ice was to protect The Rat. The Rat would sneak up behind an opponent and insert his stick up inside the jersey and rummage around in there for a while, seeing what he might dig loose. The opponent would, of course, howl and turn, and The Rat would run away and hide behind Homer.

Homer loved his job.

In one of the most epic brawls in National Hockey League history, during a game played at the Spectrum, Homer and Wayne Cashman, the Boston Bruins' enforcer, waded toward one another, engaged in battle, slugged and slugged and slugged, and then got ejected. The game was just about to resume when suddenly players leaped off both benches and charged up the ramps that led to the locker rooms.

Homer and Cashman had resumed their fight in the hallway!

Usually when players got kicked out, they'd stomp off the ice cursing and bleeding, go to their respective locker rooms, get stitched up and/or patched up, and then sit there in solitude, muttering darkly to themselves. But that night, Homer and Cashman got to the hallway at the exact same time and happened to look up and see each other. They glared. They were separated by about ninety feet. I can only imagine the *Yang* in their conversation.

And they ran at each other, which must have been pretty hilarious seeing as how they still had their skates on. In about thirty seconds the benches were emptied, the ice was deserted, and the hallway was full of Flyers and Bruins. It reminded me of those nights in my college dorm, only these guys were using hockey sticks instead of darts!

(In an ironic turn of events, Homer and Cashman ended up with the same franchise in 1997. Cashman was appointed the new head coach of the Flyers, and Homer, who had been the Flyers' head coach a few years before Cashman, was the director of player personnel.)

The next day, two black iron gates, bolted to floor and ceiling and fitted with locks, were installed in the adjoining hallway to separate the Flyers' locker room from the visitors'. It looked like a prison. They became know as The Holmgren Gates.

Homer was secretly pleased. And this was the guy I was supposed to temper and cool down and teach restraint to?

And now here he was, pounding on The Rat again, who was squealing and scooting on his hands and knees into the shrubbery in my backyard, trying to hide inside some bushes. Homer was feeling invincible about then. He invited me to take The Rat's place.

He'd made me an offer I couldn't refuse. I laced up the gloves in anticipation.

I had the idea that this would be a good chance to offer some objective evaluation and critique of Homer's fighting technique. (And it would have been a good idea, except I forgot for a moment that Homer's idea of "technique" was to come straight in and wail away with both hands.)

Just as I was about to expound on the merits of finesse, Homer unleashed one of those windmilling sledgehammers of his and cracked me flush on the jaw. I flew backward, ass over tea cups, and went right on through the post-and-rail fence at the edge of the yard. The wood splintered and it felt like my back had, too. I thought I was probably going to be pissing blood for a month. I got up and told Homer to chill. This was sparring. You were supposed to hold back on your punches. Show some restraint. Have some self-control. Yin, man, Yin!

So we began again. The Rat, meanwhile, had crawled out of the bushes and started doing what he did best—goading and inciting and agitating.

"Kill him, Pat, kill him! Knock his big block head off!"

All that did was rouse Homer again. He forgot everything I had taught him and reverted to instinct. That infuriated me. So when he came at me with his next rush, I was ready for it. I blocked every punch he threw in the flurry, and then I drew back, measured him perfectly, and smashed him square in the face with a jolting right hand.

His nose broke instantly.

There was enough blood for three transfusions. The Rat was in his glory. He was jumping up and down, yipping and laughing and squealing in glee. Homer was on his knees, his face a crimson smear. He held his busted nose in those old blood-splattered boxing gloves, looked up at me, and opened his mouth to speak. I thought for sure he was going to curse me. Instead, in an accusing whisper, almost as though he had been betrayed, he said:

"I thought we were supposed to hold back."

We both thought that over for a minute . . . and then fell to the ground in laughter.

❧ ❧ ❧

I needed help.

The injured were flocking to Haverford Community Hospital's Sports Medicine Clinic in ever-increasing numbers, but our staff was being cut in half: Joe Murphy was leaving for physical therapy school. We not only needed to replace him, we needed to add even more people. *Good* people, though. Joe and I had worked too hard to establish the Clinic and its reputation to settle for just any applicants who walked through the door.

I lucked out. Twice. First, with Fast Eddie. Then with Jimbo.

Ed Miersch was working at Rutgers University as a teacher and athletic trainer. The day he heard about opportunities in our Clinic, he was knocking on the door. For the next sixteen years, we would be virtually inseparable. He did everything at roughly the speed of sound, so "Fast Eddie" seemed a natural nickname. He was also fastidious, which appealed to the neat freak in me. For a long time he commuted from Rutgers, which was a long, long drive, and only served to demonstrate his devotion to the practice of healing.

Fast Eddie also had a lead foot, which further endeared him to me. He has had classic vans, a two-ton pickup truck, and an urban assault vehicle, and he always kept the accelerator jammed to the floor in all of them. I loved riding with Fast Eddie; it was an experience guaranteed to elevate your heart rate. Aerobics in the shotgun seat. Plus, you knew you'd never be late for an appointment. (Did I mention that I'm an anal-retentive fanatic about punctuality?)

Fast Eddie started out as a volunteer at Haverford, graduated to employee, came with me when I went on to start my own company, and finally ascended to Chief Operating Officer of that company. What he was from the very beginning and remains to this day, is a dear, valued friend.

Same with Jim Schiller. "Jimbo" was in his senior year at Temple University, about to earn his degree in physical therapy, when he too volunteered at the Clinic.

I'm big on volunteerism because I think it is an accurate measure of people—of the depth of their determination and desire. Volunteers do what they do out of genuine commitment, not for the money. They're willing to put in extra hours, long hours, just to educate themselves. That places them above all the rest. Volunteers have a shared passion, and almost always they tend to be sponges, absorbing, absorbing, absorbing. Usually they're motivated for the most noble of reasons—they want to help others.

Jimbo was best friends with my brother Joey when we were growing up. The word I've always associated with Jimbo is "jolly." He is *all* business—efficient without making a fuss or drawing attention to himself—but he's got one of those laughs that you recognize instantly and that cannot help but make you smile. Jimbo laughed a lot. And in the business of healing, smiles and laughter are worth their curative weight in prescription drugs. Jimbo would eventually become the first full-time employee of my company (Sports Physical Therapists), and he would rise to the rank of executive vice president.

  PAT CROCE POINTER
I'm big on volunteerism because I think it is an accurate measure of people—of the depth of their determination and desire. They're willing to put in extra hours, long hours, just to educate themselves. That places them above all the rest.

Others followed Fast Eddie and Jimbo. More kindred spirits.

There was Steve Mackell, known simply as "Mack." He was (and still is) one of my black belt training partners. He was as solid as a beer keg, and his character matched his physique. Like Jimbo, he laughed heartily and often, and made others do the same. Mack was also a sly, fiendish instigator and a cunning manipulator. Some of the best, most elaborate practical jokes I've ever been part of were hatched by Mack.

There was Jim McCrossin, (alias "Cochise.") And Mitch Wolf and Debbie Kuebler. They, too, began as volunteers at Haverford, became employed assistants and, once they had their degrees, were promoted. Loyalty is a precious commodity, and as such it should always be rewarded.

So I was assembling another gang. A strong bond formed as we shared many great experiences. We worked together and partied together, both with equal fervor and dedication. The energy among us consistently crackled. Everyone knew they could depend upon everyone else in the group for emotional sustenance . . . and a whoopee cushion if you dared to let your guard down. And the best part of it all was this overriding feeling that we were doing good—that what we did had real, lasting significance.

There aren't many things in this world quite as fulfilling as making someone well.

We made Debbie Kuebler well, and then we couldn't get rid of her. She first came to the clinic as a patient. Both her wheels were in a bad way—she'd had bilateral knee surgery. Her pain threshold was off the chart, but what impressed us even more was her kick-ass, *just-tell-me-what-I-have-to-do-to-get-better* attitude. She got well, which was no surprise at all, and then one day she showed up asking not for rehabilitation, but for work. She started as a volunteer (naturally), and then worked her way up to an assistant therapist out on the gym floor. When business was really percolating, she would swing over to the secretarial suite. She could do it all.

Debbie went to school while she was working, got her physical therapy degree, and became an outstanding staff therapist. And then when I left the hospital clinic to start my own business, she managed one of my centers, then became a regional manager. What an impressive journey Debbie made for herself—from a patient who could barely stand to a successful executive position, and all of that made possible by a positive attitude. Debbie also became a dear friend of our family.

As you can see, there were repeating threads that bound us all together. When you all labor in a common cause, when you all support each other, when your psychic income is boundless, and when you celebrate together, well . . . then none of it ever quite seems like work.

I did make one exception to hire someone who was not a volunteer: "Scramble Head."

Lisa Schramm should have been on the deck of the *Titanic*. It never would have gone down. She wouldn't have let it.

She was the clinic's secretary. She could restore order and sanity to the most bewildering kind of bedlam. She could unscramble chaos. Which, I guess, is why I called her Scramble Head. That, and because "Schramm" rhymes with "scram," and . . . oh, never mind, it's too complicated. Some nicknames just happen.

Lisa was plugged into the hospital grapevine and was always ferreting out useful nuggets of gossip and information. She was adept at soothing worried patients in our waiting room. The staff adored her, trusted her with secrets, and consulted her for advice. And then she had the good sense to marry Ray Pennacchia. Or maybe it was actually the other way around. Anyway, "Ray Man" would become my vice president of marketing when I started my own company, and Scramble Head would become my personal secretary.

The lame and the bruised were coming in in waves, and soon we had to renovate and expand the clinic. This time, the administration didn't need any convincing. The clinic's public perception and sparkling revenues were the deal closers. We were Haverford Hospital's rising star.

So we decided to mark the renovation with something more festive than the traditional ribbon-cutting. I invited Flyers' legend Bobby Clarke, Homer (his nose had healed and we had become great friends, spilling more beer than blood), and several other Flyers. They toured the hospital, signed autographs, and visited with patients. The reception they got—from the staff, the patients, the media, and the visitors— astounded me. That was when I first realized the hypnotic appeal that celebrities had on the public . . . and how that could be used as a marketing tool.

Later, when my own business began to flourish, every time we opened a new center we made it a Grand Opening gala awash with celebrities. We'd wheel them up in a fleet of limos, roll out the red carpet, and make sure the paparazzi—or at least the local media—were there. In marketing, perception and image are of inestimable worth. You want to make it seem as though your opening is so important that to miss it would be a tragedy.

The new-look clinic was a smashing success right from the start. We just kept growing and growing.

So did my ambition.

❧ ❧ ❧

My days were crammed with activity at the clinic. But that left the nights. Why waste them on something trivial like sleep? I wanted to establish a private physical therapy practice in a medical office building in nearby Broomall. But before I could do so, I needed start-up money. I borrowed $4,000 from my Dad. I've never asked for anything with more difficulty in my life. But I repaid him, and that $4,000 would multiply ten thousand times over.

 PAT CROCE POINTER
Ever since I graduated from Pitt, I had worked nights scuffling for extra income by doing PT work on the side. Some people call it sacrifice . . . . I call it dedication.

In 1980, I started my first business. It was called Orthopedic and Athletic Rehabilitation (OAR). I oared along three nights a week with Fast Eddie at my side. Evening employment wasn't exactly a new experience. Ever since I graduated from Pitt, I had worked nights scuffling for extra income by doing PT work on the side. Some people call it sacrifice . . . . I call it dedication.

As soon as I had my diploma, I applied to Community Nursing Service for certification to provide home health care. I was told I needed at least a year of PT experience first. A year! They might as well have said forever. Yet another door slammed—if not completely shut, then close enough. Well, if you can't go right on through an obstacle, then sneak around it. So I started seeking referrals from physicians on my own, and for the two years before I opened OAR, I did what doctors used to do once upon a long, long time ago—I made house calls.

And I fell in love with my very first homebound patient.

As fate would have it, she had also been my very first patient when I was starting out, back at TriCounty Hospital. Her name was Ruth Bradway, and a feistier, pluckier, grander old lady I have never met. If you could pick your grandmother, she'd be a first-round draft selection. She was in the insidious grip of multiple sclerosis, a despicable and disabling disease that left her arms and legs locked in agonizing semi-paralysis. The disease may have wracked her body, but it couldn't touch her soul. Or her spirit. She possessed a wonderful wit, an engaging sense of humor, and a tongue as tart as apple cider. You dueled verbally with

Ruth at your own risk, and to her immense enjoyment.

After my first week of treating Ruth at TriCounty Hospital, her husband, Howard, asked if I could come several evenings a week to their South Philly row home to further treat her. I happily agreed.

I'm not sure who treated whom. For two years I drove to their home and marveled at Ruth's indomitability. And I was in awe of Howard's devotion and unceasing patience. I listened to his stories and his wisdom, and to Ruth's ruminations on the human condition, and I got the equivalent of another education. Ruth eventually reached a point where she could get from her hospital bed to her living room with the aid of a walker and bilateral leg splints . . . and by leaning on me. It seemed like a fair exchange, considering all the life lessons I learned from them.

More than anything else, I was privileged to watch two people nourish one another, accept incredible adversity, and rise above it. They had a lifetime of love and somehow were able, through that love, to turn a wracking disease into something that, rather than driving them apart, only entwined them closer. It was a shining triumph for the human spirit.

On our wedding night, following the reception, Diane and I made a special side trip on our way to the airport. We stopped to see Ruth and Howard. We wanted to thank them for their inspiring example of what glories are possible in a union of soul mates.

❧ ❧ ❧

Shortly after I started OAR, I ceased the home care business. My private evening practice did well, even though there was a haunting distraction: one of my employees.

My secretary, specifically.

I would have had an affair with her, but we were already married.

Diane served as my secretary for the OAR business, and we developed a routine of spending some of our extra income on Friday night celebrations. It was nothing elaborate. After the last patient had left, we'd stop at a beef 'n' beer place and dare to speak our dreams out loud. It became a ritual. (And the dreams would all come true—the part-time, evening practice eventually would blossom into a full-time business with branches all around the country.) We didn't know what would unfold at the time, of course. We were just happy speaking our dreams out loud, and listening to that unbearably cute little strawberry blonde at the end of our table who was forever giggling and stacking the sugar packs.

Kelly.

I wanted to give her, and her brother soon to follow, and Diane, the kind of life I had been exposed to in recent months, and the only way I knew how to do that was to keep piling on the work load. I was managing the Sports Medicine Clinic at the hospital, conditioning Homer and some of the other Flyers, doing physical therapy three nights a week, and lecturing and writing on the wonders of fitness and sports medicine at every chance.

But I wanted more.

As my work with the Flyers and Jay Snider drew favorable reviews, Ed Snider began to introduce me to some movers and shakers. It turned out that even the wealthy and the influential are not immune to vanity or injury. Many of them wanted personalized service, either to get fit or to get well. For a change, the doors weren't slamming in my face; they were beginning to open.

One of those open doors led me to Dick Butera. He was an entrepreneur. (There was that word again. Except now I knew what it meant.) Dick had made big money developing real estate in Hilton Head, South Carolina. Then he created a public insurance company. Like most entrepreneurs, he got easily bored, and restless. I would come to understand that restlessness. What happens after you have made the money is that the need for challenge remains. The competitive instinct never really dies. Money, once you have enough of it, really is just a way to keep score.

So Dick had set his sights on Aspen, Colorado—on duplicating his Hilton Head success there. He was going to acquire the Aspen Club, a huge fitness facility in that lavish resort town. He liked my sports medicine concept and was impressed with what we had accomplished in such a modest facility at Haverford Hospital. Imagine what might be possible on a larger, grander scale. After all, in Aspen the hills were alive not so much with the sound of music as with the sound of multi-millionaires breaking their legs while schussing down the ski slopes.

I was introduced to Dick at the Snider house. Jay and I had just finished a karate session. Dick, who had just finished lunching with Ed, put up both hands in a mock martial arts stance in front of Jay, who only smiled and obeyed Yin, throwing two air punches that whistled past

Dick's ears. The breeze from them ruffled Dick's coif. He put his hands down in a hurry.

Dick's brother, Bob, had been a gubernatorial candidate in Pennsylvania, and was president of the Flyers when I first joined up to work with Homer. And Dick's then-wife, Julie Anthony, was the Flyers' sports psychologist. She had been a professional tennis player and was an avid fitness advocate. So we all shared many of the same passions and enthusiasms. It looked like a natural fit, all of us out there in the opulence of Aspen, with all that money lying around just waiting to be scooped up.

I flew to Aspen to see for myself. I had never been farther "west" than Pittsburgh. This was going to be a monumental decision, one of those life-altering decisions that had to be shared, of course. So I returned for Diane and Kelly and our newborn son, Michael, and we all flew out to Aspen. Half a day on a plane with two infants and enough equipment to keep the 101st Airborne Division supplied for a month . . . . You want to test the strength of your marriage, subject it to that stress.

On the surface, it looked like an unmatchable deal. I'd be able to create the biggest and best sports medicine center anyone had ever seen. In a gorgeous place fabled for its scenery and its smorgasbord of athletic activities. So who could possibly pass on such a dynamic and challenging opportunity?

Uh, this dummy right here, that's who.

It just didn't feel right, and I knew why. It would be a dream, but not my dream. Not totally, completely mine. I wouldn't have the final say. I wouldn't have exclusive control of my dream, my destiny.

I didn't want to have to answer to anyone except myself. And my soul mate.

  PAT CROCE POINTER
Remember this: sometimes, the very best moves are the ones you never make.

Saint Diane supported my decision. And later, she confessed that that had been her undeclared decision from the start. Bless her. But she never did forgive being subjected to that cross-country marathon. To this day, whenever she hears the word "Aspen" her right arm comes up in a

Pavlovian reflex, and she punches me with a good two-knuckle karate punch. I taught her too well.

Remember this: sometimes, the very best moves are the ones you never make.

      ❧ ❧ ❧

One move that I did make, in 1981, was accepting expanded duties with the Flyers. They wanted me even though, entrusted with the care and tutoring of Paul Holmgren, I had broken his nose in my own backyard. Or maybe that was a factor in my favor.

Anyway, I was to be their physical conditioning coach. It was like getting my own laboratory. It would give me a chance to try out my theories of conditioning and rehabilitation on people who played sports for a living. Pat Quinn, the head coach, wanted me to keep Homer and Bobby Clarke and the rest of them physically fit, on the ice, and out of the training room. And if they did get hurt, I had to help heal them. Certainly Homer knew what I could do. And so did The Rat.

But that wasn't good enough for some of the rest of the Flyers. They were established professional athletes, adored in Philadelphia, and I was the new guy. Acceptance would be slow and reluctant from some of them. That meant there was going to be an initiation. You may remember from my taping days at Pitt, I'm not big on initiations.

After one morning workout my first week on the job, I showered and dressed in a hurry, hoping to make it back to the hospital and the sports medicine clinic before the afternoon flood of patients began to arrive. (Fast Eddie and the gang took care of the morning traffic of injuries.) I was standing before the mirror, combing my hair, urging myself to comb faster, faster, faster . . . when . . . when this itching sensation began in my groin. I tried to ignore it but it didn't go away. Then I shimmied a little, but that didn't help either. Finally, mercifully, the itching stopped.

Only to be replaced by excruciating pain. I felt like I had a blow torch down my pants and a flame thrower up my crotch!

I ripped at my trousers, got them off, and then clawed at my underpants and got them off, half expecting to see flames shooting up in the air. I turned the cold water on and began frantically dousing myself, but no matter how much water I scooped, the burning raged on. And intensified!

As I was cursing and trying to put out the "fire," I looked down at the floor and saw red blotching on my underpants.

Red Hot. An analgesic balm intended to go deep down into hurting muscles and bake the pain away. But when it came in contact with certain sensitive areas of your anatomy, it was like an army of fire ants had tunneled inside you and declared war.

I heard the players whooping and laughing, and I memorized their faces. I knew the guilty ones would have stuck around to enjoy the fruits of their pyrotechnic mischief. I got the fire out at last, cleaned up, and began to limp toward the exit. That's when one of them tipped his hand.

"Hey there, Pat, what happened?"

It was Rick MacLeish, one of the Flyers' top guns. He had a devastating wrist shot, but a lousy poker face.

I walked purposefully over to him and reached down and grasped one of his fingers. He looked at me curiously. That look changed into a contortion of pain as I began to s-l-o-w-l-y torque the finger out of joint. The pain made him jerk in agony.

"Did this finger touch my clothes?"

"No! No! Wasn't me."

That particular jujitsu hold will lock anyone in place. They want to stand, but can't. The pain freezes them. MacLeish wiggled like a hooked bass.

"Who did it?"

"I don't know ... owwwwww ... really, I don't know. OWWWWWW!"

Just another turn, a bit more pressure, and ...

"Barber! OWWWWW! It was Barber."

The rest of the players laughed at MacLeish's discomfort, and also at his inability to keep from ratting.

Bill Barber was one of the all-time great Flyers. He rode shotgun on one wing with Bobby Clarke through two Stanley Cup Championships. He also liked to play practical jokes. I walked to his dressing cubicle where he was pulling off his workout uniform. I measured my words and put as much menace in them as I could.

"Don't ever touch my stuff again."

He looked at me with open disdain. Who did this hotshot karate newcomer think he was talking to? He sneered.

So I hit him in the nuts.

We'll take a brief pause where I explain that strategy. There's a story about this farmer who claimed that he could make mules talk. A newspaperman came to the farm and asked the man if what he had heard was true, that he really could make mules talk. And the man said yes, he could, and to follow him. So they walked over to a small corral and a mule ambled up and stuck its head over the top rail. The farmer bent down and picked up a two-by-four and whacked the mule right between the eyes. The newspaperman gasped. "What'd you do that for?" he asked. "'Cause," replied the farmer, "first you got to get their attention."

Well, my right uppercut directly into his testicles had certainly gotten Bill Barber's attention.

As he began to fold up like an accordion, I made a knife edge of the ridge of my left hand and put it on his throat, forcing his back up against his locker. His eyes bulged. He wanted to breathe, he wanted to scream, he wanted to puke, and he wanted to kill me, all at the same time, though not necessarily in that order. But I wasn't letting him do any of those things. I leaned in close and gritted:

"There better not be a next time."

There wasn't.

Hockey players are a special breed. I have great respect for their unquenchable work ethic and their astonishing threshold of pain, and I certainly do share their love of a good fight and their appreciation of a good beer or two. They are, for the most part, sincere and unspoiled, in great contrast to a lot of professional athletes.

In turn, they respect physical force.

What happened between Homer and me first, and between MacLeish and Barber and me later, spread quickly. I never again had to worry about my crotch catching fire.

We developed a close, lasting relationship. The only problem was that they all wanted me to teach them karate. I refrained. I knew they would have tried it on each other and then there wouldn't be enough bodies to put a team on the ice.

Besides, I was still plagued with that maddening itch that I couldn't quite scratch. No, not Red Hot in my crotch. That itch to become an entrepreneur.

And I was closer than I knew . . . .

Chapter 7
On My Own

❧ ❧ ❧

*P*eople would look at Chuck Barris and instinctively reach into their pockets for loose change. They just naturally assumed that he was a panhandler. He was perpetually rumpled and disheveled, and his hair looked as though he began each day by wetting a forefinger and inserting it into a live electrical outlet.

But he wanted to give that impression. It made people misjudge him, underestimate him. In sizing him up, they would make the mistake of assuming that he slept on a steam grate and lived under an overpass. Right away, then, he had an advantage over them.

Chuck had a genius for knowing what the public wanted—especially what television viewers wanted—and he had an absolutely unshakable courage in his convictions. He hatched *The Dating Game* when everyone told him it would never work. It was the same story with *The Newlywed Game*. Those two shows, in turn, spawned a series of hits, including *The Gong Show* (the show he's most famous for). The critics might not have thought too much of his programs, but Chuck's banker sure did.

I met Chuck because he had a bad back (probably from carrying around all that money). Shortly after I had started tutoring Jay Snider in karate, Ed Snider asked me to go to New York—in his personal limo—to see if I could alleviate the pain of a friend. I'd never been in a limo in my entire life. If Ed had told me we were driving to Hades and that Satan was the chauffeur, I'd still have been scrambling to get in. Then, when I found out who it was we were going to see—Chuck Barris!—I'd have volunteered to crawl naked over a bed of broken beer bottles just to get there!

When I was in college, the world stopped for the half hour that *The Gong Show* graced the TV screen. It was this outrageous talent contest in which ordinary lunatics would perform harebrained acts and a panel of B-list celebrity judges would rate them. When an act was really awful, one of the celebrities would slam a giant gong to oust the contestant. It was great! We'd bet each other on which of the weird contestants would get gonged and which one would end up with the incredibly cheap first prize. Chuck was our hero.

Fast Eddie came along for the ride, and we elbowed each other and grinned those can-you-believe-this grins all the way up and back. Us in a limo! Going to meet Chuck Barris!

Our hero, it turned out, was staying on 57th Street in a one-bedroom apartment that was stuffed to the rafters with . . . well, how to be polite about this?

His place was crammed with junk.

But good junk. Neat stuff. His "crazy collectibles," as he called it. Chuck had originally rented the place for a weekend. But it felt so right, so natural, that he kept it. As with his own look, appearances didn't matter all that much to him. He was interested in what felt comfortable, which in turn would relax his mind and keep it productive.

So I cleared out a space and went to work on his back. He began to feel better. I worked on his back for a short time, but it was his brain I really wanted to work on. As I was relieving his pain, I was also bombarding him with questions! He appreciated what I could do for his back, and he also understood and respected my hunger, my consuming interest in entrepreneurship. I like to think that he saw some of the driven wild man of himself in me.

Over the years we developed a friendship and a mentorship. He'd call me when his back would flare up, and as I worked on him I would ask him for counsel. During one of those conversations, I told him about the Aspen dream that I had passed up and how I yearned to do something on my own. On the spot, he invited me to fly across the country and come visit with him in his Beverly Hills home—to "think."

Come to a different environment, he said. It'll give you a whole new perspective on life. Leave where the sun rises and come to where it sets. It will turn you around and give you a fresh slant. The thought of just sitting and thinking held about as much allure for me as Red Hot in my underpants. But the sponge in me whispered, urgently: *This is your chance to learn from a genius.*

Chuck and I boarded a plane in New York the next week. Immediately he put down the seat-back tray, pulled out a cigar box, dumped the contents, and set busily to work. He looked like a mad jeweler. He took a small file and began to scrape the back of one of his expensive wrist watches. Then he took a St. Christopher's medal and began to scour the back of it. Then he glued the medal to the watch, tried the watch on, nodded with satisfaction, put it in the cigar box, got out another watch and another St. Christopher's medal, and began the whole process again. Time was precious to Chuck. I supposed that it meant so much to him that he would only entrust it to a higher authority. That, and the fact that he was ragingly superstitious.

 PAT CROCE POINTER
You never know when something that seems insignificant at
the moment might later trigger an awesome idea.

I watched this eccentric with the hairdo of a petrified porcupine, bent over a seat-back tray five miles above the earth, absorbed in trying to wed a timepiece with a religious medallion, and I thought to myself: *This is one strange whack job.*

Definitely my kind of guy.

And then I remembered what Aristotle said: "There is no great genius without a mixture of madness."

While I didn't share Chuck's superstitions, there were some of his peculiarities and oddments that I did incorporate into my own routine.

Ripping, for one.

Chuck was a voracious and scattershot reader, and whenever he happened onto something that stirred an idea in him he'd rip it out of the newspaper or magazine or pamphlet or book that he was reading and file it away. I began doing the same thing. Much to the dismay of my soul mate. To this day, Diane won't let me near a paper or magazine until she has had a chance to go through it first. Otherwise, it's liking reading Swiss cheese. But you never know when something that seems insignificant at the moment might later trigger an awesome idea. (In fact, it was an item that I ripped out of *The Philadelphia Inquirer* in the fall of 1995—about the value of the 76ers and the future potential of the National Basketball Association—that emboldened me to pursue ownership of that franchise.)

Besides ripping, Chuck was very big on noodling and doodling. He was constantly writing down random thoughts and stray ideas, so he was obsessed about always having a pen in his possession. He might wander off without his wallet, without his keys, without his driver's license, without combing his hair . . . but he was never, ever, without his pen. His explanation was that you never knew when an idea might sneak up on you, and that ideas are like butterflies—capricious and apt to flit away as quickly as they have come.

So a pen is the net you trap them with. A pen can erase a bad memory. We'd be in the middle of a meal and if the muse suddenly afflicted Chuck, he'd start scribbling on whatever was handy. He'd fill up his napkin with furious scribbling and, if you weren't alert, would snatch yours and busily turn it into Page 2. But he never had to torture himself later by trying to recall the details of that idea that had seemed absolutely brilliant back there in the middle of lunch.

I took to carrying a pen at all times, and still do. A felt tip. Pilot Razor Point. It makes a clean, surgical stroke. The nuns always liked my penmanship. They boxed my ears for my deportment (and most of the time rightly so), but they always marveled at how such a squirmy little soul could have such a precise script. It's the tidiness in me. And Chuck's dependency on the pen appealed to me because it meshed with my own natural impatience, my need to do a thing now. You write it down, you don't forget what it is you were supposed to do.

I do go through a lot of pens, though. I keep wearing down the tips because I press too hard. Who ever said writing is supposed to be Yin?

I raved to Fast Eddie once about the importance of memory-joggers, and he not only began to carry a pen himself, but also a fat pack of those tiny yellow Post-it notes. I'd turn to say something to Fast Eddie and he'd already have the pen working on a Post-it. He'd have those little tags running up one sleeve and down the other until he looked like a walking to-do list. But we'd never reach the end of a day and wonder if there was something we'd forgotten to get done.

In California, I slept at Chuck's gorgeous house on a graceful, breathtaking slope in Beverly Hills. But we did our hanging out in his three-room apartment on Rodeo Drive. It was a larger version of his New York hideaway. There was "stuff" everywhere. Pipes . . . canes . . . books . . . guitars . . . hats that he'd worn on *The Gong Show* . . . piles of stuff everywhere. Every item triggered a memory of some sort.

And sometimes an idea.

Every wall was covered with blown-up photos. Even in the bathroom. And in the very center of the living room was his desk, a sprawling three-sided thing that was a repository for the droppings of Chuck's brain. He dumped all his jottings here—the crumpled note papers, the ideas scribbled on receipts, the ripped-out articles, the inked-up napkins, the toilet paper on which he had recorded some notion, some perception, some seed of a possible television program.

The desk was illuminated by three lamps attached at different angles. It was brighter than dawn. Strewn about were hundreds of pens. The entire mess would sit there and percolate and ripen and age, waiting for him to circle round it and then reach in and pluck out something else that he could convert into dollar signs.

With lots of commas and zeros.

The most fertile thinking spot, however, was what Chuck called his "stoop." You'd climb three steps up from the street and make a left-hand turn, and there would be the front door to his apartment. And in front of it—facing Rodeo Drive—was a three-foot-by-four-foot concrete slab with a lawn chair. There we would sit and watch the creatures of California pass by. Chuck in the chair and me on the top step. It was an endlessly fascinating parade. We'd sit and observe and I'd do my sponge thing as Chuck spun tales from his past, of how he had to persist when everyone was telling him his ideas were so much garbage. He'd had more than a few doors slammed in his face. I could relate, on a smaller scale of course.

He defined a genius as someone who shoots at something no one else can see—and hits it. He would never let discouragement get the better of him, he said. Negative thoughts only drain you. So he always believed in himself, no matter how many failures piled up around his feet. The greatest pleasure of all, he said, was in doing what everyone else told you that you couldn't do, and succeeding. I had a chance to read his fictional autobiography, *You and Me, Babe.* And I spent long, captivating hours on that stoop listening to that wild-haired genius generously share his philosophies, and graciously relive all the failures that had preceded his first success.

And gradually this thought took root: *If he can do it, so can I.*

And so can you!

❦ ❦ ❦

I flew home from Chuck's knowing that I could wait no longer. It was time to act on my dream of starting a privately owned sports-medicine company.

Following my creation of a detailed business plan, and with the support of positive feedback from potential referring physicians, I resigned from Haverford. Hospital management made it difficult with enticing offers of more money, more space, more equipment, but none of those points were an issue. I wanted something of my own, that would fly or fall due to what I did, or didn't do.

I had ambition and ignition. I had knowledge and experience. I had confidence and vision.

What I didn't have was money. But I knew where they kept it.

Harmon Spolan, the president of Jefferson Bank at the time, listened attentively to my eager and grandiose plans to convert my evening OAR business into what I would call "Sports Physical Therapists." It would be a service-oriented business that would blend the sleek look of a fitness center with the pristine sanitation of a hospital and with the techniques and attitude of a professional training room. I had a 1,300 square-foot facility scouted out. It would be modest, but it would be mine.

For forty thousand dollars.

Harmon said that would be no problem, just sign this personal guarantee.

That would be a problem.

I balked because I had read too many stories of people losing their homes in pursuit of their business dreams. If I was going to fail (and I would have had to die first), I didn't want Diane and Kelly and Michael to be left homeless. On that point, I wouldn't budge.

Harmon was understanding. Instead of kicking me out of his office, he said he'd advance the money in exchange for my signature on an insurance policy for the amount I wanted to borrow. I couldn't write my name fast enough.

Fast Eddie understood my position and agreed. And in the next few years, he would explain this philosophy to lenders and enable us to borrow ever increasing amounts of unsecured money. But it became inevitable that as we opened more facilities, we would reach the point where we needed such significant amounts of money, that if I didn't sign the loan papers we wouldn't be able to keep growing. So I capitulated. But by then we were off and running, and the reward outweighed the risk.

So on January 1, 1984, my first center (the first of what would swell to forty centers around the country) opened in an office strip mall behind a shopping center in Broomall, a suburb southwest of Philadelphia. The decor was black and white, broken by dabs of scarlet. The equipment was the very latest and the very best. I wasn't about to skimp.

Jimbo and Scramble Head were my full-time staff. Mack, Mitch, and Cochise were part time. Fast Eddie would join me later, but for a while he remained at Haverford Hospital as director of the original clinic there. We didn't want to desert the hospital. They had been good to us, and vice versa. Besides, you never know when you might want to go back across a bridge, and if you've burned it, then you're stuck.

The walls of the inaugural Sports Physical Therapists were bare at first, but very soon they would be covered by enlarged color photos (à la the Chuck Barris school of interior decorating) of my celebrity patients, including Chuck himself along with Philadelphia sports stars Mike Schmidt, Julius Erving, Bobby Clarke, Charles Barkley, Moses Malone, Garry Maddox, and Maurice Cheeks.

In addition to equipment for treating the injured, we had treadmills and stationary bikes, rowing machines and steppers, muscle-pumping machines and free weights. Schmitty and Dr. J and the rest of them began to come on a regular basis—not so much because they were injured, but to prevent themselves from being injured and to prolong their careers. That little sweat palace became a gathering place for all the marquee names in Philadelphia sports.

We adhered to the three basic psychological necessities of working out: music, mirrors, and peers. The music had to be fast and blasting to keep you revved. The mirrors were for staring into to make sure that your form was correct . . . and also for vanity (they helped reinforce the good you were doing for yourself). And peers? It's always easier to work out when you have company. You can push each other along. The time passes more quickly. And shared sweat is a powerful epoxy; it can bind people together in special ways.

But still, we were very much medically oriented, and wanted to be perceived as such. We were, after all, a physical therapy center. I didn't intend for Sports Physical Therapists (SPT) to become known as just another fitness center or a typical muscle-head gym. But I wasn't opposed to expanding our financial opportunities, either.

Garry Maddox, who had been an elegant center fielder for the Phillies, asked if I could do him a favor and design an exercise and nutrition program for a guy in his neighborhood, Shelly Liss. I called Garry "Venus" because of his uncanny resemblance to the character "Venus Flytrap" on the popular TV series *WKRP in Cincinnati*. At the time, Garry was rehabilitating a lower back injury. Mack and I developed a strict 12-week program for Shelly based on guidelines set by the American College of Sports Medicine. We monitored him carefully. He lost fat weight, gained muscle mass, improved his cardiovascular conditioning, discovered new reserves of energy, and found that his entire attitude about life in general had brightened.

  PAT CROCE POINTER
I was certain that vanity and ego could be used to our advantage. There is no marketing tool quite as powerful as simple human nature.

We were onto something here. Besides maintaining our service to injured high school athletes and weekend warriors, we were on the verge of establishing a brand-new avenue of fitness—one that would cater to a market that, as yet, did not exist.

We called it the "Executive Fitness Program." We were able to use the same space, same staff, and same equipment to fashion a medically-based, telemetry-monitored, personalized fitness program for . . . well, they weren't exactly patients, so what were they? We decided to call them "clients." These were wealthy men and women who were often physically bankrupt, so to speak. No one was admitted without a thorough physical examination and an exercise prescription from their personal physician.

They were charged triple what they would have paid at a typical health club.

Didn't matter. They kept coming.

And they kept coming back—for 12 more weeks, and then 12 more after that. These guys and gals had a strong streak of masochism, obviously. They enjoyed the frenetic pace and the various and most fiendish ways we motivated them. They enjoyed the ultra-positive atmosphere and the spirited camaraderie. But most of all, they enjoyed the results. They came to learn the simple fact that, after all their hard work, they looked and felt better. Instead of fleeing from life, they rushed to embrace it. Instead of wanting to escape from the world, they wanted to participate in it.

We never advertised the Executive Fitness Program, at least not in the traditional sense. But I did hatch the idea of offering radio personalities the opportunity to take one of our 12-week fitness programs for no charge at all. They'd lose weight, gain muscle, feel re-born and, of course, would not be able to resist crowing about the program while they were on the air.

I was certain that vanity and ego could be used to our advantage. There is no marketing tool quite as powerful as simple human nature. And when people begin to receive compliments on how they look, they can't wait to babble on and on about what they're doing and, most important, where they're doing it.

My first big score was a man who happened to be my favorite deejay. Pierre Robert (pronounced "ROW-BARE") was a throwback to the age of the flower child. Like Chuck Barris, his appearance was deceiving. If you concentrated only on how he looked, then you'd miss the substance underneath. In dress and manner, he was a complete hippie. His hair hung down to his waist, and he had a Rasputin-like beard. He was as mellow as a day in May—a tie-dyed-in-the-wool Deadhead. But he was also a very bright and quick-witted guy with a silver tongue. He was absolutely charming, with a voice made for radio—soothing and s-m-o-o-o-o-t-h.

He was also a nutritional disaster. Which made him perfect for the program.

Like millions of people, he had an on-going battle with his weight. It would yo-yo wildly. He would exercise frantically and follow a vegetarian diet. But what meat he did avoid, he more than made up for with the consumption of his idea of exotic "all-natural" foods. Like tofu hot dogs. Lite beer. Reese's peanut butter cups. Ben & Jerry's ice cream by the tubful. Pierre's concept of trail mix was M&Ms, Gummi Bears, and Oreos. So he swayed between 180 and 220 pounds, and for at least a decade I had a standing wager with him: the day he reached 175 would be the day that I'd chant and dance and spin about like one of The Grateful Dead's loyal fanatics. I never had to pay up.

The year after I opened the first center, Pierre began broadcasting live fitness segments from there. He'd pedal and puff away on a stationary bike and breathlessly sing the praises of cardiovascular training. Very soon I began recording 60-second fitness and nutrition tips that aired daily during Pierre's highly rated mid-day shift. I did those for the next ten years, virtually up to the day that I consummated the 76ers deal, and I never received a penny. But of course the advertising and the publicity and the good will were of inestimable value.

Plus, I made a lifelong friend.

* * *

One step inside our kitchen door, the first pie nailed me—tossed by my princess, Kelly.

Whipped cream full in the kisser.

Twenty-nine more followed. One for each year of my life. Talk about getting plastered . . .

And I loved it! Best ambush I ever walked into. Fresh from a Saturday afternoon workout, I walked smack into a storm of pies. Flung, with love, by family and friends. Happy Birthday, Pat.

Splat! Splat! Splat!

Every family has its own traditions, and in my family one of the more revered and pleasurable—if slightly perverse—traditions, is the food fight. On special occasions we eat, we drink . . . and we throw. Some of them are elaborately planned, and some just develop spontaneously, triggered by nothing more than an innocently lobbed olive. We can see a single grape rolling down a table and that will be enough to set us off.

I don't have a sweet tooth; I have a sweet index finger. I see icing or frosting, and I can't resist taking a big swipe of it and then decorating some innocent bystander's nose. Those who know me (and my heir apparent, Michael) are always on the alert. They keep their heads on swivels.

Yes, I have my whack-job moments too. But I have a theory that there is real emotional value to a food fight. It can be cathartic. And it can act as a real ice-breaker at times. And at other times it's just downright fun.

Although we didn't throw food at our patients and clients (and we certainly didn't throw darts), we did generate excitement and laughter among them with carefully aimed water pistols every now and then.

Through fun, fitness, and fanatical physical therapy, our business was booming and our celebrity clientele list was growing.

And they kept coming back for more.

Chapter 8
Don't Throw up on My Flowers

❧ ❧ ❧

Michael Jack Schmidt hit more home runs than all but six players in the entire history of baseball by the time he retired. He played eighteen star-studded seasons for the Philadelphia Phillies, and was arguably the greatest third baseman of all time. He was a three-time league MVP. He won multiple Gold Gloves and Silver Sluggers. He was a first-ballot Hall of Famer.

And there I was, screaming at him: "You ain't Jack Shit!"

And he would look at me—the sweat running off him in rivers turning his shirt dark as mud, the veins in his temples thick as lead pencils as oxygenated blood pounded through them—and through a face contorted in agony he would . . .

Smile!

And ask me for more.

Mike Schmidt was a workout machine. He enjoyed pain and suffering so much, had such a consuming passion for conditioning, that I couldn't help but wonder if maybe we had been separated at birth.

He first came to me, limping, reluctant, and a little suspicious, one weekend in 1984. I had been recommended to him by a mutual friend. Still, he wasn't sure he wanted to entrust his body (which was his living, after all) to a stranger. My rehabilitation reputation with the Flyers helped sway him.

So he walked into my first center in Broomall with a chronic hamstring problem (that's the long, thick muscle that runs down the back of your thigh) and a strain in his rotator cuff (tiny tendons in your shoulder). By the end of the 1983 season, Schmitty had hit 389 homers and had established himself as one of the best, but his body was deteriorating to the point that his career was in jeopardy of being cut short. In his mind, though, he was far from finished with baseball. So we set to work

91

on him. And he didn't retire until 1989 (159 home runs later).

He was the perfect patient, meticulous and obedient. He would perform every rehab exercise with pristine precision, and then request more. The more progress he made, the more rehab he wanted. He ended up playing five more seasons, and in the process fell in love with physical fitness. He saw how it could lengthen his career, forestall the aging process, and fuel him with energy—emotional and mental as well as physical.

He continued to come to the center on a regular basis, and we would challenge each other, push each other along. I took to calling him "Jack" all the time. You could see the confusion on people's faces. Why is he referring to Mike Schmidt as "Jack?" We'd smile. I often wondered how many Hall of Famers would consent to being called Jack Shit? He was such an elegant cheetah of an athlete that he made the game seem too easy, and many people misinterpreted his grace for nonchalance. In Philly, we want our players soiled from effort and suffering; we want their uniforms to be caked with grime and their faces streaked with sweat and blood, preferably fresh. And Mike Schmidt, with his effortless, loping style, occasionally came off as aloof and uncaring. In fact, he was just the opposite. Especially when he was Jack.

  PAT CROCE POINTER
I think working out is as good for your soul as a moonlit walk on the beach—they both make you awesomely aware of your utter insignificance in the grand scheme. They're both very healthy for your perspective.

He became the captain of our Egocentric Team. That was a small group of professional athletes, television celebrities, and high-wire business executives that gathered at 7:00 every weekday morning to indulge in a fitness frenzy. I thought I was obsessed with punctuality, but each day I'd arrive early and there would be Garry Maddox reading the *Wall Street Journal* in his car and Mike Schmidt standing and scowling, impatiently drumming his fingers on whatever chic vehicle he had decided to drive that day. Jack couldn't wait to get going. And if somebody missed a workout, or was late, either Jack or I prescribed the punishment. It usually entailed torturing the abdominals, was guaranteed to be painful, and was always humiliating because everyone else stood around and heckled. Although it was a great way to keep your stomach flat.

Not to mention your ego.

Over the years a lot of marquee names in the fields of sports and entertainment passed through the portals of my emporium of humility. They were all treated the same. We all had to perform the same grueling work, with absolutely no exceptions. That included the host. Working out is the great leveler. You can spend all of yourself, leave puddles at the base of every machine, and then crawl home, and yet an hour later it's as though you've never been there . . . . But your dedication is rewarded—with great health and fitness, and also with the sublime sense of accomplishment that can only be achieved through discipline and hard work. I think working out is as good for your soul as a moonlit walk on the beach—they both make you awesomely aware of your utter insignificance in the grand scheme. They're both very healthy for your perspective.

From time to time, a curious rookie would join the Egocentric Team for a session. Invariably, the rookie would show up either hung over or thinking he could pull a slacker job and get preferential treatment on the basis of his reputation. Ha! What he got was double measures of everything. And as the workout progressed, you'd see his face turn the color of dirty snow, and you'd hear his belly roiling and rumbling. He'd be ready to heave, and my response was always the same—so familiar that everyone else in the group would grin in anticipation and yell along with me:

"Don't you dare throw up on the carpet! If you're gonna puke, go outside."

There would be a pause while the nauseated penitent slunked toward the door, bent in half like a wretching seasick victim. And just as he reached the fresh air, I would fire my second shot of compassion:

"And don't throw up on my flowers!"

Only one automotive executive friend of Jack's, Euse Mita, ever returned from his private puketorium to resume the vigorous workout that same training session. I was so impressed with Euse's determination, not only was he accepted immediately into the Egocentric Team, but we became close friends. Birds of a feather flock together.

Music was important for these sessions. It had to be louder than a chorus of jackhammers so that we could all hear it over the hum of the machines and the cursing and the heckling and the laughter. The Flyers, most of them still in their teens or barely out, wanted rock 'n' roll. The 76ers preferred rhythm and blues. The business suits would go compliantly along with the consensus because they were accustomed to compromise in the board room and were concerned with doing what was politically correct—and because they feared the jocks would kick their asses!

The first guys through the door would seize sound control. Pretty soon disputes would break out at the door. Remember, these were all highly competitive, classic Type-A personality people. At first I tried a rotating system. We'd alternate: rock one day, R&B the next. But then some of the hockey players—among them Tim Kerr, Dave Poulin, and Ed (Boxcar) Hospodar—took out their teeth and placed them in a voodoo circle around the stereo. None of the basketball players, including Julius Erving and Andrew Toney, would go near the sound system. They were certain witchcraft was at work.

"Pat, they're using some kind of weird hockey hex," Julius Erving said.

"Yeah, and besides that," said Andrew Toney, "it smells like shit in there."

Mike Schmidt took control. On his own, he created a series of cassettes. He would produce his version of the Top 40, with DJ impersonations and radio bits that he envisioned as incredibly witty and unbearably entertaining. That opinion was not shared by the Egocentric Team, however. The reviews of his work were brutal.

During one of the workouts, one of the basketball players winced at the latest Schmidt mix and yelled out: "You may be Mike Schmidt in baseball, but Pat's right, you ain't Jack Shit . . . not when it comes to music!"

The room howled. None louder than Jack.

❦ ❦ ❦

Within a year of opening SPT, word had gotten around about our work with Mike Schmidt and Dr. J, who was also busy extending his career and proudly showing off a sleek and improved physique. And the Flyers continued to give glowing recommendations about us as well. Our reputation had developed just as strongly and quickly as our clients' physiques had.

So one day I got a call from John Nash, then the business manager of the 76ers. He wanted to set up a meeting with himself, general manager

Pat Williams, coach Matt Guokas, and me. The purpose was to talk to me about assuming the same position with the Sixers that I held with the Flyers—as team conditioning coach. The meeting had been requested by Harold Katz, the Sixers owner (and the same man who I would, years later, end up pestering to sell me the team). I was flattered; at that time the 76ers were one of the elite teams in all of sports, and had won a world championship in 1983. Also, I would be the first physical conditioning coach of an NBA team. I was very excited about the prospect of a new challenge. But could I handle more work?

Of course! Bring it on, no matter how big a job it may be.

Well it was big, all right. Literally. My two principal projects were Moses Malone, who was almost seven feet tall, and Charles Barkley, who was about six feet, five inches, and half a slice of pizza shy of 300 pounds.

But before I could get started, I needed to test them to find out exactly from what point we were starting.

The starting point turned out to be ground zero.

First off, pro athletes regard "tests" with the same fondness they hold for wind sprints. I wanted to give them stress tests, strength tests, flexibility tests, and vertical jump tests. I also wanted to find out their percentage of body fat, although on Charles I figured it would probably be off the charts. When training camp was to open in October, they were going to be required to run two miles in a specified time. Matty Guokas called me in July of '85 and said Moses would be in Philly that weekend and that I should come up from my vacation at the Jersey shore so that we could test him at his convenience. That was my initiation to the world of professional basketball—things were done at the players' convenience.

So there I was on a steamy summer day, standing next to this giant, who stood naked (save for a pair of Sixers shorts) on a treadmill. There were ten electrodes attached to his body and connected to an EKG machine (a heart monitor). A mouthpiece had been inserted between his lips to calculate his oxygen intake. He looked downright fearsome, like something out of Dr. Frankenstein's lab. I was straining my neck looking up and explaining to him that we would start up the treadmill, and that at three-minute intervals the speed would be increased and the incline would become steeper. Because of the mouthpiece, the only way Moses could communicate that he had reached his limit was by hand signals. Thumbs-down would signal that he could go no longer.

We fired up the treadmill. At the first 3-minute mark, we accelerated and elevated it. Moses promptly gave me a signal.

With his middle finger.

Fortunately, he was a man with a sense of humor, though you'd never know it to look at him. He perennially led the NBA in rebounding, even though his hands were disproportionately small, even though there were taller players, even though he jumped about as well as a door stop. But he was relentless and indefatigable. He went after every ball. And he did so with a scowl that intimidated a lot of people. And there he was, flipping me the bird three minutes into our relationship.

The test finished, I removed the EKG electrodes from Moses' heaving chest and told him: "Moses, you're going to have to be in better shape than this to do the two miles Matty is expecting."

And he cocked his head—with sweat running off it like spring rain running off the eaves of a house—and he looked at me and smiled and said, panting: "I can run two miles. I know I can run two miles."

Pause.

"I just don't know how many days it'll take me."

Moses' sense of humor served him well. He'd be pedaling away on a stationary bike, and I'd try to do something to take his mind off the pain. So I'd start a conversation, and he would reply in a curious manner, referring to himself in the third person:

"Moses can't talk now, Pat. If Moses opens his mouth, Moses' heart gonna flop out on the floor."

I just laughed, and Moses kept on pedaling. Suffice it to say that Moses completed the two-mile run without flipping a calendar page.

My other pet project on the Sixers also had a good sense of humor, and has gone belly-laughing through life with his mouth always open so that he can insert either food or his foot. He is the only person in the history of the printed word to claim that he was misquoted in his own autobiography. Which is wonderfully ironic, since he was known throughout his career as a quote machine—always ready to say something to make people laugh, or think.

Charles Barkley was an aberration. Fat men aren't supposed to be able to play full-court basketball. Fat men aren't supposed to be able to jump up and dunk with both hands. But Charles could . . . because he wanted to. Charles was almost as wide as he was tall. He was originally listed at six feet, eight inches, but in fact he was, and is, closer to six-five. In college, at Auburn, he was tagged with one of the all-time great sports nicknames: "The Round Mound of Rebound."

Charles' idea of nutrition was pizzas and soda. And when I say pizzas, I do mean plural, and I don't mean slices. I mean plural pies. With stuff on them. In his early days, Charles always ate more than one pizza at a sitting, and sometimes more than two. Washed down with an ocean of flavored, carbonated sugar water and caffeine. The only thing Charles liked better than eating was playing basketball. And, oh yes, women.

The 76ers wanted him in the 250-pound range. I mentioned aerobics and he frowned. I mentioned lifting weights and he sneered. I sought for ways to reach him, and finally found it through massage. Not by massaging his ego (which most professional athletes expect you to do). No, I got my foot in Charles' door by stretching him out. Charles loved having his leg muscles and back muscles worked. I already had a daily stretching ritual with Dr. J, and so I knew it worked for at least one world class basketball player. Why not one more?

In fact, this sort of stretching became so popular that other teams began adopting it. And if you go to an NBA game today you'll see, during the warmups, virtually all of the players lying on the floor while trainers and therapists kneel or stand over them, twisting them this way and that.

 PAT CROCE POINTER
 Fat men aren't supposed to be able to play full-court basketball. Fat men aren't supposed to be able to jump up and dunk with both hands. But Charles could . . . because he wanted to.

So I put Charles on a similar routine as Dr. J. And after I'd kneaded him like pizza dough for a while, gradually gaining his confidence, I began to work on his mind. Slowly, patiently, I introduced him to the stationary bike, and then to a circuit of strengthening calisthenics. Almost before he knew it, I had him trapped in a workout regimen.

But his diet was still a disaster. During a game he did not play in due to injury, Charles sat on the bench in street clothes with a one-pound bag of peanut M&Ms on his lap. By the third quarter, it was empty. And he hadn't shared!

I stalked him for a week, staked him out, and learned his habits. After practice it was his habit to retreat to his home (which really was his castle), order up pizzas, and indulge another passion of his—soap operas. He mentioned to me often, in all seriousness, that it was from the soaps that he learned much of what he knew about life. That was a truly frightening revelation.

One afternoon I waited in ambush for Charles' pizza delivery man. I removed one pie from its box and replaced it with a love note. I took half the other pie, and left instructions that, from that day forward, four slices were to be his ration. I warned the delivery man—through gritted teeth and with the most colorful of Yang language—that to bring Charles more than one box at a time would be to severely endanger each and every one of those body parts of which the delivery man was especially fond. I told Charles to switch to diet liquid. Unfortunately, Charles assumed that lite beer qualified as such.

Still, he shaved off almost fifty pounds that year. I had won him over. Plus, with the physical training came a mental awakening. Charles has an incredibly strong inner drive to succeed, and it soon dawned on him that lugging around all that extra weight would ruin his back, wreck his knees, compromise his abilities, and possibly cut years off his playing career. But he could see how the training was going to prevent those things from happening—how it already was working. He liked how he looked, how he felt, and how he performed due to the training, and so to complement all that effort he switched over to a semi-healthy nutritional program.

But he couldn't resist tweaking me from time to time. We'd be in a restaurant following the second practice of two-a-days in training camp, and when it was time to order a healthy meal, Charles would look at me and tell the waiter: "Steak."

"How do you want that, sir?"

"Large!" Charles would reply, grinning at me.

One early spring evening, I came home on a desolate and hushed Flyers team bus from Madison Square Garden. They had just been eliminated from the Stanley Cup playoffs by their hated rivals, the New York Rangers. The Flyers were brooding and melancholy. Their season was over. But mine wasn't. I rushed home and unpacked.

And then re-packed.

The 76ers were scheduled to open their playoffs the very next night, in Washington. I made a pit stop at the SPT center in Broomall, then hopped on the Metroliner to D.C. There was a message waiting for me at the hotel that said to meet coach Matty Guokas and his assistant, Jimmy Lynam, for dinner at a nearby restaurant. On my way out, I saw Terry Catledge and Charles Barkley in the no man's land between the bar and the hotel lobby.

Charles, who never asked anything in a soft voice, called out: "Say, Pat, does sex the night before a game hurt your play?"

I smiled. Two large, healthy, wealthy bachelors anticipating a night on the town in a city famous for its, uh, possibilities . . . this obviously wasn't a request for permission. So I replied:

"As a matter of fact, Charles, research has proven that sex is extremely effective at relieving pent-up tensions and anxiety, and might even actually enable you to play better . . . "

Charles' eyes widened. And then, over my shoulder, I threw in the postscript:

" . . . but only if you're married."

Their laughter trailed me out the revolving door.

And Charles' laughter greeted me when I returned from dinner. He called to me from a couch in the lobby. He was seated in the middle. There was a stunning woman on one side of him, and an equally stunning lady on the other side. In all of our discussions about nutrition, the subject of this sort of sandwich had never come up.

Charles beamed up at me like a sultan surrounded by his harem. He put an arm around each woman, looked at one and then the other, and said to me:

"I plan on being high scorer tomorrow night."

It occurred to me that he had a good shot of being high scorer tonight, too.

❧ ❧ ❧

Charles was shrinking but our physical therapy business was growing. I expanded the Broomall center. And then had to expand it again. We had gone from 1,300 square feet to 4,000 square feet, and that still wasn't enough. We needed to expand again, but how?

Later, at the height of the company's success, we would build up to 10,000 square-foot centers—forty of them in all!—each one containing more than a quarter of a million dollars worth of high-tech equipment. And whether they were in Philadelphia or Atlanta or Orlando, they all had the same feel and the same look. Mainly, the centers were brightly lit and the machines were shiny—for psychological reasons. Those weren't just people coming to us, they were patients. They had something wrong with them and were usually in pain, which meant they were also depressed and frustrated. Their psyches needed healing as much as their bodies. So the brighter and more cheerful the surroundings, the better. And the brighter and more cheerful the manner in which they were treated, also the better. When you're hurting, it always feels like winter— cold and dark and bleak. So we tried to manufacture some summer sunlight for their souls. It was a fantastic formula.

And that formula—which would spawn such incredible success— was already in place at the very first center in Broomall. I always knew our center was unique, thanks to all the repeat clients and the great reputation we had achieved. But what I maybe didn't realize—in the heat of the daily battle—was the true extent of success that our formula could generate . . . .

And besides, I had already achieved my goal of becoming an entrepeneur, right?

❧ ❧ ❧

Just more than a year after the Broomall center opened, a couple of primarycare doctors on the staff of Taylor Hospital—my old stomping grounds—urged me to open a second center, in Ridley, PA, where the majority of their patients lived. I was familiar with the area and I understood and appreciated their recommendation, but for probably the first time in my life (since meeting my soul mate), I hesitated. It was uncharacteristic. All my life, I never needed encouragement to leap off a cliff. But we had gotten where we were because we always delivered, and I had some doubts whether we could ensure the same high service standards at a second facility. Even though I had finally learned to effectively delegate authority and responsibility, our staff was already pretty thin.

Jimbo would accompany me to every 76ers practice and game. Fast Eddie would do the same with the Flyers. It was crucial that both franchises come to believe in Jimbo and Fast Eddie because during the playoffs both teams could be on the road the same week, or playing games on the same night—and I couldn't be in two places at the same time.

Also, we were on call 24 hours a day, 7 days a week during the two teams' seasons, which pretty much consumed nine months of every year. Jimbo and Fast Eddie became official members of their respective teams, held in such esteem that they were even included in the team photographs.

  PAT CROCE POINTER
There is one scale on which the weights never, ever change—and that is, family measured against anything else in this life.

Family, by the way, means everything to me. Not just on the business level, where it's important that everyone feel included and have a real sense of belonging, but on a personal level. My father made me aware of the importance of family. He worked three jobs but somehow he always found time to support me, and I have tried to pass that support along to Kelly and Michael. Recitals, games, plays, whatever they were involved in I found a way to be there. And still do. Every time I'm tempted to skip one of their activities because business calls, I remind myself about priorities. Business deals come and go, but family is forever. I never needed a letter from Diane to keep me focused on this goal. There is one scale on which the weights never, ever change—and that is, family measured against anything else in this life.

We debated opening a second center. Fast Eddie swung the issue when he suggested that we open the Ridley center and he be the temporary manager. That was good enough for me, almost. That old business axiom about surrounding yourself with good people and then backing off and letting them do their jobs is sound advice. I knew what Fast Eddie could do, I knew his zest for details. I knew how committed he was. Most important, I knew I could trust him.

Yet still I teetered on the edge of that cliff. I needed one last push.

Steve Mountain, as he has been for most of both our lives, was only too happy to oblige . . . .

    ☞ ☞ ☞

I met Mountain—I never call him by his first name—the summer between high school and college. We were both defensive backs for the freshman football team at West Chester. Before school even started, I saw Mountain do something that instantly won me over . . . .

He took advantage of me.

During the first summer night of our freshman orientation, Bator and I observed that most of the freshmen were underage—they could not drink legally. And what's college without beer? Looking considerably older than he was, and decades older than he acted, Bator could pass without any trouble at all. So I scrounged up money and Bator used it to buy cases of beer, which we then sold in the dormitory parking lot out of the trunk of his Camaro. A long, eager, and thirsty line quickly formed.

Of course, we screwed them. They were captive customers, at our mercy. Our prices were ridiculously inflated and sternly non-negotiable. They could buy by the can or the six-pack. Cash only. Absolutely no refunds. There was grumbling but everyone complied. Except for this one guy.

Mountain talked fast and tried to dazzle us with a deal that would enable him to buy two-for-one. We resisted, but I admired his effort. He smiled and said he'd be back later. He waited well into the evening, by which time what beer was left had gone warm. We were tired and ready to take our profits and go home. So we had an inventory clearance sale. Discount prices.

Mountain materialized out of nowhere. He bought up our leftover beer and made himself a tidy profit. He would end up becoming my business manager.

PAT CROCE POINTER
How can you sell your services if you don't listen to your customers' needs?

We did open that second center in Ridley, in 1986, and no one pushed harder for it than Mountain. He has been invaluable to me, both as a friend and as a confidante in my professional career. In fact, he and Diane are my sounding boards. They have a way of keeping emotions at arm's length when the debate turns hot and the issue is a particularly volatile one. They are the ideal antidote, the Yins to my Yang.

I'll want to break somebody's 206 different bones and Mountain will say: "Pat, let's negotiate with him, let's buy him dinner, let's get him to agree to these terms, sign this document, initial that one, and then when we've got all that nailed down . . . then you can send the body to the morgue."

I think Mountain's a genius at evaluating situations. He is incredibly patient. He can out-wait a drought. But probably what he does best of all is keep his mouth shut.

And his ears open.

He's such a good listener, in fact, that I required every one of my Sports Physical Therapists employees who was destined for a management position to undergo six weeks of what I called "Mountain Training." There would be role-playing in work-related situations to hammer home the point that, in everything, but especially in healing people's bodies and spirits, you had to listen and you had to hear. The patient is the one in pain. The patient knows what it is that hurts. How can you effectively treat the patients if you don't listen to them? How can you successfully service the referring doctors and insurance companies if you don't listen and ask questions? How can you sell your services if you don't listen to your customers' needs?

Behind closed doors we'd have some stormy business meetings, Mountain and I, and frequently those meetings would be presided over by Pat Yang. I'd be foaming at the mouth, and I'd jump up on the conference table and do a fandango of rage, and all the while Mountain would remain seated, his legs crossed, his temper banked. He'd wait for the thunder to subside and then look up at me and ask:

"You through now?"

It took me a while, but one day it dawned on me that the louder I yelled, the more he got his way. I'd do all the screaming and he'd win all the arguments. There was a lesson in there somewhere, and like that man who teaches mules to talk, Mountain finally got my attention. We became quite a tag team in business matters, forming a good-cop, bad-cop partnership. I'd ignite, Mountain would extinguish. I'd leave a mess, and he'd walk behind with his super-duper-pooper-scooper.

And how did I repay him? Well, among other things, with a bachelor party that lives on in the record books for putting it to your pal.

Mountain was, is, a huge baseball fan. So in honor of his impending matrimony friends of his had organized a bus trip to Baltimore for a game between the Orioles and the Detroit Tigers. My first problem was that Mountain's buddies were protective of him, and they were well aware of what trauma tended to befall my bachelor party victims. The handcuffs I'd had as a department store security guard got quite a workout. Once the unfortunate bachelor had drunk himself past the point of caring, he would be cuffed and left—cuffed to his fiancée's front porch . . . cuffed to a seat on a train bound for Boston . . . cuffed to the front door of Haverford Psychiatric Hospital . . . . These were all real-life experiences of unfortunate, yet dearly loved, friends. Talk about startling wake-ups.

Word of these escapades spread, so Mountain's friends suspiciously eyed us—me and Johnny (my youngest brother) and Mack and Fast Eddie and Jimbo—on the trip to Baltimore. But we were the very models of behavior. That, of course, was only to throw them off. We stopped for dinner at a nice Italian restaurant. Fortunately, Mountain had been drinking on the bus, and continued to do so through dinner. Periodically we would toast him from our table and challenge him to slam a shot with us. How could he refuse? We bided our time, waiting for him to go to the restroom. As soon as Mountain rose unsteadily to his feet, we headed, discreetly and nonchalantly but swiftly, to the men's room.

Which we quickly converted into an operating room.

When Mountain wobbled through the door, Johnny, Mack, and I ambushed him. Mack removed orthopedic casting supplies from a black bag we had packed and handed them to Fast Eddie and Jimbo, who were filling a sink with warm water. With trainer's scissors I cut Mountain's shirt sleeves off at the shoulders, Johnny pulled his right arm out to an extended position, and Fast Eddie began wrapping wet casting from wrist to shoulder. Jimbo set to work on Mountain's left leg, casting hip to ankle. Then Fast Eddie did the left arm, casting it in a 90-degree bent position so Mountain looked as though he were about to feed himself.

He also looked like something out of *Return of the Mummy.*

We'd put the casting on extra thick so that Mountain's struggles, no matter how feeble, wouldn't interfere with the setting. For those people who tried to get in the facility, we ran water and made wretching noises and said we were cleaning up after a terribly sick, "urp," friend. With an indelible black Magic Marker, Johnny thoughtfully drew glasses and a goatee on Mountain's thoroughly amazed face. For the only time in my memory, Mountain was speechless.

We opened the door and pushed the finished work of art out. Mountain teetered, then managed to remain upright, and began to hobble back to his table.

There was a moment of complete silence. And then even his friends began to roar. If Mountain was hoping to be rescued by them, he soon found out that they were finding great humor in his predicament. So great was their enjoyment, in fact, that they helped part the crowd and carry the casted, still-drunk Mountain up the concourse of Memorial Stadium and on up into the nosebleed seats of the upper deck in left field. He had been promised a baseball game and he jolly well was going to get one.

We left him there in the bleachers, with a Tigers batting helmet cocked at a rakish angle on his head. Mountain passed out and slept blissfully through the game, snoring noisily. It took the vendors several trips before they realized that the guy in the top row wasn't motioning them for a beer or a hot dog—his arm was stuck out like that because it was in a cast. We kept hoping some slugger would belt a pitch near him and he'd show up on TV.

My boys and I wanted to leave him there for the clean-up crew. Imagine awakening to a monumental hangover in a deserted ball park, with both your arms and one leg in a cast. But his gang out-voted mine. So we carted the heavy load home.

I know he forgave me because he's the one who kept urging me to expand the business, and open another center, and another one, and one more after that . . . .

So we did.

Chapter 9
The Triangle

❧ ❧ ❧

*T*here are love triangles. There are dinner triangles. There's the Bermuda Triangle . . . .

And one day while I was doodling, drawing my usual assortment of pinwheels and lightning bolts and stars and pirate flags, hoping to be struck by random inspiration, I sketched a triangle.

An equilateral triangle. I looked at it for a while, then continued to doodle. But I kept thinking about that triangle.

I operate on the theory that putting a pen on a pad is like rubbing two sticks together. Rub long enough, hard enough, and you can make fire. Doodle long enough, hard enough, and you may be able to coax an idea into life. Of course for every good idea, you're apt to fill a trash bin with discarded hieroglyphics. But at least doodling keeps your fingers moving and your brain idling. And I always want to be alert enough to snatch any stray idea that might come floating past.

That equilateral triangle would become the philosophical foundation of my business—and of my business approach—from that day forward. I looked at the three equal sides and tried to boil down what I wanted Sports Physical Therapists to be. What were my goals?

Well, I wanted to provide exceptional patient care—in other words, quality service.

I wanted to have fun. Work and fun shouldn't be mutually exclusive. Work doesn't have to be drudge. In fact, if it is, chances are you won't do a very good job. Some of the sourest, sorriest souls I've ever encountered are people who get up each morning and dread going to work because they detest their job.

And I wanted to make money. We all do, of course, but in the physical therapy profession in the mid-1980s, you didn't dare say that out loud. If you did, you were ostracized. Healing is a noble profession. The profit motive was regarded as some sort of perversion. But why? None of us ever took a vow of poverty. I was turning patients and clients into customers. I was one of the first to advertise our PT services. Up until then, the standard operating procedure was to hang out your shingle and depend on word of mouth. But as my mother once said, churches ring their bells just to let you know they're there.

So I wanted to provide quality. I wanted to have fun. And I wanted to make a profit.

Quality. Fun. Profit.

It would be our mission statement. In three words. Seven vowels, nine consonants. No verbs. No clutter. None of the three more important than the other. None of the three possible without the other. Just like the three sides of an equilateral triangle. . . .

 PAT CROCE POINTER
 There's nothing so simple that someone can't misunderstand it. Almost always, the problem can be traced to communication.

I didn't want to make money but not have fun doing it. And I didn't want to make money at the expense of my patients; the profit wouldn't come from shorting them on the quality of service.

I also didn't want to have fun but not make money. Laughing is good for the spirit, but you can't pay your bills with yuks. Besides, my conscience wouldn't permit me to have fun while skimping on service.

And while I wanted to provide quality service, I sure wanted to get properly paid for it. And when you provide quality service, your patients appreciate it and your business blooms. And that is fun.

You may remember that mission statements were all the rage in the 1980s. Corporations poured a lot of money and manpower into developing them. Problem was, they tended to be wordy and pretentious. And pretty much useless because most employees didn't understand them.

So I used the principle that is applied in weight-lifting: kiss. In other words, "Keep It Simple, Stupid."

Fun. Quality. Profit. You didn't have to understand geometry to understand my triangle. Or did you?

There's nothing so simple that someone can't misunderstand it. Almost always, the problem can be traced to communication.

The best illustration of this I've heard involves a college student who got a summer job on a farm. The farmer stopped by the barn to ask his new hired hand: "Where's that horse I asked you to have shod?"

"Did you say shod?" the student asked nervously. "I thought you said shot. We just finished burying that sucker."

The moral is, no matter how carefully and completely you think you have explained something, the very last words out of your mouth should always be:

"Does anyone have any questions?"

And anyone who does ask a question should not, under any circumstances, be ridiculed. All mockery does is produce resentment in every employee, guarantee that no one will ask questions, and provoke the staff to perform their duties with a total absence of pride. Instead, every question should be taken seriously, given proper consideration, and answered in full. In fact, every question should be treated as an opportunity to increase the quality of service. (Which, in turn, would increase the fun and the profit!)

To that end, I was big on motivational and bonding meetings. Not the kind of meeting that is convened just to "have a meeting," nor the kind that those in upper management arrange in order to justify their jobs. No. These meetings had to have a purpose. Mine were more like high school pep rallies—noisy and boisterous and spirited. But there was substance, too.

I took to hosting monthly company staff meetings for everyone—all managers and staff were invited. The managers of each center, in turn, would hold weekly staff meetings, and then meet with each employee, one-on-one, once a month. That probably sounds like a lot of meetings, but I never wanted an employee to feel left out of the loop. If you had a complaint, you had the chance, frequently, to voice it. Same for suggestions. Same for compliments. Same—most important of all—for any questions.

You hear a lot of corporate blather about employee empowerment. In fact, many businesses only want robots—obedient, subservient, and unquestioning. Such businesses only cheat themselves.

But if you expect your employees to listen to you, then you ought to listen to them when you ask for their input. Every time I've ever felt puffed up with confidence, certain that I needed no help, I've always collided with reality.

Once it was nearly fatal. . . .

❧ ❧ ❧

In 1989, I had got it in my head that earning a helicopter pilot's license would somehow fill a hole in my life. I should have been worried about filling the hole in my head.

I took hours and hours of lessons. My instructor was Frank Hudson, a veteran of the Korean War, who knew as much about flying as birds do. Frank taught me at the Wilmington Airport in Delaware. The day for my solo flight arrived. Frank felt I was ready. I, of course, was positive I was ready. I always wanted to have the controls and I chafed under supervision—not just in a chopper, but in anything.

As a warm-up, we took a trial flight—I had the controls and Frank sat to my right in the co-pilot's seat. It was late-afternoon on one of those extraordinarily clear, crisp days that convince you that anything is possible. Following Frank's instructions, I headed west into the sunset and toward a small mountain ridge several miles away where I was to make a U-turn. On the return trip, five miles from the airport, I radioed the control tower for clearance to land. (Flying is not like driving—you don't just drop out of the sky and into the first open parking space you can find.)

My landing was soft as a baby's breath, and right on the center of the helicopter pad. Frank got out, gave me a thumbs-up of encouragement, and moved away to watch his pupil take his first solo flight.

Solo? Suddenly I never felt so alone in my life. No co-pilot, no security blanket. I was the bird. And I got very weak in the wings. Droplets of liquid anxiety began to crawl down the back of my neck. The helicopter got airborne, though how it did I'm still not sure. I must have been flying it from memory.

Without the 180 pounds of co-pilot next to me, the chopper began to list to one side. I had to make immediate adjustments. But gently, carefully. A chopper has to be flown with both your hands and both your feet, and their subtle pressure on pedals and handles produces instant alterations. You have to fight the tendency to overreact. Sudden, sharp movements can cause things to happen that you really would rather avoid.

Like crashing.

My solo flight was to take the same course as the warm-up flight. I flew into the sun, over the ridge, and made my turn. My misgivings began to evaporate. This was actually going quite well. Maybe I was a natural. Me and Lindbergh. Me and the Bird Man.

And it was about then that I looked down and noticed a series of high-power electrical lines. You know how sometimes your mind will produce some terrifying image out of nowhere? Well, the image my mind elected to present to me at that moment was of a sudden mechanical failure, the chopper careening out of control like a wounded hawk, and locking into a slow death-spiral right onto those wires.

Which then would fry me into a crispy critter.

I began to sweat. The inside of the chopper reeked with the smell of fear. But I steadied myself. Deep breaths. Positive thoughts. Yin. Yin. Yin.

Then I saw what I was certain was the landmark for the five-mile radius around the airport's runways. Sweet relief. I coaxed my tongue back up into my mouth and cleared my throat and worked the radio:

"Wilmington Tower, this is helicopter 53 Papa Charlie," I croaked, straining to be calm.

After identifying yourself, you are to inform the tower of your altitude, position, and purpose. I did:

"Six hundred feet. Five miles to the west. Requesting permission to land."

I resisted the impulse to add: "And scared shitless!"

The tower controllers told me to keep on coming, and to inform them when I was a mile out. I looked down and saw cars, and more of those deep-fry power lines, and school buses with kids pouring out of them on their way home from school, and . . . wait a minute! That wasn't right. None of this looked familiar.

Panic squeezed my colon. The beads of sweat on my brow formed rivers that poured over my sunglasses. And then it hit me: What I had believed to be the airport's runway—when I was at the five-mile landmark—turned out to be, instead, a huge K-Mart parking lot!

I was lost!

I was lost in space!

I had misplaced an entire airport! (And all because I hadn't been pay-ing strict attention.)

The moment that realization hit me, it felt as though I had per-formed, involuntarily and simultaneously, every single bodily function that a human being is capable of.

I looked frantically for something familiar on the ground. I looked frantically in the cockpit for something to wipe the sweat out of my eyes. I also looked frantically around for air traffic. What if I had wandered into the flight path of another craft? I'd be roadkill. My hands and feet seemed to have a life of their own. They worked by themselves while my brain inanely screamed: "Pull into a gas station and ask for directions!"

A ghastly scenario raced through my mind. I'd run out of fuel and crash in a bright ball of flame. What they'd find left of me wouldn't be enough to fill a thimble. At my funeral, the priest would say: "Poor Pat, if he'd just been listening . . . if he'd just been paying attention . . ."

It was at that point that the folks at the Wilmington Tower, bless 'em, radioed me, wondering why I hadn't checked in when I was a mile out as they had instructed. I was never so happy to have been missed.

"Wilmington Tower," I said humbly, "I'm a student pilot and I have flown off course."

If I wasn't so scared, I might have added: "Can I pick anything up for you while I'm over K-Mart? They're having a blue light special."

The tower people were nice. They didn't make remarks about a pathetic rookie pilot who didn't know whether to wind his ass or scratch his watch. They turned on the rotating beacon. (Leave a light on for me, Ma, I'm comin' home.) The beacon was bright, even in daylight. It was also only about two miles away to my left.

I landed safely. Actually, considering my emotional state, it was a remarkably precise landing. And then I sat there while the last of my confidence formed a puddle of sweat at my feet.

I looked out. There came Frank, smiling, ready to congratulate me on my first solo flight. What he should have done was what my Dad would have done—box my ears in for not listening.

Maybe the very first thing I remember my father being stern about was listening. If you didn't keep your mind and both ears open, he'd close them for you. Somewhere along the line I'd forgotten the importance of paying careful attention. My maiden helicopter solo had been a sledgehammer of a reminder. From then on I became a world-class listener.

To ideas, suggestions, grievances, directions, and instructions.

Especially instructions.

❦ ❦ ❦

We kept opening new centers, first in the Philadelphia area, then in New Jersey, and then farther out—up to Minnesota and down to Florida. I was always mindful of something I'd heard said by Zig Ziglar, the motivation guru: "If you help others get what they want, then you'll get what you want."

I found this especially applicable to employees, and it was reinforced when Diane and I went to Japan.

  PAT CROCE POINTER
Somewhere along the line I'd forgotten the importance of paying careful attention. My maiden helicopter solo had been a sledgehammer of a reminder. From then on I became a world-class listener.

The Cybex Corporation had invited me to be a guest speaker, probably in appreciation of all the computerized testing equipment I bought from them—literally boxcars full. We spent a week in Tokyo and Osaka. I gave four four-hour presentations on the concept and practice of sports medicine and fitness in America. I was aided by a translator who was so adept that not only was her Japanese better than mine, but so was her English. To show my respect, I spent six months prior to my visit studying Japanese so that once there I could speak a reasonably coherent paragraph during my presentation, and so I could use everyday phrases in conversation. I had also convinced my tutor, Kuniko, to provide some choice words for use during "saki" happy hour.

The neat freak in me responded instantly to the Japanese reverence for cleanliness and discipline. I was pretty successful in the service business, but I was overwhelmed by their concept of service. They had a knack of not only serving you, but of conveying the impression that it was their great pleasure to do so. And in so doing they made you, the customer, feel truly special. That was precisely what I wanted to instill.

And everywhere you looked there was such attention to detail—cab drivers wore white gloves, the backseat headrests were covered with white doilies, and when we reached our destination the back doors opened automatically, even before you would start to turn your body. The overall impression was that they were always one thoughtful step ahead of the customer. And, unfailingly, they would tell you: "Domo arigato." Thank you. They were doing the serving and yet they were the ones doing the thanking. That, too, was worth emulating.

We traveled from Osaka to Tokyo via the famed Bullet Train, the Shinkansen. We had heard that it was never late. We couldn't help but smile at that. Never late? Sure. Still, to be safe we were at the station early. And here came the Shinkansen, a virtually noiseless missile. Ten minutes early, yet. The train hadn't even stopped and the platform was overrun by brigades of cleaning women, who lined up and waited for the Shinkansen to disgorge its passenger load. When the last passenger was safely off, a whistle blew and the cleaning women grabbed their equipment and sprinted on board. Their work done, they exited and we boarded. The train began to pull out of the station—precisely on time—and I looked out the window only to see the cleaning brigades lined up in a row, smiling cheerily and waving farewell.

They behaved as though it had been a great honor to have cleaned for us. But at the same time they did not have the posture of slaves. It dawned on me that here were people who took great pride in what they did and how they did it. They didn't feel their work was menial in any way. They realized that they were performing the best kind of service— they were making other people feel good. I brought all that back with me and incorporated it into our Triangle.

Fortunately, our employees took to it instantly. In turn, I consistently let them know they were appreciated. I made sure our managers lavished compliments, both verbal and written. And I averaged about fifty personal notes a week myself. Positive reinforcement is a wondrous thing. It begets itself.

And as we all know, a compliment and a dollar will buy you a cup of coffee. So I was big on bonuses and surprise gifts. "Tips," I called them. We were, after all, in the service business. I remembered from my days delivering newspapers and shining shoes how a tip made me feel—not only appreciated, but also self-fulfilled. It gave my work meaning. So starting with the very first center in Broomall, we would establish long-range goals and quarterly objectives, and when we met or exceeded them, the tips would come. Sometimes, money. One time, watches. Another time, cell phones. And one evening a truck backed up and out poured color TV sets for everyone.

The Japanese had it exactly right. There is no unimportant job. And the jobs you tend to take for granted as a manager are actually the most crucial to your business. Two examples:

1. Receptionists.
2. Secretaries.

They make your first impression for you, and you know what they say about first impressions: You never get a second chance to make a first impression. Either by phone or face-to-face, they are your first contact with patients or customers. They set the schedules and they collect the payments. They can, by attitude alone, make your clientele feel satisfied and happy, or frustrated and angry. They have the first hello and they have the last goodbye—two very powerful links.

At our centers we designated the secretaries and receptionists as our windows to the world. From the start, I scheduled special evenings on Hallmark's wonderful creation, "Secretaries Day." When the Broomall center was an initial hit and continued doing so well that I was encouraged to open more centers, I wanted to show my appreciation to Scramble Head and to Punky (Beth Schwartz, whom I named "Punky" in honor of her new-wave hairdos). I decided to turn each of them into Cinderella for a night.

Their coach was a limo, long and luxurious and equipped with champagne. They were picked up at their homes and presented with striking floral arrangements. Diane and I drank a toast to them en route to the restaurant. After dinner, one of those belt-looseners, we retreated to the limo for dessert.

But not just the usual dessert. Special, individual treats. Punky's was a pair of diamond earrings. When her shrieks of joy shattered the glass in the limo, I knew that it had been a good choice. The limo crossed over the Walt Whitman Bridge into New Jersey and purred into a shopping center in Cherry Hill. It was late and dark and deserted. We got out and walked to the nearest building, a fur salon. It was midnight. I banged on the door. Instantly, all the lights, inside and out, flared on. It was bright as dawn. Scramble Head blinked. The owner of the salon opened the door and grandly ushered us in.

"Pick yourself a coat," I told Scramble Head.

Her shrieks broke what windows Punky's hadn't. I think she tried on every coat in the entire fur bank. But she found exactly the right one.

So had I, I told them both. So had I . . . .

       ❦ ❦ ❦

Looking to exploit my energy level and expand my pulpit, I asked Mountain what he thought about me taking on a one-hour, live, call-in sports-medicine radio talk show. He thought I was stretched too far as it was. I told him I still had untapped Spandex in me. I could stretch to the moon and back. Okay, he said. He understood my need to preach what I passionately believed in, and he had connections at an AM station in Philadelphia that had just changed to an all-sports format. The call letters were WIP, and the dial spot was 610.

I came on at 10 each weekday morning. I answered questions about exercise and diet and sports injuries. But that alone wouldn't be enough to hold and entertain an audience for an hour, so I usually invited a guest—an athlete, doctor, inventor, author, or some sort of sports celebrity. I cranked up my own exuberance each and every day, which isn't hard at all when you believe in what you're selling. (And I was also able to indirectly promote our Sports PT centers.) I wanted plenty of P & V—piss and vinegar—in the show. I was so worked up that they could have opened the windows at the station and turned off the transmitter for that hour.

A signature line quickly evolved. I would greet every caller with an enthusiastic "How are you?" And I had a stock response whenever I was asked the same question:

"I feel great!"

So that had to be the caller's response, too. No lame "okay." No tepid "good." No lethargic "so-so."

You'd better feel great and say it as vibrantly as bells chiming, or else I rudely hung up on you. I would give you a second chance in case you forgot the first time. But after that, it was "great" or you were gone—or gonged! It's in the mind, really it is. If your mind says it feels great, your body will listen. And even if you don't truly feel great, lie to yourself anyway. You'll be pleasantly surprised at what may follow.

PAT CROCE POINTER
I cranked up my own exuberance each and every day, which isn't hard at all when you believe in what you're selling.

I tried to boost the energy level of every caller. And I was so persistent, so anal about getting that "I feel great!" response, that sometimes bizarre conversations seeped out onto the airwaves. To wit:

Me: "Good morning, John, and welcome to the show. How are you?"

John: "I'm hanging in there, Pat. How are you?"

Me: "I feel g-r-r-r-e-a-t, John. But your answer wasn't acceptable. Now, how are you?"

John: "I'm doing okay." Gong! (I had a slew of chop-busting sound effects at my disposal.)

Me: "John, John. Come on now, work with me. One last time, John, how do you feel?"

John: "I feel great!"

Me: "Attaboy, John. Good job. That's the attitude. Now, how can I help you?"

John: "Well, I was in a skiing accident this past weekend and I broke my back and my right ankle and I tore up my right knee. I'm here in a hospital bed and I was wondering what isometric exercises you could recommend."

Me: "Wow, John, you're incredible. Just think, you could break all those bones and still feel great . . . . "

Mostly we had fun, the callers and me. The show had a good run— four years. We made a lot of friends and helped a lot of people.

I only received minimum union scale to do the show, and Mountain and I decided from the start that I wouldn't personally endorse any product or service on the air. That would preserve my integrity, and so when I recommended a specific piece of exercise equipment or running shoe or dietary supplement, the caller would know I wasn't on the take—that I hadn't been bought off. Like all of our patients and clients, the callers were entitled to an honest, unbiased opinion.

But I did have fun tweaking some of the show's sponsors, much to the delight of the listeners, and to the riotous enjoyment of my producer. Every once in a while the last spot coming out of a commercial break would be an ad for something that ran directly counter to my message about fitness. Sometimes I thought maybe the producer of the show deliberately scheduled the commercial sequences in that order just to hear my reaction, knowing it would make the listeners howl.

For example, a certain well-known fried chicken franchise seemed to run an inordinate number of commercials during my hour. As soon as I opened the microphone back up, I'd say: "And if you eat that fried chicken, make sure you tear off the skin first, throw it up against the window, and watch it stick there for a while until it starts to slide down in its own grease. That's what it does to your body! You might as well slap it right on your butt or paste it to your thighs or mount it to your spare tire!"

On the other side of the glass, the producer would be rolling on the floor.

PAT CROCE POINTER
I firmly believe that the earlier you can get started working out and eating right, the better. We tend to form habits for a lifetime when we're young.

During my tenure at WIP, there was a period when bee pollen was in vogue. It was touted as having the power to give you great spurts of vitality. There were commercials for it during my show that made glowing claims of how it would give you the energy of a nuclear reactor. I bit almost completely through my lip, but kept silent about this alleged magic potion . . . until one day when a caller asked me about its alleged benefits. As a healer, I had to be honest. I could see the producer's eyes bulge in anticipation.

"It's your choice if you want to ingest bee pollen," I told the caller.

"But in case you aren't sure what it is exactly, let me explain. A worker bee flies up to a flower and sits on it and rubs his ass on it. Then the company that makes bee pollen wipes the bee's ass and gives it to you to swallow."

By now the producer had broken three ribs from laughing. But I wasn't done:

"Now if you're a queen bee and you produce 48,000 eggs, to the great pleasure of all your worker bees, then maybe eating ass-wipe pollen might have some appeal to you. But if what you're looking for is a good roll in the hay, I'd just invest my money in a water bed."

The last echoes hadn't died away when the station management called me on the carpet. Either I tempered my remarks or my radio days were numbered. By then, however, the "I Feel Great" slogan had become as permanent a part of me as my pirate-ship tattoo, and with it I created a spinoff—a traveling motivational fitness show for grade-school kids in the Philadelphia area.

I firmly believe that the earlier you can get started working out and eating right, the better. We tend to form habits for a lifetime when we're young. So Ray Man and I would visit a couple dozen public and private schools each year with the "I Feel Great Show." I charged nothing. I had only two requests—one, that everyone wear sneakers (to get in the proper mood), and two, that my presentation would include the entire student body and would take place during the last hour of the school day. Because by the time I was done with them, they'd be so wired that they'd be useless in class and the teachers would never forgive me.

Ray Man and I used music, slides, prizes, and surprises. We had those kids hopping around like crazed kangaroos. The show became so popular that we had a three-year waiting list. I didn't want anyone to have to wait, especially if it meant forming good habits, so I had to find another way to reach them all.

I approached Carl Hirsh, the president of the Spectrum (a popular venue for assorted concerts and ice shows, and at that time the home of the 76ers and Flyers) to propose an "I Feel Great Show" in that arena. Instead of preaching the fitness gospel to a few hundred kids a week, I could reach 15,000 at a pop. Carl agreed, though not without some misgivings. But he became a quick convert. The first show was a smash, and we ended up doing an annual show for the next four years.

We cranked up music to a decibel level approaching a 747 at takeoff. We set off indoor fireworks. We had strobe lights flashing like prairie lightning. We brought in huge names—Michael Jordan, Billy Joel, Evander Holyfield, DJ Jazzy Jeff and the Fresh Prince (a.k.a. Will Smith)—

live or via video to further excite the crowd. These inspirational guests told their own stories of hopes and dreams . . . where they had come from and how they had gotten to where they were.

The kids were from third grade through eighth grade—8 to 14 in age. They never sat down during the show because we never gave them a chance to. The message itself was fairly subliminal (even though it came wrapped up in an explosive spectacle of good-natured mayhem). I wanted them to learn without beating them over the head and alienating them. "GREAT" came to be an acronym for:

G—Give compliments!

R—Read!

E—Exercise!

A—Avoid drugs!

T—Think positive!

Actually, those five points are worth following your entire life. If you go back and read the acronym again, you'll see that there are absolutely no age or sex limitations to any of these principles. Anyone can choose to embrace and enact these standards for living. And by doing so, you are certain to increase your own personal standard of living.

We'd have big-name stars from each of Philadelphia's four major professional sports franchises make surprise appearances. Some of them would suddenly materialize in different sections of the audience. Others would emerge from darkened ramps into spotlights. We gave away hats and buttons and pencil cases, and fifteen mountain bikes which the celebrities, usually led by the Flyers' star, Eric Lindros, would ride around the arena floor.

The show was carefully choreographed, but there was always one athlete who would show up and improvise:

Charles Barkley.

I was always nervous because you never knew what Charles was going to do. But he genuinely loved kids, and they were always drawn to him—probably because they sensed he was still one of them.

One year, Charles told the kids how his younger brother had suffered a stroke as a result of drug abuse. It was a heart-wrenching moment. The only sound in the jammed arena was Charles' voice. If he managed to scare even one kid off drugs that day, then the whole show had been a rousing success.

Another year, Charles took a microphone and roamed through the audience, plopping down amid giggling kids and interviewing them. He sat down next to one pudgy boy, who probably reminded Charles of himself, and asked him to speak his dreams out loud.

"I want to be a pro basketball player, just like you," he told Charles. Charles told him "Fine, go for it. But not at the expense of your education. Do that first." And then Charles took off his game jersey and gave it to the boy. It was a poignant moment, reinforcing what I've always believed in and tried to pass on:

Always shoot for the moon. Even if you miss, you might grab a star as you go by.

Chapter 10

The Ten Commandments
of Customer Service

❦ ❦ ❦

*T*he great Eugene Ormandy once dislocated his shoulder while conducting the Philadelphia Orchestra. Dislocated!

Think about that. Isn't that wonderful? We've all heard of pitchers firing with such fury, with such abandon, that they throw their arms out of their sockets. And quarterbacks who occasionally get pile-driven to the turf with such fearsome force that their shoulders are wrenched out of joint.

But a symphony conductor?

A man who wears a tuxedo, not pads? A man whose only weapon is a thin sliver of a baton that's not much bigger than a knitting needle?

This man dislocates his shoulder?

Indeed, he did. And all because of passion. All because he got so caught up in his work that he was driven to wring from himself and his musicians the very best that they had to give.

Ormandy was leading the orchestra in a performance of a symphony by Brahms. It was going, according to all accounts, quite splendidly. Ormandy was demanding and the artists were responding and it was all building to a perfect, shattering crescendo.

Then they got to the part where, in the margin of one page, Brahms had written the instruction: "As loud as possible!" And so Maestro Ormandy, with great punches of energy and sweeping flourishes of his baton, summoned tidal waves of sound from his musicians.

A few bars later, Brahms had written another instruction: "Louder still!" Dutifully, Maestro Ormandy hurled his whole being into one last violent spasm of a request for even greater volume, for one final gust of symphonic eruption.

He got it.

And in so doing, dislocated his shoulder.

Remember, this was a certified genius. He could have coasted on his reputation. If he had been even a little less demanding of himself and his musicians during this performance, who in the audience could have detected? Who would have known?

Well, *he* would have known, for one. And his musicians would have known. And none of them could abide that. So pride drove him, and them. Pride and passion. A passion for their work.

And that is exactly what we tried to spread among our employees at Sports Physical Therapists, and continue to spread among our 76ers staff and players—an exuberant, infectious passion for their work.

But inspiration does not come without effort, and it definitely does not come without guidelines and principles to work by.

When Sports Physical Therapists began, I was (as you know) hellbent on providing the absolute best customer service possible. I did what I suspected was the right thing to do—be nice to people, be positive, be proactive, be prompt, etc. At first, it was all just instinct. Then, little by little, the actions and postures and tone of our overall service philosophy began to take shape. Eventually, we came up with ten standard principles of language, action, and attitude that were to become our virtual playbook.

We called our principles the "Ten Commandments of Customer Service." And we found over the years that you can apply them to any business, as well as to your personal life, to create an atmosphere of success. And so here they are. Feel free to make them yours . . . .

1. HELLO ... AND GOODBYE

If you were a patient at one of my Sports Physical Therapists centers, we'd get you coming . . .

And then we'd get you going.

There was no escaping a hearty "hello" at the sound of your first footstep, and an equally cheery "goodbye" the moment you turned for the door.

Every staff member was required to greet you and then to send you on your way . . . and they were required to do the same to each other as well. Without exception. Regardless of personality, mentality, or disposition. No matter if they were shy or introverted, or even if they had laryngitis!

And a mumbled "hello" did not count. Neither did a tepid "goodbye." You had to say it like you meant it, even if you didn't. It had to be robust, hearty. Boom it out. Try it yourself for a day. You're apt to be surprised by the results.

Most of us mutter our greetings out of reflex. They come stumbling out of our mouths, nothing more than insincere asides devoid of genuine feeling. We pass each other and exchange these limp salutations, and for their scant effect we might as well have saved our breath.

So try some sonic booms on for size! Greet everyone with exclamation-splattered, bell-ringing, echo-chamber *HELLOOOOOO!!!* thunderclaps, and then watch what happens.

You're likely to startle the people you meet, and they'll probably give you a quizzical look at first. But inside they'll feel a stab of guilt, thinking, *Geez, he knocked me backwards and I only gave him the usual whisper.* Then something magical happens. They are apt to resolve right then and there to hit the next person they meet with a sonic boom themselves. Just the thought of preparing for such a greeting is enough to straighten them up, to put a little pep in their step, a little glide in their stride. Why, if they're not careful, they may even feel the need to smile.

PAT CROCE POINTER
Goodbye, delivered with the proper enthusiasm and energy, implies that you look forward to the next opportunity to tell the customer "hello" all over again.

Make them smile. Make them work out those facial muscles. And all from one word, from one simple little five-letter word that was the very first word most of us ever learned. You see, it's all in the presentation.

Goodbye, however, is a little trickier. Goodbye takes some work. Hello is a reflex, but goodbye has to become a habit. Goodbye seals the deal. Goodbye tells them you still care just as much as you did when you told them hello (and were anxious to take their money). Goodbye says you mean what you've said. Goodbye, delivered with the proper enthusiasm and energy, implies that you look forward to the next opportunity to tell the customer "hello" all over again.

Goodbye, well-meant, sends them out the door feeling appreciated and respected, as opposed to feeling totally alone or abandoned. It tells them there will be a next time. The right goodbye will help make them want to come back.

One of the first things I did as the new owner of the 76ers was to schedule a monthly meeting with the event staff of the First Union Center, our arena. These are the ushers and ticket-takers, about 250 in all, and while they are not technically employees of the Sixers, the patrons perceive them to be. And as we all know, perception can be more important than reality—especially when you're selling and servicing.

At the monthly meeting I remind them of our Ten Commandments of Customer Service. I remind them that in many respects they're every bit as important as the players because, while the fans want to see a win, they want to be treated well, too. The Sixers can pull out a thrilling win at the very end of a game, but if the patrons have had an unpleasant experience with a surly usher or a rude vendor, then their glow from that victory is going to vanish. They won't enjoy themselves. And they might not come back. So I emphasize to the staff the importance of the hello, and the equal importance of the goodbye or good night.

The first such staff meeting I had, one usher raised his hand and asked: "How do I react when we've lost and some fan tells me where I can stick my goodbye?"

The rest of them laughed. So did I. We'd all either been born in Philadelphia or we'd become accustomed to the Philly "atty-tood." We tend to devour our own in this town. The scenario he was suggesting wasn't just plausible or possible—in Philly it was virtually guaranteed.

I told him, and all of them, that for every bird flipped to them, for every crude response to their goodbyes, they should lick their index fingers and mark one up in the air for us. That's a small victory for our team.

Being nice is a game in itself. It's a game we want to win.

You can, too.

Think of someone you don't especially like—never have and never will—but whom you have the occasion to see often. Maybe you don't speak. Maybe you only exchange cursory nods. Well, that's all going to change. Starting now, hit that person with the sonic-boom hello. *Every* time you see them. Yes, it will be an effort at first. Yes, you will feel hypocritical. Yes, they will probably sneer at you. But keep at it. It will get easier. And almost from the start, you're going to feel good about taking this new approach. Maybe you'll even feel great! You should. This is a triumph over yourself, and there is no tougher opponent.

You're going to feel the teeniest bit smug. Maybe a little superior. But that's pardonable. Indulge yourself a little. You're going to make them feel petty, and perhaps even guilty. Eventually, they may even feel compelled to reply likewise. They may feel they have to answer back.

And who knows then what magic might evolve. Why, it might even lead to the start of a friendship . . . .

2. FIRST-NAME BASIS

Is there a lovelier sound in the whole wide world than the sound of your own first name being spoken aloud?

Of course not. Silk on satin is not nearly as smooth. A soft spring rain on parched ground is not as sweet or as welcomed. It is a basic vanity to which we are all susceptible. It is the first identity we learn. It is the first thing that separates us from everyone else. It is what we carry for our entire life.

So, at our Sports Physical Therapists centers, we used a patient's first name at every opportunity. Except when a person wished to be addressed by title—Doctor, Reverend, Father, Your Honor, etc.—or if he or she preferred the respect and formality of Miss or Mister.

Whatever pleased the patient pleased us.

Of course, if I were around them long enough, they were going to get tattooed with a nickname.

And, incidentally, I think a nickname is something that most people secretly enjoy because it's even more personal than a first name. Providing, of course, that it isn't perceived as cruel or demeaning by the person who gets it.

I'll never forget my school days, and the start of a particular new school year with a very strict teacher. A nun, no less.

"You, sir," she said, pointing to me, "what is your name?"

"Pat," I answered cheerfully.

She shook her head in rebuke and made a sour face of disapproval.

"No," she corrected me. "We do not use nicknames or contractions. So then, your full name is Pasquale."

She pinched her lips, and primly moved on. She pointed to the boy sitting next to me.

My buddy Bator. Born, of course, Joe Masters.

Now the whole class was braced. Bator was always a wild and crazy guy, and the class anticipated some serious entertainment.

"And you, sir, what is your name?"

"Joesquale!" answered Bator, who always was quick to catch on.

To this day, there is a spot inside me that still hurts from holding in the laughter as the nun smacked Bator for his insolence!

During our karate workouts, Master Fred Scott and I talked frequently of the oriental philosophy that the quality of your practice, play, and work come to represent who you really are. To maintain the respect that your name commands should be paramount in your every endeavor.

Yao Shiuo, the famous Chinese philosopher, said: "When a tiger dies, it leaves its skin. But when a man dies, he leaves his name."

I was so struck by this saying that I asked Master Scott if he would use his family contacts in Japan to engage a calligrapher to inscribe it on rice paper. My intent was to frame it and then present it to Mike Schmidt in celebration of his induction into Baseball's Hall of Fame. It would be a unique commemoration, yet it seemed simple enough to secure. But after a year, an entire year, I still didn't have it.

The Japanese are very superstitious, especially when death is concerned. They shy away from using any form of the verb "to die," or any other word that suggests expiration.

Master Scott's friends finally found a calligrapher who was willing to risk bucking the superstition, but he balked (no pun intended) as soon as he learned the identity of the recipient. Baseball is enormously popular in Japan, and Mike Schmidt's name is revered there. The calligrapher felt unworthy of such a momentous request and, with all courtesy and respect, declined.

  PAT CROCE POINTER
We live in a world that's often cold and impersonal. Anything we can do to de-ice that world is helpful to all of us. When you use a first name, you personalize your experiences with people.

There was a happy ending, though. It got done, finally. And by none other than Kyoshu Imai, one of the official calligraphers to the Emperor. In the process, I came to have a whole new appreciation for the importance of a name.

Every employee at Sports Physical Therapists wore a name tag. I think that's vital. We greeted the patients on a first-name basis, and we wanted to make it easy for them to respond in kind. We wanted them to feel comfortable, at ease. It's the same goal I have for the fans on game night at the First Union Center. The entire Sixers staff is identified and ready for service.

And I try to extend this courtesy outside of my own business, as well. Take restaurants. If I am waited on by a server without a name tag, I always ask: "Excuse me, but what's your first name?" I'll probably forget it as soon as I leave the restaurant, but at least for that time the person serving me won't have to hear "Hey you!" Or "Excuse me, Miss." Or "Pardon me, Sir." No. They will hear their name.

We live in a world that's often cold and impersonal. Anything we can do to de-ice that world is helpful to all of us. When you use a first name, you personalize your experiences with people. There are enough instances in life where our identities are already condensed to numbers. Any time you can oppose that impersonal attitude by using a person's first name, you help make the world a better and brighter place.

The patients who came to us at SPT were feeling down already. We needed to work on their spirits as well as their injuries. A hearty hello and a booming goodbye, coupled with the use of a patient's first name, tended to be the best kind of medicine—simple to administer, easy to swallow, and with immediate effects.

Greeted, wished farewell, and called by their first name, patients were more inclined to come back for more therapy (even though it was mostly pain and drudge to which they were returning). Anything we could do to make it more intimate not only helped them, but helped us—they became more cooperative and receptive to our treatment (i.e. pain and drudge).

As with hello and goodbye, the important part of using first names is consistency. It can't be applied once in a while; that's worse than never. Because if you've got a patient just about cheered up, and then one day they come through the door (anticipating the warmth of hearing their first name) and there is no greeting and no first name, the effect can be devastating. Then your sincerity would—and should—be seriously questioned. The patient will be thinking: *Oh, so I'm really just another piece of meat around here, after all.*

This scenario illustrates the most important element of these Ten Commandments of Customer Service: consistency.

Every day, every way, call those first names out loud.

3. LISTEN. LISTEN. LISTEN.

Anatomical fact: We have twice as many devices for hearing as we do for speaking.

Two ears. One mouth.

It is logical, then, to suspect that our maker intended for us to listen twice as much as we speak.

Unfortunately, it is a vice of human nature to fall in love with the sound of your own voice. And as with any vice, there are pitfalls that come with the territory. If you speak long enough, the odds are pretty good that you'll get around to saying something you regret. Also, in speaking so much, you throw away the chance to learn.

There's an old Italian proverb that makes that point perfectly: *From listening comes wisdom. From speaking comes repentance.*

I've heard a couple of variations on this:

You never have to regret what you don't say.

And . . .

If you're listening to someone else, you're giving yourself the chance to learn something new. But if you're only listening to yourself, then you're not learning anything that you don't already know.

Every rehabilitation session, every workout, every staff meeting . . . I ended them all with the same important request: "Any questions?" And that was followed by my most important job of all—listening. While maintaining eye contact. While making notes, either mentally or on paper with my trusty Pilot Razor Point 2.

We don't want to hear what we don't want to hear. That, too, is human nature. So in the service business, we naturally don't want to listen to complaints. But when we do listen to complaints, then it's possible to turn a negative into a *double* positive. I found that when we listened to a patient's complaint about our service, and then moved to rectify the complaint, first we helped ourselves by improving ourselves, and then we helped ourselves all over again because we turned the complainer into a convert, and he or she would spread our praise.

"I told them they were doing it wrong," the patient would say to friends and family, feeling self-important as their explanation continued . . .

"And you know what? They did what I said! I won't go any place else now. They're definitely the best. They actually listen to you!"

People are so accustomed to being tuned out, to being an unheard voice, that they are always shocked, and then quite pleased, when you do listen to them. And *respond* to them. With the 76ers, my senior vice president is Dave Coskey. He oversees marketing, public relations, and community relations, which are pretty standard departments in most franchises. But he's also in charge of a unique department—*fan relations*—and his lieutenant is none other than Bator. Their job is to make the customers feel great. They're our ears to the public.

The credo of the Fan Relations department is: *What we don't want to hear is exactly what we should listen to most.*

The complaints may be something that are easily fixed, like an unstable armrest on an arena seat. Or they may be beyond fixing, like a father writing to ask if we could change the 76ers home schedule to avoid a conflict with his son's bar mitzvah. So our philosophy is to fix what we are capable of fixing, but absolutely do not ignore what we are not capable of fixing. It would have been easy enough to toss the bar mitzvah letter into the circular file and dismiss it as a quack request. But that is not what top-shelf service providers do.

So Bator made sure the young man and his father received a letter of sincere apology, explaining that the NBA schedule was drawn up by the league office and could not be adjusted. Enclosed was an autographed photo of our superstar, Allen Iverson, congratulating the young man on his passage.

I'd like to think we made a couple of Sixers fans for life.

The neat thing about listening is that it empowers you. It is true that people who talk and talk and talk can monopolize the conversation. But it is also true that people who listen and listen and listen—and then ask strategic questions—can *control* the conversation. Never underestimate the power of silence.

Merv Griffin, the businessman and entertainer, has said that when he bought Resorts International (the Atlantic City hotel and casino) from Donald Trump, he was purposely mute, determined to listen and to let the other man do all the talking.

"We sat down to negotiate," Merv said, "and he talked and I listened. He almost collapsed because I just sat there staring at him. He didn't know what to do. He talked for thirty minutes and I never said a word."

Donald's continuous monologue provided Merv with the time and information he needed to form the appropriate answers when it was his turn to counter in the negotiations.

It's true: The best way to persuade people is to just listen to them.

One of the greatest temptations in conversation is to interrupt someone and finish their sentences for them. This is not only rude, but it's also a sign of great arrogance. And, it's self-defeating. Instead of really hearing what the person is saying, you're smothering their ideas and their knowledge with your own prejudices. But if you listen—and try to comprehend—then you're demonstrating that you're less interested in having your own way than in finding the best way.

 PAT CROCE POINTER
The best way to persuade people is to just listen to them.

When Jay Snider was president of Spectacor, the corporation that owned the Philadelphia Flyers, he had the occasion to listen to the concerns of several Special customers. He listened attentively. And after hearing them, he ordered the removal of several clusters of seats throughout the Spectrum. Those conventional seats were replaced by wheelchair-accessible seating. This was done before passage of the American Disabilities Act.

Jay's measures went even further than expected. He ordered the new seating areas installed on the first level—closer to the action, but in the high-rent district. However, not only did he position security ushers near those areas, but he also charged these Special customers the equivalent of the lowest-priced seats in the house.

These people didn't have the opportunity to select their own seats. So he did it for them.

He was able to do this because he listened to them in the first place.

4. COMMUNICATE CLEARLY

There is a wonderful book by Robert Fulghum entitled *All I Really Need to Know I Learned in Kindergarten*. The title speaks the truth. For example, we learn at a very early age that if we make a mess, we should clean it up. We learn to say "please" and "thank you." We learn that a nap is always nice. We learn that when we go out into the large and sometimes frightening world, it is always comforting to hold hands.

But somewhere in the process of growing up, we tend to forget these simple truths. But they're still in there, living inside us. They never die because they are so deeply ingrained. We learn these truths so completely as children because they are communicated to us with great clarity. Think about it: have you ever been spoken to more clearly than when you were a small child? Do you ever speak more distinctly yourself than when you speak to a small child?

I'm not suggesting that in business you should address everyone as though they were four years old (although, come to think of it, there are times when you need to do precisely that). But the principle of clear communication applies. You cannot make things too simple. You cannot be too specific.

Making a clear and full explanation is like going around closing windows—the windows that might otherwise be left open to misunderstanding. Because when windows are left open, people make assumptions. And as you know, when you A-S-S-U-M-E, you make an ass of you and me.

 PAT CROCE POINTER
Making a clear and full explanation is like going around closing windows—the windows that might otherwise be left open to misunderstanding.

So when somebody says to me, "How about a lunch meeting next week?" I start closing windows.

"Okay. Next Wednesday." That's one window.

"At 12:30." That's another window.

"At Norm and Lou's Deli." That nails everything down. That closes all the windows. No assumptions are possible!

In our physical therapy sessions, we were always very specific with patients. By the time we got finished closing all the windows, our explanations were air-tight.

"You do the exercise, like so. You hold and count to ten on each repetition, like this. You do one set of fifteen repetitions in the morning. You do a second set of fifteen repetitions in the evening. Do you have any questions?"

If a patient doesn't understand, if all the instructions haven't been communicated clearly, then there is a possibility that the therapy exercises will be done wrong and may end up causing damage rather than healing. The potential for harm is always there if you do not make yourself perfectly understood.

Consider this typical scenario: You're driving along and the person in the shotgun seat is giving you directions . . . .

"I make a left up here, don't I?"

"Right."

"Oh, a right. I was sure I was supposed to make a left."

"No, you're right."

"Right?"

"No, I don't mean you're *right*. I mean you're *right*, you do make a left."

Of course by then you're five blocks past where you were supposed to turn because the navigator said "right" when what he really meant was "correct." Ah, but "correct" sounds so formal, doesn't it? "Correct" sounds so, you'll pardon the expression, *correct*. And who wants to waste the time or energy being so *correct* when you can just be casual?

But if you are not correct, then you're wrong.

Take, for example, the man who rang the doorbell of a mansion and asked the lady of the house if he could do some work in exchange for a hot meal. "Well," said the woman, "it just so happens I have two gallons of green paint in the garage. If you paint the porch, I'll give you dinner."

Two hours later the man reappeared, his clothes covered in green paint. "I finished the job, ma'am, but I'm afraid you've been ripped off."

"What makes you say that?" asked the woman.

"That's not a Porsche in the garage, that's a Chevy."

The woman did not communicate clearly. And neither did the man. She lazily made her request, and he did not ask any questions.

The most important part of communicating clearly is enunciating distinctly. It takes a measure of discipline to achieve, but it's an important habit to cultivate. For example, I force myself to give any answer that is in the affirmative as "Yes."

Not "yeah."

Not "yep."

And not the sheepish old "uh-huh."

Those are sloppy. And the reason people speak like this is simple:

verbal laziness. It's the oral form of slouching. Try "yes" on for size and see if it doesn't make you sit up straight, both physically and mentally. Now put some zest in it:

YessssssSSSSSS!

It's contagious, too. You keep saying "yes" with energy and passion, and pretty soon the people you're talking to will begin to feel like slobs. They'll start responding in kind. You'll feel the enthusiasm circulating.

My father trained me. He was strict about a lot of things, and saying "yes" was one of his pets. I learned soon enough that saying "yes" made home a much less painful place to be. And later, I learned that the tips tended to be larger when you were dispensing a vibrant "yes" to any customer's request.

Your message must be clear not only in speech, but also in memos, faxes, letters, e-mails, smoke signals—in all forms of communication!

And when you are putting together a management team or a staff of employees, be sure to match up individuals who complement each other's communication skills. If one person is vulnerable in the area of remembering customers' names, for example, match them up with a person who's got a photographic memory and can spot (and *name*) a customer from a mile off in heavy fog.

The simplest explanation of this concept that I've heard is from a snippet of dialogue in the movie *Rocky*. I love that movie! You may remember that Rocky Balboa (another Philly guy) was thick of tongue and thin of brain but full of true grit. His girlfriend, Adrienne, was as shy as he was extroverted, as quiet as he was brash. They seemed terribly mismatched, and yet they made a seamlessly welded couple.

"I got gaps, she's got gaps," Rocky explained. "But together, we got no gaps."

They understood each other. They sensed each other's thoughts. They communicated. They just *knew*.

And that's when the true magic occurs.

This kind of magic occurred a few years ago during the Special Olympics in Seattle. There were nine contestants at the starting line of the 100-meter race, and each of the nine athletes had either a physical or mental disability. They shared the experience of living a challenged life. What they also shared was the great blessing of being able to communicate with each other.

The starter's pistol cracked and all nine took off. Only a few steps out of the blocks, however, one of the runners got tangled in his feet and fell. He landed in the dust, lay there, and wept—partly in pain, partly in frustration. The other runners heard him, slowed their strides, and then stopped. They looked at one another, turned, and then ran back up the dusty track to the fallen boy. Not just a couple of them . . .

All of them.

And when they reached the boy, they helped him to his feet. A girl with Downs Syndrome kissed him on the cheek. "That will help make the hurt go away," she told him, and he smiled a little.

One of his knees had been twisted in the fall and so he couldn't run on that leg. So the other eight lined up alongside him, four on each side, and the nine of them linked arms and walked together down that dusty track. They crossed the finish line as one.

Here they had come to compete against each other, and instead they finished as one entry, united as one entity, and no one was left behind to cry in the dust.

What a glorious triumph for the human spirit.

What a shining moment for communication.

5. BE NEAT, CLEAN, AND FIT

Let's say you're being encouraged by a physical therapist or trainer to start a daily walking regimen.

"It'll whittle away some inches from your waist," he tells you, "and that in turn will help alleviate that lower-back problem you've had for so long.

"And walking is great for your heart and your lungs and your circulation," the therapist goes on. "It can help lower your blood pressure and give you more energy. You'll get more oxygen to the brain, and that will help you think better. Your entire outlook on life will perk right up. All that from just putting one foot in front of the other!"

You're sold. And then you look at the therapist. Wrinkled, baggy pants. One shoelace untied and flopping like a dying worm. Belly bubbling over the belt. Shirt tail creeping out.

One word flashes in neon above his messy hair: "Hypocrite!"

Followed by another: "Slob!"

I think it's true of every endeavor—but especially in physical therapy and physical fitness—that you have to practice what you preach. People just naturally respond more readily to someone who takes an obvious pride in their appearance. Being neat, clean, and fit automatically establishes you as a person who can be trusted, as someone who knows of what he speaks, and as an authority who should be given due respect.

There's an old saying in physical therapy: "If it's physical, then it's therapy." I wanted all my staff benefitting from that kind of therapy, because wellness makes good business sense. Healthy employees are naturally more productive. So I instituted the two-hour rule. Each employee should perform a minimum of thirty minutes of cardiovascular exercise or complete a strength-training circuit, at a moderate intensity, at least four times a week. That's a modest investment of one hour per pound for that truly extraordinary muscle that goes *thumpa-thumpa-thumpa* up to 100,000 times every day, and in the process sends some 1,800 gallons of blood zinging through 62,000 miles of vessels and veins.

  PAT CROCE POINTER
Being neat, clean, and fit automatically establishes you as a person who can be trusted, as someone who knows of what he speaks, and as an authority who should be given due respect.

Two hours a week—just *two* out of 168—to take care of your pump and its plumbing. A reasonable request of my employees. And one that required no special effort. The facilities were right there where they worked, after all, and outfitted with all of the best in exercise equipment. Most did more than two hours, not to suck up but because they either already knew or they quickly found out that the wonder of fitness is the return on the investment. The more you put into it, the more energy you generate. This increases endurance and improves attitude. Not to mention having a positive effect on both your waistline and your *bottom* line.

We also followed a uniform dress code. No sequins or spangles or beads. Pants and SPT logo shirt only—simple fare, but functional. I was more relaxed than some businesses regarding hairstyle and facial-hair growth. As a man with a mustache and goatee myself, and as a man whose hair once was a cascade of curls down to the shoulder, I couldn't very well demand buzz cuts of all the troops. I just didn't want anyone looking like they'd slept in their clothes or been shipwrecked for six months.

Office sanitation was, however, an obsession.

It was when I owned Sports Physical Therapists and it is now that I own the 76ers. I wouldn't want to work out with barbells that had rusted or on a Nautilus machine that was wet from someone else's sweat. And I wouldn't want to pay my way into an arena to watch the greatest athletes in the world, only to find something sticky on my seat.

It's a good philosophy to walk a mile in another man's shoes before you judge him. But I think that we all want those shoes to be dry and fumigated before we ever slip them on.

My father was a cleanliness fanatic, and his four sons were delegated specific responsibilities to keep the house shipshape. I inherited my father's mania for cleanliness, too, and it persists to this day. But I look like a bum alongside by brother, Vince. V will clean the kitchen with a zealot's intensity as soon as he's done cooking. Nothing unusual about that, you say? Well, V does his cleaning *before* he even eats the meal. When I go to his house, I get down and roll around on the carpet in his living room just to mess up the precise patterns made by those perfect vertical lines that he intentionally left with the vacuum cleaner. Sometimes I'll continue to stand just outside the foyer even after he's opened the door . . . .

"Come on in," he'll say. "What are you waiting for?"

"I'm looking for them . . . ."

"For what?"

"For those surgical slippers you'll want me to put on before I'm allowed to set foot in your house!" I know to duck his right-hand punch after that one comes out.

We may have been raised with an overzealous craving for cleanliness, but I don't think that was ever a handicap. On the other hand, if we hadn't been raised this way, then I think that could have hurt. In my profession, there was not only the simple issue of cleanliness, but there was also the continual concern about germs. Also, with the arrival of AIDS, people were more conscious about such things.

It was my daily habit—when not taking an early-morning run in the streets or training in the dojo—to visit different SPT centers and work out. I could kill two birds with one stone, get my morning sweat in and also check out each center in action. Early one Monday morning, just after finishing a workout at the center in Wayne (which at that time housed our corporate offices), I entered the men's room to shower and . . . was appalled!

The place was a mess!

The mirror was smeared with smudge marks. The sink was clotted with the remnants of someone's shaving efforts. The dirty towel basket in one corner was overflowing with damp, soiled linen. One fluorescent light had burned out. The shower was dripping and the door wouldn't close all the way. I looked up to the heavens in exasperation, seeking divine help . . . and I immediately spotted two ceiling tiles that were stained!

I didn't need hot water by then. I was already steaming.

And I was still steaming when I stormed into the room for the usual weekly corporate meeting. I called it to order and then I called them all into the men's room. Women included.

The staff watched curiously as their bosses' bosses filed contritely into the little boy's room. Possibly never to emerge again, judging from the look on Pat's contorted face.

The management session lasted an hour. In the bathroom! I chewed and chewed until there were only bits of bone and hanks of hair left. You could say we got at least one issue cleaned up.

Your environment, your appearance, your attitude—make them as pristine as possible and let them permeate your being and your business.

No environment is safe from my obsession. Not even outdoor businesses, like the miniature golf courses that I own in partnership with my buddy Mark Benevento. They are located in the South Jersey shore towns of Avalon and Sea Isle. They are all called Pirate Island. Marky Mark is a golf aficionado and also the brains of the business. Me, I'm just nuts for all things pirate, and have been since I was little. If I'd been born a few centuries ago, I'd probably have sailed with Blackbeard.

The golf courses carry the same pirate theme—tropical foliage, 40-foot rope bridges suspended over 20-foot high waterfalls, with holes weaving through a series of treasure chest caves in which there are Disney-style pirate animatrons. The 18th holes are on-board 38-foot-long replicas of pirate ships. Marky Mark has the courses patrolled. They are continually walked by monitors. Not because we expect trouble or need policing. But to make sure everything is clean. That the caves haven't been soiled with graffiti, the foliage hasn't been trampled, and the water isn't littered.

The cashiers take your money when you come and the putters when you leave. And they are supposed to be as careful cleaning those clubs as they are counting the money. No lollipop residue on the handles. No chewing gum on the blades.

"No self-respecting pirate would put up with such cleanliness," you say?

Yes, but no customer comes back without it . . . .

6. BE PROMPT AND PROFESSIONAL

If you're late, you're rude.

You're also inconsiderate, discourteous, thoughtless, unorganized, and lacking in discipline.

And, you have lots and lots of company. More people are late than early.

But I'm not talking about one extreme or the other here. I'm talking about high-noon punctuality. I'm talking about the simple act of being on time. Promptness is another fetish of mine. If I'm such a fanatic about cleanliness, then you know I'm going to be a stickler about promptness, too. The two are connected after all, in that each requires self-discipline. Dirt and tardiness result from laziness, and laziness almost always stems from lack of discipline.

We can't control time, obviously. But we can budget it, manage it, and save it. And we can keep our word about it. And that's what you do when you set a date, make an appointment, or arrange a meeting—you give your word to the other person.

"Two-thirty? I'll be there," you say.

And when it gets to be two-forty-five and you're not there, then how many people have you inconvenienced? They may force a polite smile when you finally show up, and they may even graciously wave away your apology, but you have already made an impression—one that won't be going away any time soon, one that may be costlier than you'll ever realize.

Being habitually late creates the impression of being unreliable: *If he can't even get to a meeting on time, then how can I trust him with the details of this contract?*

And we all know what it feels like to be on the receiving end of someone's thoughtless tardiness. How many times have you sat and seethed in the doctor's—or dentist's—waiting room? You can only thumb through so many year-old magazines, you can only watch fish endlessly prowl a tank for just so long before you want to stand up and vent your rage at being so disrespected. You look at the sign at the receptionist's desk: "Payment is expected upon receipt of services." And you want to deliver your own conditions: "And I'm deducting 30 percent from my bill for every hour you keep me waiting."

Being on time is a habit, nothing more. It requires a little organization, a little discipline, and a little planning. The physical and mental demands are minimal. If you can count, and you can walk, then you can be on time.

Even as a college student I had a thing about promptness. I was never late for class or practice, for a meeting or party. No, wait . . . there was one class that I was late for. Because I waited for Bator. But I never did again! The one semester that Bator roomed with me at West Chester, he found out about punctuality. If it was time to go, then the door never even had a chance to bump up against my scrawny ass, regardless of his condition or state of dress at the time. Sometimes he'd be running after me trying to dress at a gallop, hopping along on one leg while pulling on his pants, his shirt open, his tie trailing behind him like the tail of a kite, and he'd be turning the air blue with his thoughts about "these %*&#% obsessions of yours . . . ."

PAT CROCE POINTER
Being on time is a habit, nothing more. It requires a little organization, a little discipline, and a little planning. The physical and mental demands are minimal.

I always started my meetings on time at Sports Physical Therapists, and I still do with the Sixers. And I set strict time limits—no meeting lasted longer than ninety minutes. Any longer and they became counter-productive—attention spans would waver. My theory was that everyone attending the meeting could then plan his or her schedule accordingly. If you were scheduled for a nine o'clock meeting with me, you didn't have to wonder whether you could make your eleven o'clock. Punctuality breeds productivity.

Punctuality is also a climate-control device. It makes employees feel they are working in an environment thriving with confidence and assurance. There are firm schedules and they are followed. Uncertainty is removed. You don't have to ask: "Is this going to happen?"

However, what does tend to happen, despite our best efforts to prevent it, is . . . *shit.*

Shit happens.

And with disconcerting regularity.

Tires really do go flat. Kids do get sick. Dogs really do eat homework (though only if it is first rolled in raw hamburger). So if you had a genuine emergency, if there was a mitigating factor why you were going to be late or couldn't make it to a meeting, you were expected to give us the courtesy of a phone call, with a valid excuse. I was demanding but I was not an unreasonable tyrant.

Being late for a meeting, an appointment, or a class is a selfish, self-indulgent act. You make innocent bystanders suffer for your tardiness. It is simply unprofessional.

When we had expanded into New Jersey and Delaware, we held tri-state staff meetings once a month, in the Broomall center, on Wednesday evenings.

Seven sharp.

As soon as the little hand locked on 7 and the big hand clicked on 12, I instructed Fast Eddie to lock the front door. No admittance. No exceptions. No phone calls accepted.

One by one the stragglers would arrive. They would pull on the door handle. They would knock. They would press their noses up against the glass and look forlornly in, using their most pathetic, pleading, adopt-a-puppy faces. They would look at their watches in disbelief, trying to will time to reverse. Finally they would submit to the inevitable. They would turn and trudge away, shoulders slumped in defeat, knowing that in the morning they would have to face the wrath of their managers. At their cars, they would look up at the night sky and you could almost hear their prayers of supplication for divine inspiration: "Gimme an excuse . . . puhleeeeezeeee!"

Later, when we had centers stretching from Green Bay to Miami, I hosted a managers' outing in the Pocono Mountains in Pennsylvania. The first day was a full one. Everyone worked hard. The night was a full one, too. Everyone partied hard, following our credo: *Work Hard, Play Hard.* The second day began with a breakfast meeting.

Eight sharp.

A disturbing number of managers were late. Maybe they were hung over. Maybe they were lackadaisical. Maybe, worst of all, they decided that time was merely relative. When they finally staggered into the restaurant, Fast Eddie met them at the door and told them to return to their rooms.

"And do what?" they asked.

"Wait."

The wait lasted the better part of eleven hours. They were recalled to the restaurant for the dinner meeting.

Seven sharp.

No one was late. They apologized to everyone they had inconvenienced. How often have we heard it said, or said it ourselves: "Time is fleeting." All the more reason to respect it.

7. BE POSITIVE

His name was Theodore S. Geisel and he had a fertile imagination, with a special gift for inventing words, putting them to rhyme, and creating the most captivating kinds of creatures. Armed with his first book—which was ostensibly written for children but which actually possessed an ageless appeal—and brimming with high hope, he knocked expectantly on the door of a publishing house.

His manuscript was rejected.

He went to another publisher. And was rejected.

He went to a third publisher. And was rejected again.

Number 4 said no. Number 5 said no. Number 6 said no. Number 7 said no. Number 8 said no. Number 9 said no. Number 10 said no.

Number 11 said no. Number 12 said no. Number 13 said no. Number 14 said no. Number 15 said no. Number 16 said no. Number 17 said no. Number 18 said no. Number 19 said no.

Number 20 said no.

Number 21 said no.

Number 22 said no.

When would *you* have given up? After the fourth rejection? Or would you have persisted through ten rejections and then quit? Would you have knocked on fifteen different doors before surrendering? Would you, like Theodore S. Geisel, have gone on to Number 23, and, hearing yet another rejection, then said, "That's it, I'm done"?

Well, you would have really been sorry then. But not nearly as sorry as the first 23 publishers who rejected him.

Because he kept on. He went to Number 24.

Who said: *"YessssSSSSS!"* That sweet sound that the salesperson in all of us craves. *"YessssSSSSS!"*

And Number 24 went on to publish six million copies of that first book written by Theodore S. Geisel, whose pen name was . . .

Dr. Seuss!

The author of *Green Eggs and Ham* and *The Cat in the Hat.* Do these titles ring a bell?

He went on to write more than fifty books that have sold more than 200 million copies, and which are still selling to this day in seventeen different languages.

Dr. Seuss is my hero. He is my motivational role model. Not only because he was read to me, not only because I read him to Kelly and Michael, and not only because—God willing—I'll be privileged to read him to my grandchildren. No, it is because he redefined the word "perseverance" for me. His story is the epitome of being positive, and even more important, of *staying* positive. We are all capable of starting out in a positive frame of mind. But to be able to sustain that through failure upon failure, and defeat after defeat—23 rejections!—*that* is the true measure of a positive attitude.

Life has a way of becoming a self-fulfilling prophecy. If you always expect the worst, then you'll hardly ever be disappointed.

The first motivational book that really got my juices percolating was Zig Ziglar's *See You at the Top.* I read it in the late 1970s and then began to buy and absorb his audiocassette tapes. His message reinforced my long-standing belief in the importance of approaching everything with a positive attitude. There have been a lot of scoffers and cynics along the way, but their ridicule has never affected me. In fact, the more sour and skeptical these naysayers are, the happier and more confident I am. If you can load up on the positives—without losing perspective or ignoring reality—then you have a huge built-in advantage.

Our Sports Physical Therapists centers hummed with this sort of thinking. When interviewing prospective employees, Fast Eddie and I looked for positive-thinking people who smiled easily and often, and who looked at every negative situation as an opportunity rather than as an obstacle. In therapy, if you treat only the patient's body, then you're only doing half the job. While we tried to recondition their bodies, we also tried to recondition their minds. The first stage in getting better is believing that you *will* get better.

This revised outlook does not come without effort on the patient's part. But you could see it working gradually. A patient would come to us grumpy and dejected. He would be greeted with a hearty hello and called by his first name. He would be surrounded by smiles. He would be treated by a fit, neat, clean, chipper therapist who was glowing with health and optimism. After treatment, he would be sent on his way with a robust round of goodbyes. After a few visits, it would begin to dawn on him that he was the only sour one. Soon, he would begin to feel a twinge of guilt for complaining, complaining, complaining about being too tired, too ached, too stiff, doing too many exercises, getting too few calories, etc.

 PAT CROCE POINTER
We are all capable of starting out in a positive frame of mind. But to be able to sustain that through failure upon failure . . . *that* is the true measure of a positive attitude.

I'm not going to con you and say everyone became a convert. Human nature wouldn't allow such a mass conversion. But while we were mending knees and straightening shoulders and strengthening spines and substituting fat with muscle, we also cranked out some reformed attitudes and helped people change the way they looked at life.

And that was probably the most rewarding part of it.

As a 60th birthday present for my mom, I sent her and her two sisters, my Aunt Corinne and Aunt Mary Jane, to Ireland, home of their ancestors. When they returned ten days later, my mom told us about this one particular woman who was in their tour group. She was shot through with negativity. Here she was on a lush, enchanting isle, home of leprechauns and all sorts of other beguilements, and yet for every rainbow you pointed out, she could find two dozen cold and drenching downpours. She hit the floor in the morning complaining and she hit the pillow at night still complaining. The weather was too wet, the hotels too chilly and damp, the food too bland, the beer too warm, the lines too long, the prices too high, the people too rude, and so on. The woman was a veritable Bitching Machine.

But, my mom said, their Irish tour guide never allowed the woman to get to him. Not so much as a suggestion of a frown. Not even an arch of an eyebrow. Inside, he probably wanted to hurl her from the bus out into the sea. But he maintained a positive attitude. He was determined that one bitter old biddy wouldn't prevent him from giving the rest of the group their money's worth.

They toured Blarney Castle, and everyone was impressed with the bedroom chambers, awed by the great dining hall, left gaping in the antique weapons room. But in the heart of every Irish descendant there is an overwhelming longing for one thing and one thing only in this castle—the Blarney Stone.

To kiss it, according to legend, is to be granted eloquence and to be guaranteed good fortune. The day my mother's group toured Blarney Castle, however, the Blarney Stone was roped off for repairs and access to it was forbidden.

Naturally, the Bitching Machine went ballistic.

The rest of them were all disappointed, of course, but they accepted the situation, realizing there was nothing they could do except remain positive and enjoy the experience.

But the Bitching Machine was firing on all cylinders. She cried and moaned, claimed that she had been defrauded, and even demanded her money back. The tour guide remained patient. He tried to soothe her. He tried to transfer his positivity to her. She bitched on.

Finally, in a last effort to placate her, the guide said: "You know, ma'am, legend has it that if you kiss someone who has kissed the Blarney Stone, then it's as though you actually kissed the Blarney Stone yourself. Your luck will be guaranteed."

The woman, her face still twisted in its familiar scowl, snorted her skepticism.

"And I suppose you're now going to tell me that *you* have kissed the Stone?" she said humorlessly.

He smiled ever so politely, and told her: "Why no, ma'am, I've done even better than that."

He paused, pointed to his buttocks, and said, "I've sat on it."

The group broke into cheers.

A long time before that trip, my mom had taught me a quotation that I carry with me always. In fact, I recited it for the world to hear at the memorable press conference introducing me as an owner of the

Philadelphia 76ers:

"Two people look out through the same bars . . .

"one sees the mud, the other sees the stars."

You see, I think it's inherent in all of us to be positive. Certainly we all start out that way. Just observe little children. They laugh and they play and every day is a wonderful new adventure, every day is awash in possibility.

And then what happens? We grow up. We allow the positive to be drained from us. We succumb to the negative. Negativity—like deception and prejudice and all the other ugliness of human nature—has to be acquired, it has to be learned, because it does not come naturally. We aren't born with it. We are born being naturally positive.

So it requires effort to remain that way. More than that, it requires a term you hear all the time in sports: second effort.

And, sometimes, remaining positive requires a third and fourth effort. Sometimes, a 14th and 15th effort.

And sometimes, why sometimes it even requires a Dr. Seuss effort . . . .

8. GIVE COMPLIMENTS

Better to light just one candle than to curse the darkness.

That's what compliments are—candles in the dark. It can be a cold, daunting world out there, as dank and foreboding as the bowels of a cave. But a compliment . . . ah, it casts a glow and drives away the shadows, and in doing so seems to soften and smooth out our day.

Have you ever petted a cat, rubbed your hand along its spine, starting at the neck and working on down to its tail? Notice how it arches in pleasure? Feel how it rises, like yeast baking? The cat would stand there all day if you'd just keep stroking it.

We all have the cat in us. Our egos arch like a cat's back when we're stroked with praise.

"Great job on that financial report, Andy."

"You really killed them in that marketing meeting, Dave."

"Susie, you been working out? You look marvelous."

More, more. Please, please. Pile it on. I can take it! I love it!

A compliment is truly the one gift that fits all. The gift that everyone will appreciate. The gift that no one will want to return for refund or exchange.

And it's a gift that costs nothing.

One of my best pieces of advice to the staff was to combine two of the Ten Commandments—give a compliment followed immediately by the person's first name. Even the most dour grump will have a hard time suppressing a smile or keeping his ego from arching in ecstasy.

Our people were instructed to look for the positive in their patients, their vendors, their co-workers, and themselves, and when finding it, to reinforce it with praise. A slap on the back. A lusty high-five. A chest bump. Applause. A handwritten note. A thank-you. What never fails to amaze me is the enormous impact that small gestures can have.

I think it's because when you compliment someone you tend to catch them by surprise. Most of us are used to complaints and gripes, and so when we are approached by someone saying, "Hey, I just want to tell you . . ."

Out of reflex we brace ourselves for what's surely coming. But what if what we hear next is:

" . . . this is really great work you've done."

Ohhhhh. How unexpected. How delicious. Gimme another and I'll arch my back right out of alignment.

PAT CROCE POINTER
Praise tends to reproduce itself. Compliments tend to get passed along. When someone has elevated your spirits with a compliment . . . then you're apt to have an encouraging word for someone else.

One small stroke can be a powerful stimulus. We found in rehabilitating injuries that patients desperately needed encouragement and reinforcement to continue to work through the pain and the discomfort, to achieve short-term goals, to recover inch-by-sure-inch, and to become convinced that in the long run, all of their effort would be worthwhile. There's something to those Mary Poppins lyrics: "Just a spoonful of sugar helps the medicine go down . . . ."

If it's true that man does not live by bread alone, it's also true that he needs buttering up from time to time.

There is a school of thought that states the best sort of emotional nutrition is the "compliment sandwich"—you put criticism between two slices of praise. But I don't like that approach. A compliment should be, above all, sincere. If you always precede criticism with a compliment and then end with another compliment, then soon the praise becomes meaningless. The person you're praising begins to dread hearing praise, knowing what is coming after it. The compliment becomes nothing more than an air bag deploying just before the crash. Or the silencer on a pistol. Instead of making someone arch their back, this sort of compliment is more likely to draw a hiss.

Similarly, there is an important distinction between praise and flattery. I've heard flattery defined as telling a man what he already thinks of himself. Flattery is transparent and insincere, an obvious attempt to ingratiate, and all but the most hopeless egoist can detect it. But heartfelt praise, a genuine compliment, should come with no strings attached, with no deception, and with no ulterior motives in mind.

Compliments are a lot like birthday presents—everyone loves them no matter how much they protest that they've gotten too old for them. And it's not the size or price of the gift that matters, it really is the thought. You'd be astounded at what a simple card of congratulations— signed by you with three or four words of encouragement—can mean to an employee.

Want to know another great way to let an employee know how much you value him or her? Try unleashing the power of these four words: "What do you think?"

Praise tends to reproduce itself. Compliments tend to get passed along. When someone has elevated your spirits with a compliment, and you're feeling better about yourself and the world in general, then you're apt to have an encouraging word for someone else.

And if everyone goes around lighting just one candle, we could make the darkest cave look like high noon in July.

One of the most profitable and widespread businesses around is Mary Kay Cosmetics, which is dependent upon the commitment of its pink-clad salesforce. And Mary Kay Ash, the founder, believed that compliments will do more for a disposition than the brightest lipstick or the most velvety lotion. Her company's motto is: "Praise People to Success." Also, she has said that in her company, the initials P&L did not stand for the customary Profit and Loss, rather they stood for People and Love.

Mary Kay encouraged her sales staff to imagine that everyone they meet has a sign hanging around their neck that implores: "Make me feel important."

What a terrific concept!

Mark Twain distilled the potency of praise into this one sentence: "I can live for two months on a good compliment."

All of us can, no matter our station in life, no matter what our status. Like the cat arching its back, we all respond to praise. We cannot help ourselves.

Any time is appropriate for a compliment. So don't hoard them. Spend them freely, and spend them now. As a poet once explained:

> When the pleasure you are viewing,
> Any work that one is doing,
> And you like him or you love him, tell him now.
> Don't withhold your approbations,
> 'Til the parson makes orations,
> And he lies with snowy lilies on his brow.
> Now's the time to show it to him.
> 'Cause a man can't read his tombstone when he's dead.

9. HAVE FUN

In the movie *Oh, God!*, George Burns plays the lead role. I mean, *the* lead role—The Big Guy himself. He laments about the way people react to him and to life in general. He laments over our grimness in all things. He frets that we are frightened of fun, that we're reluctant to really enjoy ourselves.

"Sometimes," he says, "I feel like a comedian playing to an audience that's afraid to laugh."

It is, indeed, grim enough here on the third rock from the sun. All the more reason to take fun where you can find it; and if you can't find it, then manufacture it. Of all the traits I admire in people, I think I prize a sense of humor most. A good sense of humor makes most of the other good things possible—a positive attitude, passion, pride, productivity, a sense of well being, and compassion for others.

Did you know that laughter is aerobic? Good for the heart, good for the circulation. A few strong belly laughs can do you as much good as several minutes worth of moderate exercise. That alone is enough to recommend it, let alone what it can do for your attitude and your outlook.

Personally, I like facial wrinkles. They're badges of living. Every furrow, every rut, every crinkle stands for something. Mostly, they identify you as a survivor. So I respect them, especially the ones that are called "laugh lines." I see them and I know their owner has found a way to muddle through this mess—probably his or her secret is to laugh at every opportunity—to squeeze all the juice out of life. Never trust someone without wrinkles; it means they haven't laughed enough.

There is an old adage that goes, "Years wrinkle the skin, but having fun prevents wrinkling of the soul."

PAT CROCE POINTER
A good sense of humor makes most of the other good things possible—a positive attitude, passion, pride, productivity, a sense of well being, and compassion for others.

Most of us agree that life is short. Many even agree that it is meant to be enjoyed. And then there's the school of thought that believes *this* is really hell and that the good part comes next. These people are content to just sit back and let life pass by. I couldn't agree less.

A long time ago I read that life is a cup and we should drink deeply from it. I took that expression to heart. As you've seen, there have been times when I've tried to drink so deeply that it's choked me and dribbled down my shirt. Still, I believe it is better to make a mess than to become dehydrated.

At SPT, my philosophy on fun was simple. Since I was expecting my employees to give me at least one-third of their day, then they should have some fun along the way. So I tried to foster an atmosphere where expressing yourself, laughing, and having fun were not just accepted, but encouraged. In the end, they would be more productive, there would be less employee turnover, and patients would find the setting more conducive to getting well. When I was younger, my fun was more about mischief than anything else. As I got older, I channeled most of my energy, enthusiasm, and passion into work, and the fun came in accomplishment.

Obviously there are going to be dark days. There are going to be occasions when laughing is totally inappropriate. But if you can make having fun one of your guiding principles, it can cushion some of those whiplash-causing collisions with reality that we all have from time to time.

When I bought into the 76ers, I acquired a team that had become accustomed to losing. And had forgotten what fun looked like. What fun *felt* like.

So I looked for reasons to celebrate—when we sealed the deal to buy the team; when we won the draft lottery; the night of the draft itself. We hosted a draft party for our fans that was second to none. We would celebrate all the small triumphs in hopes of instilling a new attitude, creating an *expectation* of success instead of failure. Knowing that it would take some time to get the losing reversed and the winning started, I wanted the fans to have fun every night, regardless of the outcome. I wanted them involved. So in the spring of '96, after we had bought the team but had not yet officially taken over, I invited all the season ticketholders to a meeting, a kind of town hall gathering. I wanted to hear what they didn't like, and what they did like.

About a hundred showed up. Each one had a complaint. Or ten.

Some could be easily rectified, some couldn't. One fan wondered why the ushers at Flyers games wore Flyers lapel pins and were courteous and pleasant, while the same event staff at 76ers games *also* wore Flyers lapel pins *(not* Sixers pins) but were rude. Prior to the first game of the 1996–97 season, my first official game as owner, Bator assembled the entire event staff and I handed out 76ers lapel pins and introduced them to our Ten Commandments of Customer Service.

Try, I said—no matter how unpleasant things may get—to have fun.

I needed to remember my own advice a few months later. I had promised the fans at that first meeting that we would have a follow-up meeting midway through the season. Two months in advance, invitations were mailed. The meeting was scheduled for February 20, 1997, at 6:00 PM, ninety minutes before tipoff of a game against the Los Angeles Clippers. The doors to the First Union Center were opened thirty minutes earlier than usual to accommodate the meeting.

The timing was catastrophic. It was the day of the NBA trading deadline. And we had no trade to announce, to the fans' great displeasure. Our season, which had begun with some promise in the first month, had deteriorated at an alarming rate. The night of the meeting, our win–loss record was dismal—12 wins and 39 ugly losses—and we had lost our last five games in a row. Trade rumors had been rampant during the previous week. Derrick Coleman, who had been a lightning rod for controversy his entire career, had just returned from an extended absence due to, of all things, a cut pinkie. He was also overweight. Our locker room seethed with tension. That morning's *Philadelphia Inquirer* had a story that contained the coach's first public criticism of the players. The finger-pointing had only just started. We were on the deck of the *Titanic* and the scramble for lifeboats was on. And now I had to go out and meet season ticketholders.

Have fun? Yeah, right. This'll be a barrel of monkeys.

I stood alone in the tunnel. I thought furiously: *How can I bail out of this?* But no convenient excuse came to mind.

And then Fran "The Man" Cassidy, my vice president of sales and one of the original SPT gang, tapped me on the shoulder. A mischievous smile split his face. He held up his cell phone and made me an offer:

"Pat, I could call in a bomb scare and we could empty the building."

The scary thing was that it sure sounded tempting. But I declined. It was time to face the music, and they were playing my song.

It was time to heed Emerson's motivational advice: Always, always, always, always, always do what you are afraid to do.

At six sharp, I strode out.

And my knees buckled at what I saw.

There were hundreds of fans. They filled two entire sections. TV cameras were everywhere. Newspaper reporters were lined up with their note pads and tape recorders ready to record this fiasco. This was particularly alarming because the media hadn't even been invited, but I could hardly tell them to leave. I began to sweat like I had when I flew the helicopter and lost the airport.

Was I having fun yet?

I welcomed everyone. I thanked them for coming out on a cold winter night. Then I reached into a bag and pulled out the mask that Ron Hextall, the Flyers goalie, wore. I put it on, hoping that it would break the ice. Or at least melt it a little.

"I'm ready for you to fire away," I told them, awaiting their laughter.

Silence.

So I tried again:

"But no hitting below the belt."

Almost immediately a heckler shouted:

"Why not, Pat? You hit us below the belt."

By then I was sweating the Mississippi River. I spent the first fifteen minutes detailing all of our progress off the court—the creation of a fan club, an alumni association, a free newsletter, our community outreach programs, the new fan-friendly atmosphere, and the entertaining show that surrounded our games.

It didn't impress them a lick. When it was their turn, they lashed out at me for forty-five minutes. What a mess you've got here. Coach can't coach. General manager can't manage. Players can't play. One woman in the front raised her hand. As she waited for the portable microphone to be brought to her, I sighed. But she was polite. Maybe this would be the start of a cease-fire.

"Pat," she asked, "what will it take to get Derrick Coleman to play?"

I never got a chance to answer. Another heckler answered for me: "Jenny Craig!"

The crowd actually laughed. Finally, some mirth! Even I laughed.

At seven sharp, they untied me from the stake and put out the last of the flames. I started to limp toward the exit ramp and then saw fans, dozens of them, blocking my exit. In Philadelphia, our version of the Welcome Wagon is the Lynch Mob. I was prepared to be the guest of honor.

But, no, these fans had stayed to thank me for listening and for caring. I got some high-fives. Some hugs. Even some kisses.

Twice now I have scheduled fan meetings that were supposed to be fun gatherings, but which became instead vociferous uprisings. And yet both had endings that, if not particularly happy, were definitely productive. I learned a lot. I learned more than I would have if I hadn't gone into these meetings with the "have fun" approach to listening to our customers.

A couple days later, my mom, the eternal clipper and encourager, sent me this item she had found in her church bulletin:

Words To Live By

In Calcutta, India, there is a children's home that
was founded by Mother Theresa. On one of the
walls hangs this sign:

Sometimes, people are unreasonable, illogical,
and self-centered.
LOVE THEM ANYWAY.

Often, if you do good, people will accuse you of
selfish, ulterior motives.
DO GOOD ANYWAY.

There is a risk that if you are successful, you will
win false friends and true enemies.
SUCCEED ANYWAY.

There is always the possibility that the good you
do today will be forgotten tomorrow.
DO GOOD ANYWAY.

People will remind you that honesty and frankness
make you vulnerable.
BE HONEST AND FRANK ANYWAY.

There is a chance that what you spent years building
may be destroyed overnight.
BUILD ANYWAY.

10. DO IT NOW!

I do everything in a hurry. That includes waiting.

As far as I'm concerned, a deadline is not something you meet, it's something you *beat*. It's called a deadline for a very good reason—it leaves no room for excuses, not even death.

You're familiar with the acronym, *ASAP*, that managers and supervisors are always scrawling across the tops of memos they send along to their underlings. It means, of course, "As Soon As Possible."

Well, at SPT our working motto was ASAPITL:

As
Soon
As
Possible
Is
Too
Late.

Most motivational books and tapes suggest that the way to be a success is to do what successful people do. Sounds simple. Is simple. Is true. But like a great many true and simple things, people seem unable to do it. They *know* what they should do, so ignorance is not the problem. But for whatever reason—laziness, fear, lack of organization, lack of discipline, lack of motivation—they simply refuse to just do it.

Read the last three words of that last paragraph. Sound familiar? In one of the great marketing coups of our time, Nike has managed to make that slogan part of our everyday language: "Just Do It!"

I love it, of course, for all that it implies—no excuses, no alibis, no procrastinating, and no waiting for someone else. It's a Yang kind of mantra. It's a throttle-open, accelerator-mashed, splinter-a-two-by-four-with-your-forehead sense of purpose.

But I added one word . . . tacked it on the end like an extra turbo-booster strapped to the ass of a rocket.

"Now."

Just Do It *Now!*

It adds the proper urgency.

Visualize the Nike swoosh. Now visualize the Nike swoosh with an exclamation point after it.

  PAT CROCE POINTER
If you do not immediately implement what you learn today, then the world will have changed by tomorrow and you will be two steps behind.

Through our years of success at SPT, as we expanded through the East and into the Midwest and South, we were visited by competitors, potential acquirers, and industry copycats. We granted them full access. They were free to snoop around and ask all the questions they wanted. Imitation really is the sincerest form of flattery, after all. And yet no one could duplicate exactly what we did. I always felt that there were a couple of reasons for this. First, they didn't do everything exactly as we did, and that's certainly understandable. They wanted to modify some things, adapt others. And second, even though they may have known *what* to do, they just didn't do it *now*.

You see, our calendar was just a little different. We appreciated that there was a yesterday, but we regarded it as ancient history, valuable only in that from it we should learn what mistakes to avoid in the future. We knew that there was a today because that was what we lived and worked for. What didn't exist for us was the concept of tomorrow. As in, *we'll get around to that tomorrow.* Oh no, we won't. Tomorrow is too late. Tomorrow is unacceptable. Tomorrow is the lazy man's greatest labor-saving device.

If you are waiting for tomorrow for your ship to come in, my advice to you is to start right *now* by working days, nights, holidays, and weekends building the dock.

Yes, I exaggerate. But only slightly, only to make this point: If you do not immediately implement what you learn today, then the world will have changed by tomorrow and you will be two steps behind. You'll be playing catch-up. And that's always a losing game.

Hospitals have it right. Their code for urgency is "STAT." In their world, STAT means, literally, "life or death." It conjures up visions of those electric shock paddles, and white-coated physicians straddling motionless bodies, delivering great thumping punches to the sternums, trying desperately to pound life back into patients . . . to pull them back from the other side. Well, goals and objectives and ideas can expire, too. If you wait, even a day, and sometimes even an hour, they can slip away.

You wait . . . too late.

One of the standing rules at SPT was that we called all new patients the same night of their first visit. Not only was follow-up important to make sure there had been no complications or questions, but also to let them know that our concern was genuine and that our care and interest didn't end when they walked out the door. But the clincher was doing it that same night. Hopefully we had made a good first impression during their visit, and the call served to cement that impression.

There were two other STAT rules: All phone calls had to be responded to within 24 hours. All written correspondence had to be responded to within 48 hours.

That didn't mean you had to have a solution to every problem or an answer to every question within 24 or 48 hours. What it meant was that a simple acknowledgment had to be made. You were responding to the caller or the writer: Yes, I got your message. I'm working on it.

Often a simple acknowledgment is as important as a solution. How many times have you waited for a phone call to be returned, or a memo to be answered? Frustrating, isn't it? It's like you threw something "over the transom" and you don't know if it landed on a desk or in a waste-basket. You sit there and stew in your own juices. Did they get that fax? Do they know I called? The longer you are left waiting . . . well, you know what happens.

I apply STAT to everything. I go through life with a cattle prod between my southern cheeks. I have never believed in waiting for some-one to knock on my door, or to give me a call, or even to return my call. Take the initiative yourself, and take it now.

If not sooner.

You know that song from the musical *Annie*? The one about tomor-row . . . the one that assures us that the sun'll come up tomorrow? The one that tells us tomorrow is always just a day away? Well, what they don't mention about tomorrow is that, more times than not, tomorrow is just *too damn late!*

By *tomorrow*, deals will have died. Promises will have been broken. Ideas will have been stolen. Dreams will have gone bust. All before tomorrow ever gets here.

And, yes, the Yin part of me concedes that there is virtue in patience.

And then the Yang screams at me Abraham Lincoln's line: "Things will come to those who wait, but only those things left by those who hustle."

It's much better to be the one leaving the leftovers than the one pick-ing through them.

POSTSCRIPT

Our Ten Commandments of Customer Service, as I mentioned, are pretty much the stuff we all learned in kindergarten. Or maybe on *Sesame Street*. We never really outgrow these simple truths, we just misplace them temporarily.

The Commandments are helpful mainly because, in one way or another, they help you to empower other people. They help us all feel like we're not alone, that we're not without help.

That we're not all blind mules . . .

Let me explain:

A motorist was driving on a lonely back road when he blew a tire, skidded into a ditch, and turned upside down. He managed to get out but knew he was miles from nowhere. And about the time he was ready to panic, a farmer came down the road with his blind mule, Gus. The farmer hitched Gus to the car, cracked his whip in the air, and clucked:

"Yaaaa, there, Sam! Pull, Sam, pull!"

The mule didn't move.

The farmer cracked his whip again and yelled out:

"Yaaaa, there, Jake! Pull, Jake, pull!"

The mule still didn't move.

Once more the farmer cracked his whip and shouted:

"Yaaaa, there, Pete! Pull, Pete, pull!"

Still, Gus did not move.

And then the farmer cracked his whip and shouted:

"Yaaaa, there, Gus! Pull, Gus, pull!"

And at that, Gus dug his hind legs in and churned up big clods of dirt, and he planted his forelegs and surged forward, and soon enough the car turned right-side up and came trawling out of the ditch and back onto the road. The motorist was astounded and appreciative and curious.

"Why," he asked the farmer, "did you call out all those other names?"

"Gus is blind," said the farmer, "and if he thought it was up to him alone to pull that car out, he wouldn't even have tried. But when he thought he had help, well, he was stronger than he knew."

We've all got some blind mule in us.

If we're lucky, we've got some of that farmer in us, too.

Chapter 11
Going for Number 1

❦ ❦ ❦

The word is "Ichiban."

Pronounced IT-CHEE-BAHN.

Say it with force. Say it with your whole being. Say it like you are sneezing.

Say it now:

ICHIBAN!!!

It's Japanese, and the very sound of it exploding out of your mouth makes you think of Samurai warriors. Ichiban is the intense feeling that sports fanatics experience when they paint their faces in their school colors and pump their index fingers and scream into the TV cameras: "We're Number One!"

I decided to make Ichiban part of our everyday vocabulary at Sports Physical Therapists. It was a motivational prod, a way to remind everyone to keep their eyes on the prize. And the prize was the coveted Malcolm Baldrige National Quality Award. After one of our karate workouts, Jay Snider had shown me a *USA Today* front-page article about the award and its recipients. We shared an affinity for quality, agreeing that it mattered far more than quantity. Anyone can make a lot of inferior stuff. We had an appreciation not for sheer volume but for precise quality.

The Baldrige Awards celebrated that philosophy. Instantly, I wanted one.

Jay said he hoped that one day his company, Spectacor, could strive to achieve such an award. And then he added: "Pat, I think your company could compete for one of them right now."

Well, that got me juiced good and proper. The winners received their awards from the President of the United States. Right away my fantasy synapses fired at warp speed. I saw myself, my family, and my staff strolling through the White House and then, in the Rose Garden, being honored just like Super Bowl champions and the Ichiban warriors of collegiate football and basketball. Mr. Yang himself shaking hands with the Prez. How about that?

As soon as I had showered and dressed, I drove to the corporate office and immediately convened a meeting with Fast Eddie and Jimbo. The second they heard my turbocharger they knew we were about to set off on another crusade. They were always ready for a wild ride, and the Baldrige campaign had them revved immediately. We had been looking for a common cause to unite all the employees, to build their pride, to keep their competitive juices percolating. It was fine to keep opening new centers, to keep increasing the number of patients healed, and to continue servicing a wide range of high school, college, and professional sports teams. But I wanted something that would give us all added motivation and focus—and perhaps some national acclaim.

I wanted us running into the wind. Uphill. At full throttle. And then, having reached the summit, to be able to scream out: *I C H I B A N !*

And then hear it echo in all directions.

So I created a sign, simple and direct, one word, no flourishes—a flaming red ICHIBAN on a background of white. That sign was hung in every center in every visible spot. No matter where you stood, sat, knelt, squatted, or sweat, you saw it. It was a constant reminder to every employee of our goal. Of *their* goal. And, of course, it piqued curiosity. So when any patient, vendor or visitor saw it and asked what it meant, the employee could answer: "It means 'Number One.' It's our company goal."

PAT CROCE POINTER
Quality assurance surveys are vital for any business. I believed that we shouldn't wait to hear from clients or patients. If they had bricks or bouquets to throw our way, we needed to know.

But we didn't just want to be Number One in our own industry. We wanted to be Number One in the entire country—to compete against all the elite companies in the world of business . . . and win. We wanted to be the national champions. Pretty ambitious, huh? Perhaps unrealistically so, right? No! That's negative thinking—but it's also human nature. So I knew that to pursue this crusade everyone would have to have the focus of a laser beam. The Ichiban signs would help keep that focus.

It is the habit of the brain to drift. It's an extraordinary organ, the brain—three pounds of gray matter with a conscious mind and a sub-conscious mind that, kind of like Yin and Yang, are always fighting for control of you. One does all the scheming, the other does all the dreaming. You have to keep the conscious mind in line or the subconscious will seduce you into taking a holiday.

So as part of the Ichiban standard, we began to monitor ourselves closer than ever. If I was anal before, I became *sphinctal*. Was the telephone answered within three rings? Was every patient seen within 24 hours of his or her first phone call to us? Was every patient greeted, cheerfully, by a staff member within five minutes of entering? Was patient waiting time always kept under 15 minutes? In addition to questioning ourselves profusely, each week we randomly called ten patients at each center and asked them seven questions about the quality of their treatment.

Quality assurance surveys are vital for any business. I believed that we shouldn't wait to hear from clients or patients. If they had bricks or bouquets to throw our way, we needed to know. The fact is, some people are reluctant to complain. They may be shy, they may be uncomfortable making a fuss . . . for whatever reason, they do not volunteer criticism or compliments. If you wait to hear the complaints, your quality of service only deteriorates. And by the time you hear them it may be too late—you may already have lost business. So we obeyed our Latin. *Carpe diem!* Seize the day! Even if it turns out to be a rainy, sleety, gloomy day.

I'm such a believer in finding out what the customer thinks that since the first game of my first season as the Sixers owner, I asked Bator to call ten randomly selected season ticket holders each week and ask them a dozen very specific questions. That information was, and is, distilled and tabulated and shared with the staff. There were some things beyond our control—winning games being the biggest, and most frustrating, example. But everything that was in our control should be exactly that—in *our* control.

To help implement Bator's fan relations department goal of consistently exceeding our fans' expectations, I hired Joe Marrella as a consultant. Joe was my "phantom fan." He and his wife Ruth and their teenaged son Joseph attended games in the guise of a typical family and they secretly evaluated everything from entering the parking lot to the bathrooms to the refreshments. Joe has performed his unique service for Disney World repeatedly, and I'm a believer in doing what the successful people do. He and his family could find out things that a hundred phone surveys couldn't uncover.

To make Ichiban a reality, I felt we needed an overall plan. A blueprint. Something specific. Something in writing. Something that was always there to remind you. Like the Ichiban signs.

I wanted us to go running up that hill and into that wind at full throttle, but even in my exuberance, I knew that if we didn't have a road map of some sort we'd be liable to run off the edge. You know that old saying: "The bad news is that we're lost, but the good news is we're making great time." Well, without a map you might make great time but you might also end up taking the longest, most inconvenient route.

My tattered, torn, and tattooed biker buddy T-Bone explained how having a plan—a road map—can actually save someone's life. One time, while on his way to a Sixers game, he pulled his motorcycle over to the side of the road to ask a kid how far it was to the First Union Center. The kid looked T-Bone over, and then looked down the road T-Bone was heading.

"If you keep going that way, it's 24,901 miles, give or take a rotation of the earth."

T-Bone curled his upper lip into a sneer.

"But if you turn around and then make a left at the corner, it's only a mile."

The kid was lucky. T-Bone decided he was funny and not just a wiseass. So he let him live.

A plan keeps you headed in the right direction, and as all my top staff can testify, I need them to keep waving the plan in my face because I tend to react on the Three-I principle:

Impatience.

Impulse.

Instinct.

Marketing wasn't a problem with us. Marketing was my forte. I like to think I can sell ice to a bartender and sand to a lifeguard . . . but only if I truly believe in what I'm selling. I don't spend my passion indiscriminately.

As a kid, I can still remember walking into a bakery that was in a small strip plaza around the corner from our home. An elderly woman ordered a dozen donuts. The baker carefully counted out the twelve, and then with a little flourish put a thirteenth in the bag. No charge. I still remember the look on that woman's face. When I got older, I came to understand that look. It was the look of somebody getting something for nothing, and in the process being made to feel special. When I was a kid, I thought thirteen for the price of twelve just looked like a good deal. When I got older, I realized that it was a terrific marketing concept.

On some level, everyone—*everyone*—responds to the notion of getting something for free.

PAT CROCE POINTER
I was called a shameless promoter, a huckster, a Barnum & Bailey disciple. But I was passionate about what I was doing, and I was positive about what I was doing, so I continued to do it—and with great success.

So at every SPT center, we began handing out a free tee-shirt to each new patient, client, and customer. The shirts were black and over the heart proclaimed in white lettering: "I Survived Pat Croce." The back of the shirt was occupied almost entirely by the company logo. We couldn't give them out fast enough. People came to regard them as badges of honor. Professional athletes, media celebrities, patients . . . they all took to wearing the T-shirts, parading around like peacocks. Of course, in the process they were walking billboards for the business. It was like having your own Yellow Pages strutting down the street. As we opened more centers, I made one change in the inscription in front: "I Survived Pat Croce's Team." I could hardly take all the credit as we grew and grew. And, ironically, the new shirts became even more prized, the attitude of the wearer being: See, it took more than Crazy Croce himself—it took a whole damn team to handle *me!*

What is important to know is that this kind of marketing was considered taboo in my field. Or any field related to the medical industry. I was called a shameless promoter, a huckster, a Barnum & Bailey disciple. But I was passionate about what I was doing, and I was positive about what I was doing, so I continued to do it—and with great success. Having had my ass bambooed by Master Kwon, names weren't about to make a dent in me. I must confess to succumbing to my ego here—when I see the aggressive marketing campaigns mounted by the health care industry these days, I feel vindicated.

I feel, too, that if you're selling the pig, you ought to sell all of it, including the oink. Prior to the 1997–98 NBA season, we used the "baker's dozen" concept to help stimulate 76ers season ticket sales. And after that dismal '96–'97 season we needed lots of help. Every season ticket holder who renewed and every new one who signed on received a black T-shirt emblazoned with a stylish, newly designed 76ers logo. We put 76ers caps on cabbies and toll booth operators. We replaced broken backboards on city courts and playgrounds. And we sold 39 percent more tickets than the year before (and a total of 79 percent more tickets as of the 1999–2000 season).

And that was the kind of aggressive attitude we used at SPT in our Baldrige Crusade. The quest for Ichiban began in 1992 with Jimbo being appointed our quality guru. He attended national quality seminars. He interviewed past winners of Malcolm Baldrige Awards, found out what their entries had looked like, learned what the selection committee tended to favor. Then he put together our 75-page entry. Seventy-five pages precisely. Not a paragraph more. Not a sentence more. Not a comma more. You see, the instructions that accompanied the application forms were very specific. Any page that numbered over 75 would be ripped out and burned. And any application that was received by the selection committee one minute—no, one *tick*—past the due date would be summarily tossed out.

I loved it, of course. These people were as anal about punctuality and precision as I was. They felt that if a company couldn't follow very specific instructions, then how sloppy and careless was it in servicing its customers? No detail should be considered too small.

The selection committee had suggested that bar graphs and pie charts be used as support. Dutifully, we had bar graphs and pie charts. We used the type the committee specified. We used the font the committee specified. There was not an undotted "i," not an uncrossed "t." And as our own little personal flourish, we designed a sharp, cool looking color-coordinated cover superimposing the Sports Physical Therapists logo over the Malcolm Baldrige National Quality Award. It was like subliminal advertising. It looked dynamite. We looked like a winner.

And then on the morning we were going to entrust our entry to Federal Express (a previous Baldrige Award winner), Jimbo looked it over for the thousand and first time and, on the bound cover, read that we were submitting Sports Physical Therapists for consideration of a quality award named "Baldridge."

The name was misspelled!

An extra "d." Shit! Shit! Shit!

No detail too small? This wasn't a detail! We had misspelled the name of the man who was honored by the award we were trying to win.

Talk about a turd in the cut-crystal punch bowl!

Jimbo scooped up the six copies of our entry and sped to Cetlin Design, our advertising designer, for emergency surgery. Larry Cetlin went to work with his scalpel. He removed the mistake. He redesigned a new cover page on the spot. Somehow, when he was done with his graphic plastic surgery, not a hint of our earlier error was visible. Jimbo drove at roughly the speed of sound to reach the nearest FedEx pickup site. Our entry was on time. More important, it was accepted. This was a huge victory in itself because most applications were disqualified at the door for failure to follow directions.

We made it to the second round before being eliminated. That was disappointing, but it was also a terrific learning experience. Our centers had benefited from the whole Ichiban campaign. In 1993, we tried again. There were requests for applications from 159,999 other businesses. Almost all of them failed to apply or were shot down immediately. Again, we survived the first round. Yes, there was honor in that, but you know what you hear every year at the Academy Awards, about how it's just an honor to be nominated? That's a crock. That's a brave front. The truth is, we all want to win.

Well, we made it past the second round. We made it all the way to the semi-finals. We were in the Top 10 in the service category. We needed to survive one more cut to qualify for closer scrutiny—surprise drop-ins, on-site visits and inspections, and interviews with staff members by the Baldrige judges. We were ready. In fact, we were hoping to be put under the microscope; the closer and more critical the look, the better.

But it wasn't to be. We lost out to the Ritz Carlton Hotel chain.

But the experience had been enormously rewarding. We had all rallied around a common cause. Our well-oiled machine was revving like never before, and pride was at an all-time high.

Also at an all-time high was interest in us by other members of the physical therapy industry. We had been receiving considerable national attention, but now our corporate office was besieged by inquiries from large publicly-held companies and venture capitalists. The culture that we had cultivated appealed to them. They wanted to incorporate much of what we had done, including our Ten Commandments of Customer Service, into their own corporate cultures.

And some of them wanted to do more than just incorporate our culture. They wanted to buy Sports Physical Therapists.

@ @ @

In the process of developing a distinct culture in SPT, I thought from time to time that I ought to instill some culture in myself.

I know what you're thinking: *Culturing Pat is like putting an earring on a pig.*

But I was well-intentioned and sincere. I was willing to try to better myself, and shouldn't that count for something? Maybe I could smooth off some of my rough edges. Cultivate some Yin, suppress some of that Yang. I had immersed myself in the martial arts, but what about the fine arts? I had heard that saying about how "music hath charms to soothe the savage beast." I couldn't paint. I had become a voracious reader but I wasn't much of a fiction writer. So how about music?

I settled on the saxophone. I like the way it sounded, mellow and soulful, and I admired the way it could, in the properly skilled hands, express a wide range of emotions. I was a big fan (eventually, a friend) of Grover Washington, Jr. I felt like I had the moves and I knew I had the hot air. So I began taking sax lessons.

From a big fat music man.

Following a month of lessons, I agreed to buy an instrument from him—for $400. I figured I was getting screwed because he'd charge me a dollar just for a little reed, which are usually a dime a dozen. He always seemed to be nickel-and-diming me to death. I gave him two hundred bucks, with the rest to follow the next lesson. Then shortly afterward he called to tell me he wanted his saxophone back.

He caught me off guard. I figured, weasel that he was, he had probably found someone he could screw for even more money.

"Okay," I said, "but I want my two hundred bucks back."

"Gotta have it right now," he said. "Bring it over."

I said that I would get it to him over the weekend. Diane and V and I always worked out together on the weekend, and still do. So on the way to our workout at one of my centers, I stopped at the guy's house and knocked on his side door. His navel got there a couple of feet before the rest of him.

"Gimme my sax."

"Yeah, but gimme my money first."

"I said, gimme my sax," said the music man.

And with that he came out the door and grabbed my windpipe and started squeezing like it was a bagpipe. He grabbed the sax with his other hand.

Of course, I hit him. Knocked him ass-over-appetite through the door.

"Go get my money!"

His wife came to investigate and she started screaming. Sounded like someone strangling a cat.

I went around to the car to tell Diane and V what had happened, and suddenly the garage door slowly opened and here came the music man.

Swinging a shovel!

He was ready to decapitate me. I stepped in and to one side and blocked his blow. Now I was properly pissed. Now Yang was demanding to be fed.

"Now, I'm gonna have to hurt you," I told him, almost apologetically.

I saw V coming up behind him, with his hands extended to each side. He was going to clap the music man's ears. That, incidentally, will make you feel like a 747 is taking off inside your head.

"V, no!"

I knew this could only end badly.

So I exhaled and told the music man: "Just go inside and get the cops."

We ended up in court. The music man represented himself, and in his arrogance and drug-induced state managed to expose the asshole that he was. I had the receipt from my first $200. The judge told me to give the music man the other $200. The sax was then mine.

But not for long.

Tommy Conwell, who had a great rock-and-roll band called "The Young Rumblers," and who worked out at one of my centers, admired that sax. So I lent it to him.

In almost no time at all, it was stolen.

Figures, right? My continuing search for cultivation always seems to end up in frustration. I try to develop some Yin, and end up *Yanging* a music teacher.

❦ ❦ ❦

Of all the remarkable athletes who passed through our centers, the three most dedicated were Michael Jack Schmidt, Julius Erving, and Dave Poulin.

Jack and Doctor J were especially in tune with their bodies. That's one reason they're both in the Hall of Fame. They worked out to extend their careers, and in the process they came to love the lean, hungry look and feel of supreme fitness—the sensation of being right on the edge physically.

But the strongest and fittest of them all was a hockey player we all called Moose.

Dave Poulin had played hockey at Notre Dame. But the talent scouts of the National Hockey League were not especially impressed with American players in the early '80s. Moose was deemed to be sturdy and willing, but not skilled enough for the NHL. He went undrafted. He also went undeterred.

Like Dr. Seuss, Moose kept knocking on doors. He went all the way to Stockholm before he found one that didn't close in his face. He made one of Sweden's elite hockey teams—made it on pluck, grit, determination, and a killer work ethic. The coach of that team, Ted Sator, eventually became an assistant coach under Mike Keenan with the Philadelphia Flyers, and he convinced management to bring in Moose for a look as soon as the European season ended.

Moose not only made the team, but he was eventually made captain of the Flyers. The black "C" that a hockey captain wears on his sweater is not given out lightly. It is hockey's version of the Medal of Honor. Moose valiantly led the gritty Flyers into the 1987 Stanley Cup finals, where they pushed the star-studded Edmonton Oilers—led by the great Wayne Gretzky—to the seven-game limit before finally succumbing.

With all the celebrity endorsements (unsolicited) from people like Doc and Jack and Moose, and with the national attention generated by our performance in the Baldrige competition, and with our centers showing a healthy bottom line, suddenly SPT was attracting much attention from Wall Street. I was being urged to go public, but I didn't like the idea of accommodating the stock market at the expense of our customers. My expertise and my interest was in starting, growing, and running things—not in answering to shareholders.

And then the large national public health-care companies came calling. They all kept whispering the same word in my ear:

Merger.

 PAT CROCE POINTER

Selling SPT wasn't nearly as emotionally wrenching as I thought it might be. I'm not one for looking back. I prefer to see what's coming.

Meanwhile the industry was changing, and not for the better. The insurance companies were starting to determine the fees. They haggled over everything, which compromised service to the patients. I could see our triangle—fun, quality, profit—beginning to disintegrate. I had gotten in the business at exactly the right time, and now it felt more and more like this would be the right time to get out. Merging, being acquired, looked more and more tempting.

So I met with a succession of health-care industry CEOs.

But it had to be the right fit. It had to have the right feel. I didn't want just anyone assimilating our culture into theirs. And I wanted to make sure all my people were taken care of—that they didn't just survive, but that they would have the opportunity to thrive. I felt that NovaCare might be a good fit after talking to John Foster, the CEO. NovaCare was headquartered locally, in King of Prussia, Pennsylvania, and had already begun acquiring other physical therapy centers—they had 120 before acquiring my 40. Today, they have more than 500. After much encouragement and input from Mountain and my financial advisor, Isadore "Issy" Friedman, we sealed the deal in September of 1993. All my people kept their positions in good standing, and my top guns were promoted to top spots.

Selling SPT—the business I had started from scratch and cultivated for more than ten years—wasn't nearly as emotionally wrenching as I thought it might be. I'm not one for looking back. I prefer to see what's coming. I like to anticipate.

I stayed at NovaCare for two years, to help with the transition. I still had a proprietary interest, and so I wanted to make sure that things went right. I also wanted to protect my people. And I suppose I was a little curious to see what life was like in the high-powered corporate world ... to see how I'd react to a life of four walls and a desk.

I found out soon enough. I was the square peg being jammed unsuccessfully into the round hole. I felt like a captured wolf who furiously refuses to be domesticated. Meetings would drone on and on, but after ninety minutes my alarm would go off and I'd just up and leave. Entire days would go by and nothing exciting would occur, nothing significant would get done. There was a gaping void in my life. I have a fundamental need to constantly challenge myself, to prove myself *to myself*. Now all my venting outlets and competitive channels had been closed off. Yang was going berserk inside me.

So I gave in to Yang. I threw myself into the martial arts. I had never stopped karate training, but now I had more time, I wasn't traveling as much, and ... I was turning 40. Was this my mid-life crisis? Was this my middle-age rage? I don't think it was quite that, exactly. It's just that I don't like being comfortable. I need to feed my hunger. I have to indulge my addiction to danger. I have to face the fact that I've got a serious habit ....

And my drug of choice is adrenalin.

I made the U.S. Tang Soo Do Karate team that qualified for an international tournament in the United Kingdom. No one on any of the competitive teams was over 25, which of course made me geriatric. Or Jurassic.

My first opponent was from Greece. I annihilated him.

My second opponent was from Germany. I obliterated him.

My third opponent was from Malaysia. I disintegrated him.

My fourth opponent—in the gold medal match—was from the UK. A stud. He was about six-two, 180. I was six feet, 165. He was shaved bald with a ponytail. I had Yang in my eyes. It was like the movie *Bloodsport*. We killed each other. He scored, I scored. We went back and forth. It was a great match.

And then I cold-cocked him with a spinning wheel kick to the head— it was a direct hit that felt incredible, but it would cost me. You see, in competitive karate you're allowed slight contact, but not *full* contact. Otherwise, the corpses would pile up. My exuberance had gotten the best of me, and I suffered a point deduction. As added penance, I had to face the audience, kneel down, and bow in contrition and apology.

I ended up with the silver medal.

I know what you're thinking: Pat, you should have pulled your kick!

And I'm thinking: *Damn, he should have ducked!*

❧ ❧ ❧

Years earlier, I had come home late one night after working a Flyers game to find Diane crying. A helicopter leased by Donald Trump had gone down. Three of his people were on board. All three perished in the crash, two of whom we knew. I told her on the spot that I'd get rid of my chopper. (That's right: that first solo flight where I lost the airport didn't faze me—I had bought a chopper and flown it many times since then.) But in all honesty, I was just trying to placate her—I was hoping I really wouldn't have to give up my bird.

But I did. And I switched to something "safer."

Motorcycles.

I remembered how part of the fun of hangin' at the high (more than 25 years earlier) had included tooling around on Corky's 350 cc Honda. So I talked Diane into letting me buy a bike. Not just any bike, naturally. I wanted the jumbo jet of bikes—a Harley Davidson 1340 cc—a 750-pound get-the-hell-outta-my-way hog. But the waiting list to get one of these rare beauties was anywhere from six months to a year. Which was six months to a year longer than I could wait.

So I settled for a slightly used 1990 Harley Fat Boy. But before I made the purchase, I wanted to secure the services of an instructor, just as I had for karate and for Japanese and for the helicopter (although most definitely *not* like I had for the saxophone). I know what you're thinking here, too: *The perfect man to teach you how to ride a motorcycle would be Evel Knievel.* But no. I enrolled in the State Police's motorcycle safety course.

I immediately picked up on the four basic rules of what to do when turning at an intersection—slow, look, lean, and roll. The first two speak for themselves. The lean is what gets the bike turned. The roll is what you do to the throttle to power the bike through the turn.

During the first full day of riding my newly acquired Fat Boy—a monster compared to the 100-pound, 125 cc Yamaha I'd used during the State Police training—I had a little incident. I hadn't paid enough attention to instructions and I didn't respect the increased power of the hog, so I *deserved* exactly what was coming. There was a car gliding to a stop sign on my right as I entered an intersection. I slowed, but not nearly enough. I didn't lean enough, either. And I didn't get a chance to roll the throttle because *I* was the one doing the rolling! I jumped off the bike and pulled it down on top of me, kind of like a rodeo cowboy wrangling a calf.

That desperate maneuver kept us—the hog and me—from hitting the car. It didn't, however, keep us out of dents, nicks, and assorted scratches. The biggest contusions were the ones on my ego. The incident was another helpful little reminder, though. Every time I don't pay proper attention, every time I get ahead of myself . . . well, remember that farmer who could make mules talk? "First, you got to hit 'em between the eyes with a two-by-four to get their attention." The hog had gotten my attention, no doubt about it. The very next morning, I limped out of bed and straddled the bike and spent more than an hour in an empty school parking lot doing what I should have done before my first ride—making turns.

Practice doesn't make perfect. Practice makes permanent. *Perfect practice* is what makes perfect.

It was about this time that I hooked up with Steve O'Kula— "Steve-O." He owned a one-bay garage on a corner of Main Street in Manayunk (a Philadelphia neighborhood). It was a perfect dive. It reeked of engine grease and atmosphere. It was a middle-aged adult's trip back in time . . . to hangin' at the high. Biking is a unique subculture. There are rules and ways, and you abide by them. And if you don't, well, there's a very good chance you can get killed—either by accident or by gunshot.

  PAT CROCE POINTER
Practice doesn't make perfect. Practice makes permanent.
***Perfect practice* is what makes perfect.**

Biking attracts a rainbow of characters, and at any given time you can find Yuppies, doctors, plumbers, accountants, and legitimate nomads and Hell's Angels types all waiting for bikes at Steve-O's. Soon enough we had formed a group. Not a "gang" in the destructive sense. Just a group of disparate personalities who shared a passion for biking and good laughs. Besides Steve-O, there was our road captain and enforcer, T-Bone (Tom Weisbecker), and Meat (Mike Comfort) and KO (Kevin McCracken) and Doc (Dr. Jack McPhilemy) and Spanky and Piggy and Happy. Talk about a human zoo. Even Disney couldn't sanitize these characters. Eventually Fast Eddie and Fran joined the fun of our rolling thunder.

Every other Tuesday evening for three years, I went to Steve-O's and learned all I could about motorcycles. I wanted to be as familiar with the innards of a Harley as I was with the human anatomy. I ended up restoring a couple of them, a 1947 Harley Flat Head which sits in my office in the First Union Center, and a 1946 Knuckle Head. They're magnificent beasts. Restoring these beasts was like putting dinosaur bones back together into a skeleton. It gives you a real appreciation for their heritage.

I drove a Harley Bad Boy that we had doctored up until the summer of '99. And whenever there was a day that I didn't need to dress up, I cruised to work with a smile. There's a visceral appeal to biking; it tempts you on a lot of levels. There's the sense of freedom. There's the seduction of the open road. There's the pure rush of incredible speed. There are the sights you just don't see from your car on the interstate. There are the people you just don't meet any other place (we've gone to rallies in Sturgis, South Dakota; Daytona, Florida; and Lincoln, New Hampshire).

And there's the danger. Fear can seep clean into your bones.

What you really learn to appreciate, and to pay close respectful attention to, is the weather. You may notice it in your car if there's a hard rainstorm or sleet or snow. In a helicopter, you notice it ten-fold. On a bike, you notice it a *hundred-fold.* We nearly went through a twister crossing the Badlands in South Dakota, and I can tell you for certain that a twister is a serious expression of Yang. There is an old wartime saying that there are no atheists in foxholes. You won't find any on the seat of a bike during a storm, either.

There are also bugs—bugs that hit you with the force of bullets. There's grime that coats you like tar. There are pebbles and little shards of rock that tear into you like shrapnel. And for all the discomfort and danger, and probably *because* of the discomfort and danger, you find that all your senses are heightened.

On a motorcycle, you are most assuredly alive.

During my immersion into karate following the sale of Sports Physical Therapists, I'd find myself awaiting a bout, sitting in the proper cross-legged position (fists on knees, spine straight as an arrow), preparing to fight some hotshot killer twenty years my junior, risking my bones for some chunk of metal, and frequently the same question would occur to me:

What the hell am I doing here?

It's the same question that I ask myself when I'm sitting on the seat of a hog trapped in a slashing rainstorm. The same question that I asked myself when I was alone in a helicopter lost in space. And the same question that I asked myself twenty-five years earlier when I was sitting in the back of Bator's car about to play "chicken."

Always the same question: *What the hell am I doing here?*

And my answer has always been the same: Living life to the fullest. Not always the smartest, admittedly. But at such moments I sure wasn't bored. The problem was, there were never enough of those moments.

And once again, I needed an outlet. I needed a new challenge.

Like maybe buying a bad basketball team . . .

Chapter 12
The Will of the Soul

❦ ❦ ❦

*I*n October of 1995, I found myself in the worst possible position that an obsessive-compulsive Type-A workaholic can be in: I had lots of money and no responsibilities.

I know it sounds like heaven. But for me, it was hell. No job, no challenge. Forty years old and cut adrift. Forty years old and I still didn't know what I wanted to be when I grew up. I had fulfilled my two-year obligation to the NovaCare merger and now I felt like a mountain climber who has successfully scaled a daunting summit and, after the initial exhilaration of conquest has passed, is overcome by melancholy and a curious hollow feeling, and this haunting question:

Now what?

I had a series of brain-picking meetings and lunches with high-powered businessmen—creative tycoons like Ed Snider and Chuck Barris, my venture capitalist buddy Eddie Antoian, and Ron Rubin, a highly successful Philadelphia real-estate developer. I was searching for an answer; the problem was, I wasn't quite sure what the question was. The unscratchable itch had returned. Mr. Yang needed to be fed again.

And then I had lunch with Harold Katz. Harold was a self-made multi-millionaire who had gotten rich off the fat of the land. Literally. He started up a weight-loss business that he ran out of his home (the first files were kept in the bathtub). He ended up with a nationwide franchised business, NutriSystems, that made him gobs of money. He used 12 million of those dollars to buy the 76ers. Harold was a hopelessly addicted hoopaholic. He played basketball in high school, had a full court built in back of his house, and had been a long-time 76ers season ticket holder. He prided himself on how much he knew about the intricacies of the game.

He bought the Sixers in July of 1981. They were already good. He made them even better. In 1983, in only his second season of ownership, they won the NBA championship. And for that entire decade they were among the elite teams of the sport. But then came a series of injuries, bad trades, worse drafts, assorted miscalculations and mistakes, and the Sixers started to slide. They muddled through the 1990s in a prolonged slump. The losing seasons mounted, and so did Harold's frustration. He was very much a hands-on owner, and he took far more than a wealthy dilettante's passing interest in his team. For many owners, a professional sports franchise is simply a rich man's toy. But this was Harold's consuming passion, his baby, and the persistent losing ate at him. And the media consistently scalded him.

So it was against this background that Harold and I had lunch. And even though I had no specific business ideas in mind that day, I instinctively obeyed Number 3 of my Ten Commandments: Listen, listen, listen. I was aware that opportunity sometimes knocks very softly, and what I heard that day was a very unhappy man. He complained about the ominous financial implications in the new collective bargaining agreement between the NBA and the Players Association. He moaned about the commute he now had to make to see his beloved 76ers play—he had just purchased a lavish mansion outside Boca Raton, Florida, where the sky seemed all the more blue and sunny compared to the bleak gray cloud that hung over his team in Philadelphia. And he seethed at how the media vilified him—his frustration was magnified because he had no recourse, no way of retaliating. He went on and on, pouring out venom and frustration and anguish.

In short, this was a despondent man.

And then the "On" switch clicked in my brain. I didn't even put down my fork.

"Harold," I blurted out, "let me buy 10 percent of the team from you."

I'm not sure who was more surprised—Harold, listening to the guy who used to tape and stretch and rehabilitate his players now offering to buy a chunk of his team, or me, thinking: *Yo, Pat, where the hell did that one come from?*

I didn't give him a chance to even hiccup.

"I'll infuse culture," I told him, breathlessly. "I'll restore team spirit, I'll pour in all my business philosophies. I'll get the team involved in the community and get the community interested in the team again. I'll stand on the roof of the CoreStates Center and take all the flak, and you can play golf in Florida and fly up for the games and smoke cigars and enjoy yourself."

"Harold," I concluded, leaning across the table, "let me take the *agita* for you."

He took the cigar out of his mouth slowly. To his credit, he didn't just laugh in my face and sneer: "Go tape an ankle, trainer."

Instead, he smiled. A weary smile, I remember thinking. And he said: "No, Pat, I don't take on partners. When I sell the team, it will be all or nothing."

I drove home from that lunch with my face split wide open by a grin. Lottery winners aren't as happy as I was at that moment. You may think that I had just been rejected. Ah, but the Be Positive commandment (Number 7) told me that I had been presented, however obliquely, with an opportunity. You see, Harold had heard himself say "no," but it sounded more like *"maybe"* to me. His response was not a flat-out refusal, rather it was a qualification. A provision. I had heard "all or nothing."

The word that I *didn't* hear—the one that, had I heard it, might have stopped me then and there—was "never."

Harold had not said he'd never sell to me. All he had done was set boundaries.

"All or nothing."

It's vital at this point to emphasize that we already had a ten-year relationship. Had I not known Harold Katz, that lunch probably never would have happened. Had I called him cold, he probably wouldn't even have taken my call. Under different circumstances, I would have had no entree at all. I didn't smoke cigars with him. Didn't play golf with him. Didn't shoot hoops with him. I wasn't one of his franchisees. But I *was* the physical therapist for his team for almost ten years. He knew me. I wasn't a stranger. The first time I was in the office of John Foster, the CEO of NovaCare, I was riveted by a three-word plaque that stated:

"Relationships Determine Results."

Exactly! Almost every success or opportunity that I have had can be traced back to a relationship. Knowing this, I immediately started considering who I needed to talk to about this sliver of an opportunity, this tiny opening in Howard's defenses.

The next day after my lunch with Harold, I called Ron Rubin. He was the consummate deal-maker and an avid sports fan. I had met him through his gorgeous wife, Marcia, whom I had first treated fifteen years earlier when she'd suffered skiing injuries. Many of my relationships grew from meeting people as patients. Their misfortune often turned out to be my good fortune, just in getting to know them. I told Ron about my lunch with Harold, and that I sensed some vulnerability—that now might be the time to buy the 76ers.

He laughed.

"You don't want to be an eager buyer from a reluctant seller," he said. "Especially if the seller is Harold Katz."

Sage advice. But I had the scent now. I was wired. I was going to track him down, even if it meant I had to wade through a thousand miles of Florida swamp to do it.

PAT CROCE POINTER
Almost every success or opportunity that I have had can be traced back to a relationship.

"Let me take care of Harold," I said. "Are you interested in coming in with me if he is willing to sell?"

Ron said: "I'm in. But good luck."

I'm sure he felt this was all a pipe dream that would blow over, that I had let my optimism and enthusiasm get the better of me.

Forty-eight hours after my lunch with Harold, I stood in our kitchen, about to have lunch with Diane, and tried to pick up the phone. I couldn't. It might as well have weighed three tons. Remember Commandment Number 10? Do It *Now!* I didn't want Harold to catch a breath. I wanted to repeat my interest in buying, and to let him know that now I had Ron Rubin on my side. I had some clout behind me, some serious financial muscle.

I kept walking to the phone . . . and then walking away. I had that queasy feeling you get when you think about asking out the prettiest girl in class. Or the queasy feeling that girls must get just thinking about dating the high school hunk. I feared rejection. I feared dejection. I feared Harold might laugh at me. I feared . . . well, I had a thousand fears. And fear can paralyze you.

I walked to my office and looked at the motivational sign I had bought at an open-air arts and crafts show on the Ocean City boardwalk one summer. The Emerson quote:

"Always, always, always, always, always do what you're afraid to do."

I took a deep breath, turned around, and headed back for the phone. I could hear my dad's voice: "If you never ask, then the answer is always 'no.'"

"Hi, Harold, Pat Croce. I wanted to thank you for lunch the other day (even though I paid for it). I've been thinking about our conversation regarding the Sixers. Since you won't own the team with me, Harold, I'd like to buy the team from you. All of it."

My heartbeat sounded louder than Big Ben tolling high noon.

Fortunately, he didn't hang up. Fortunately, his laugh was one of indulgence.

"No, Pat, when I sell the team, it'll be for a lot of money. At least one-hundred-twenty-five million dollars. And I'm not ready to sell yet."

We chatted for another minute, then rang off. I put the phone down very carefully, then did a whooping war dance through the house.

True, once again his very first word had been "no." But words came after that. Other words that, to me at least, made the "no" insignificant. Now I had a price. Now I had more encouragement because once again he didn't say he'd "never" sell to me. He said he wasn't ready "yet." That suggested to me a weakening of his position, however slight. That suggested to me that he had been thinking more than casually about selling since our lunch. Perhaps I had planted the germ of a thought in his mind.

I was revved now. If you maintain a positive attitude, then you can turn a seed into a bloom with just one drop of rain. I sensed an opening, and now it was up to me to start prying that opening a little wider each day. The best way to eat the elephant standing in your path, remember, is one bite at a time.

I went after Harold like a wolf pack hunts. I was going to run him into the ground. I dreamed up a million excuses to talk to him. I called him at his home in Philadelphia. I called him at his 76ers office. I called him at his new home in Florida. Now that I think back, I all but stalked him.

But I wasn't rude. I didn't badger him. I just didn't make it easy for him to forget about me and my eagerness to buy. For days and then for weeks and then for months, I was the drip-drip-dripping that over enough time turns a rock to sand.

"Please remember, Harold," I told him, "when the time does come that you're prepared to sell, I want to be the person you call."

At the end of one of our telephone conversations, he said that if I was ever in Florida to stop in to see him.

Bang! Another opening. I called him a couple days after that to say I'd be in Florida on business the following week, and he repeated his gracious invitation. What I didn't tell him was that the only business I had in Florida was to see him!

We were out by his pool—Harold, his wife Peggy, and I—and when I got up one of their two Rottweilers came at me and bit me right on the ass!

"Geez, Harold, if you don't want to sell you don't have to sic your dogs on me!" I joked.

At least there was no blood. Harold was embarrassed and very apologetic, and I think he felt the least bit guilty. If I'd thought it would have helped sway him, I'd have let those dogs gnaw on just about any part of me they wanted.

But I did sense a shift. Things weren't getting any better for the Sixers. In fact, they were getting worse. The team kept losing, which was, perversely, of great benefit to me. I didn't wish them ill, but I didn't mind that they were helping my cause, either. Out of 82 games that year, they would end up with just 18 wins. Harold became more and more depressed.

After my visit in Florida, I called Ron Rubin and said, "I think he's getting ready to go."

If he was, I'd need financial help. Ron suggested Comcast Corporation, the communications giant headquartered in Philadelphia. I concurred, and so Ron immediately called Ralph Roberts, the founder of Comcast. Yes, he was more than interested. How much might we be talking about? "One-hundred-thirty-million dollars," I replied, figuring I should give myself a five-million dollar cushion.

I called Harold to let him know that I had extra backing. Real money. Bottomless pockets kind of money. Could we, I asked, start the preliminaries? Harold agreed, reluctantly. I could hear the fatigue in his voice. And also the surprise. I was wearing him down!

It took four months of intense persistence and commitment to get to the *preliminary* stage of the deal! But I wasn't counting at the time. Persistence has no time limits.

It was the start of a new year—1996. I had been pursuing Harold relentlessly since October. And at last I had him up a tree. Tim Broadt, my lawyer, drew up a two-page letter of confidentiality that Harold had demanded. Ron and I signed it. My accountant, Andy Z (Zelenkofske), who would perform my due diligence, signed it. And I sent it to Harold.

"What's this?" he asked.

"The confidentiality agreement you wanted."

"Oh."

He tinkered with it. He wanted this, he wanted that. Then he rejected it altogether and had his accountant's lawyer create a new document. That incident set the pattern. Over the entire course of the negotiations Harold would find any pretense he could to get upset and make demands. And I understood. In his heart of hearts, he still didn't think he would ever really sell.

PAT CROCE POINTER
It took four months of intense persistence and commitment to get to the *preliminary* stage of the deal! But I wasn't counting at the time. Persistence has no time limits.

His emotions were being pulled this way and that way. In moments of depression, he'd think: *What the hell do I need this aggravation for? I'm better off selling; take the money and run.* And then the sentiment would tug at him. The team was his pride and joy, and had been a huge chunk of his life for a decade and a half. The emotional umbilical cord that tethered the team to the owner was a strong one.

Harold was also obsessed with keeping all of this a secret. That is never easy in business in general, and in Philadelphia, where leaks abound—especially in sports—it's damn near impossible. Harold didn't even notify his personal lawyer of the potential sale until we got to the negotiations stage.

With Ralph Roberts buying the Sixers on behalf of Comcast, the corporation's lawyer, Art Block, also signed the confidentiality agreement. They faxed it to my house. I faxed it to Harold in Florida.

"Who's this?" Harold screamed.

He was pissed because now another person had become involved and knew about the pending deal. He demanded to know who else would be involved. Well, Bob Pick, the accountant for merger and acquisitions for Comcast, for one. He signed the agreement and faxed it to me. I faxed it on to Harold.

Another yelp of dismay and anger. Another threat to pull back and not sell.

For half a day in January of 1996, I was busier than a cat covering crap. Comcast people were faxing things to me and I was relaying them to Harold and then answering his questions, trying to mollify him, trying desperately to keep this deal from unraveling, knowing all the time that he was looking for the slightest excuse to bail out. My fax machine sounded like a hailstorm on a tin roof.

And suddenly in the middle of it, while I stood there in paperwork piled up to my kneecaps, my mind took a sudden detour and . . .

I was lucky that day—talking into two phones at once, my fax machine smoking—lucky in that Mr. Yang, for once, had succumbed to the influence of Yin. I simply couldn't afford to lose it at that point. I didn't dare scream at someone, didn't dare hit someone, didn't dare threaten someone. I was tap dancing through a mine field. Harold was increasingly skittish. When Ralph's son Brian Roberts signed on—he was, after all, the president of Comcast—Harold was furious. Yet *another* person had become involved.

I lost count of the number of times he said the deal was off, he was done, he wasn't selling, goodbye, sayonara, it's over. Each time, though, patiently, ever so carefully and delicately, I was able to reel him back in. I kept praying that Mr. Yang would continue to snooze peacefully. Comcast decided that since it was buying content for its television cable systems by buying the 76ers, it should add even more content. How about buying the Flyers, too? Well, heck, might as well buy the two arenas they play in, as well—the Spectrum and the new CoreStates Center that was scheduled to open that summer. Ed Snider, the owner of the Flyers and the two arenas, agreed to sell a controlling percentage to Comcast.

Which created a new, and potentially disastrous, problem: Harold and Ed were mortal enemies. They despised each other with a passion that was boundless. They had feuded, publicly and privately, for years. When I informed Harold of Ed's participation, he almost had a seizure.

"Ed Snider isn't going to end up owning my basketball team, is he?" Harold demanded.

No, no, I assured him. Comcast, by a large margin, will own the majority of everything.

After more than four months of pursuit and perseverance, after all the clandestine meetings and hushed phone calls and top-secret faxes, I was stressed. And the stress soon entered the realm of paranoia. Ron had informed me that Ralph and Brian Roberts, Ed Snider, and he had scheduled a Sunday meeting. I had been excluded. The street corner survivalist in me was immediately suspicious.

Were they trying an end-run? Were they plotting to go ahead without me? What the hell was this?

I was mad and I was scared. I tried to be brutally honest with myself: *Maybe they still think of you as just a trainer, a taper of ankles and mender of bodies. Maybe they don't regard you as a card-carrying member of their exclusive club yet. Maybe they're going to ace you out and have a big laugh.* If you give your mind half a chance when your emotional state is in proper chaos, it's amazing what it can conjure up.

There's an old saying about paranoia: You're not paranoid if they really are out to get you. My first and fiercest instinct was to protect my back.

So on the sly—on the very day I heard about their secret meeting—I lined up a meeting of my own with a big investment house on Wall Street. The next day, I went to New York to lunch with them. We met at the 21 Club. I knew I was playing at the top level of the financial game when the bill came. There were three of us—I'd had a fish sandwich and water, they'd each had a cheeseburger and an iced tea.

Total tab: *One-hundred-twenty-one dollars.* Not including the tip.

"How much backing would you need?" one of them asked between bites.

"One-hundred-forty million dollars." I tried to sound casual.

I figured I ought to give myself even more of a cushion. Just in case. I was finding out that business is full of "just-in-cases."

One of them excused himself to make a phone call. He was back before I could finish my water.

"Yeah, we can do that," he said. "No problem."

He was so nonchalant that you'd have thought he was telling me nothing more than, "Sure, no problem, we can give you a ride to the train station when we are done with lunch."

It turned out that I didn't need the backing and I needn't have worried about that Sunday meeting that I hadn't been invited to . . . but the whole experience was instructive and worthwhile. It reminded me again just how long that walk from the training room to the boardroom really was. I still remember how it felt sitting in the Comcast boardroom for the first time, a room that appeared to be only slightly smaller than the palace at Versailles. It was an office in the clouds on the 36th floor, finely appointed with tasteful decor and an unmistakable atmosphere of power. I looked around, tried not to let my jaw drop, awed at the magnitude of the people assembled, and asked myself that same question I had asked on the seat of the hog and on the karate mat and in Bator's car:

What the hell am I doing here?

My pulse answered for me. It sounded like the cannon during the finale of "The 1812 Overture."

Comcast was—is—extraordinarily professional. And there's a genuine family atmosphere that begins with Ralph, the mentor, and Brian, the wunderkind, and extends on down. But they, and I, still weren't done. We had gotten Harold to the negotiating table and at long last he seemed ready to sell. And then . . .

And then one cold night in February, Harold's lawyer called. It was 10 o'clock. He had some points of concern in the final contract.

Seventy-two separate and distinct points of concern.

So Art Block and Bob Pick (I called them Block and Tackle) and I went to the lawyer's high-rise condo in center city Philadelphia. We plodded through all seventy-two points of concern. We recessed in the hallway. We came back in and haggled some more. Then we went downstairs and caucused outside in Bob Pick's car. We called Brian Roberts about some of the stickier points. Even with the motor running and the heater on, it was still cold. I remember thinking that even in the Wharton School of Business, I bet they don't mention that among the dangers in a six-hundred-million-dollar deal is that you might lose some of your extremities to frostbite, or succumb to carbon monoxide poisoning while making phone calls from inside a parked car during negotiations.

One of my favorite things about business is the fact that creativity and personality are important factors—it's not just all figures and charts and dollars and cents. A good deal maker will do whatever it takes, and use every facet of their character, to get it done.

It was after midnight when we got done, and there were still a few points of concern that hadn't been resolved. Eventually though, they were.

Finally, we were ready to formally announce the deal. The date of the press conference was set for March 19, 1996. The story had broken four days earlier. We all agreed that it was pretty remarkable that we'd managed to keep such a secret for so long in a town that is right there with Washington, D.C. when it comes to loose lips.

 PAT CROCE POINTER
One of my favorite things about business is the fact that creativity and personality are important factors—it's not just all figures and charts and dollars and cents. A good deal maker will do whatever it takes, and use every facet of their character, to get it done.

The night before the formal announcement, I reflected on how the ripple effect from just one phone call—the call that I had been so afraid to make, that first call to Harold Katz five months before—could be so great. One pebble tossed hesitantly into a pool had swelled from ripple to wave to tsunami. Two teams and two arenas had changed hands. A 24-hour sports television network would follow. So would a minor league hockey team, the Philadelphia Phantoms. It's truly astonishing—all that from one phone call. It reminded me of the poem about how a war had been lost all for the want of a single nail for a horseshoe.

And about that time I got a phone call.

Block and Tackle were just finishing up the last of the paperwork when Harold had changed his mind at the last minute.

It was almost 3 o'clock in the morning of the day that I was going to be introduced as part-owner and new president of the 76ers.

Harold had had a serious, last-minute attack of second thoughts.

I was wide awake now. And so was Mr. Yang. *This* close, hours away, and it was all going to collapse?

No, we had all agreed, we were done making concessions. We had a clean, clear deal. If Harold wanted to walk now, then no one was going to stand in front of him, no one was going to slam the door and not let him out. We had reached our limit. There would be no more negotiating.

He capitulated. We all exhaled. That morning I went with Harold to the 76ers offices, which then were located in the bowels of Veterans

Stadium, home of the Eagles and Phillies, and across the street from the Spectrum. As we walked through the offices, I couldn't help but think that here, right *here*, is where I used to sneak over the fence to get into Eagles games with Jakester. Now I would have an office here. Now I would have a team here. Now I was the president. An owner. Do dreams really come true? Oh my, yes. A thousand times, yes. A thousand times a thousand times, yes!

Harold gathered his staff and thanked them. He cried. Right up to the very end he didn't think he'd sell, and now that he had, he still had a hard time believing it. We went to the formal announcement and press conference in the Spectrum. Ralph Roberts spoke. Brian Roberts spoke. Ed Snider spoke. I introduced Harold, and I kissed him.

He was asked by one of the media what had made him sell. He looked down the dais, pointed to me, and said, "Pat Croce called me fifty times."

I laughed aloud with the audience. But I couldn't help but think to myself: *Damn, I had to double Dr. Seuss' determination to make my dream come true, and then some.*

I can't tell you how many people told me afterwards that if they'd known Harold was ready to sell, they'd have bought the team from him. How come I had been the lucky one? I attributed it to Commandments Number 3 (Listen, Listen, Listen), Number 4 (Communicate Clearly), Number 6 (Be Prompt and Professional), Number 7 (Be Positive), and Number 10 (Do It *Now!*).

It came my turn to speak. I had more pent-up emotion, more energy that needed to be released, than Three Mile Island. I got up behind the microphones and then I did something totally spontaneous, giving in completely to Mr. Yang. I flung my closed fists to the heavens, threw my head back, and let loose a barbaric yell. And like my first day on the radio program years earlier, the media in attendance could have turned off their microphones and the whole city would have heard me nonetheless.

Damn, but it felt good.

And then I grinned and shouted the three-word motto that had become my signature line:

"I feel grrrrrrrreat!"

Local radio and TV played that sound bite over and over. The networks picked it up. My howl was on ESPN's SportsCenter, on CNN, all over and around the dial.

I'm no poet. I don't read much poetry. But there's one poem, only eight lines long, that I committed to memory a long time ago. I thought of it continually that day, the day of perhaps my greatest triumph, and I recite it in every motivational speech I give. If ever it applied, that was the day. It was written by Ella Wheeler Wilcox, and it goes like this:

> *One ship sails east, and another west*
> *With the same winds that blow;*
> *'Tis the set of the sails and not the gales*
> *That decides the way we go.*
> *Like the winds of the sea are the ways of fate*
> *As they voyage along through life;*
> *'Tis the will of the soul that decides its goals*
> *And not the calm or the strife.*

We are all capable, every one of us, of far, far more than we realize. Look at all that was wrought by one phone call, by just one finger tap-tap-tapping out a seven-digit number.

The only thing that is ever foolish about a dream is to not act on it.

'Tis the will of the soul . . . how bad do you want it?

Chapter 13

Where's the
Owner's Manual?

❧ ❧ ❧

*M*y first official act as the owner of a professional sports franchise was to become a shoplifter.

And if you're going to steal, then steal only from the very best.

So less than 48 hours after having been formally and publicly introduced as the new president of the Philadelphia 76ers, I was bound for New York and the offices of the Commissioner of the National Basketball Association.

To kiss his ring.

David Stern is arguably the most powerful and influential man in sports. Since 1984, he has presided over the rebirth and revitalization of professional basketball. On his watch, the NBA has metamorphosed from a league with severe image and financial problems (with several members teetering on the brink of bankruptcy) into a truly successful international venture. Basketball is second only to soccer as the most-played sport in the world—and it's closing the gap fast.

It seemed only right to me that I formally present myself to Mr. Stern. Kind of like the way a new ambassador to Great Britain would present himself to the court of King James.

David Stern remembered me from my days as the Sixers' physical therapist. We had encountered each other frequently in the corridors of the Spectrum whenever he was in town for the playoffs back in the Sixers' glory days, when being in the playoffs was regarded as a birthright. He used to call me the "trainer for the stars" because of my notoriety with the likes of Dr. J and Moses Malone, as well as Mike Schmidt and Bobby Clarke.

As he welcomed me enthusiastically into the fold, it dawned on me that this was a fairly exclusive club. It has only twenty-nine members. That's a heady thought if you dwell on it. But as far as I was concerned,

I'd never had much use for fraternities of any kind, and I definitely wasn't a joiner. And all I knew about the other twenty-eight owners was that I wanted to kick their asses up and down the court.

I think the Commissioner was pleased that a guy off the street corner had joined the league. Give it the commoner's touch. But he also recognized my impatience, and when I asked him if he had any advice for a brand new owner, he smiled and gave me some great counsel:

"Don't try to do it overnight."

I nodded my understanding. Mr. Yang, of course, sneered. Patience? *Ha!*

I looked around. The offices are up there in the fourth tier of clouds, higher than the offices at Comcast, higher even than Michael Jordan can jump. It occurred to me that this was a fairly momentous day. Me, the trainer-turned-owner, with the commish and his deputy, Russ Granik, just kickin' back and talkin' hoops up there in the sky.

"You know what I need? I need a memento of some kind to commemorate this moment," I blurted out.

I looked around the room. My gaze fell on the Commissioner's desk and a small but handsome Champion basketball clock. Stern's eyes followed mine, nervously. When he saw what it was that I was coveting, he reached to protect it.

Too late.

I suggested a bargain.

"I'll give this back when you give me the championship trophy," I said, waving the clock.

I was fortunate. He smiled. The Commissioner has a sense of humor. I think he appreciated my passion. Certainly it would be good for the league if the team in one of the country's top five markets could be turned around and at least be made competitive again. So, the visit came to a cordial conclusion and I took my leave.

And on the way out I made a pig of myself. I helped myself to every souvenir in sight. An NBA T-shirt here, a cap there. A video. A schedule. I thought about asking the Commissioner if he had a shopping cart I might borrow while I loaded up. But I figured I had pressed my luck far enough.

That clock, incidentally, sits on the desk in my office. I can't wait to trade it in.

❧ ❧ ❧

Now that I own the 76ers, I get interviewed on TV all the time in front of millions of viewers. But my message wasn't always in demand . . . .

My public speaking experience started when an audience of five came to listen to an energetic 23-year-old kid marvel about the magical benefits of exercise and nutrition at a fitness club's wellness night. Either there weren't many people interested in being well, or more likely, no one wanted to risk their evening listening to a no-name speaker named Pat Croce.

But I can guarantee you that those five in attendance told at least five others of their moving experience. Literally.

Slowly and steadily the audience grew. Venues got larger. Rotary Clubs, Lions Clubs, and even Mothers Clubs throughout the region lined up to pay absolutely nothing for my fire and brimstone sermon, usually accompanied by my amusing stories and physical antics.

No one was beyond my reach. From AARP meetings to the "I Feel Great Show" in grade schools, no one could escape my motivating message. Eventually, and surprisingly so, I was offered a fee to speak to a group of insurance salesmen. That engagement, and others like it that followed, generated the word-of-mouth endorsement that has led to today's list of speaking engagements for Fortune 500 companies.

During my speaking engagements, I talk about dreams and goal setting. I always talk about how one of my dreams—ever since I met Ed Snider—was to own a professional sports team. And then I explain how it just so happened that I had gotten my heart set on one team in particular: the 76ers.

And invariably the response of the people I was speaking to *was* always the same:

"Why them? They suck!"

Maybe that was part of the appeal. If they had already been successful, then where would the challenge be? My challenge was to turn that "suck" into "luck," and to turn that team into a champion.

So I had the prize, now what would I do with it? For starters, I needed someone to run the franchise: A general manager. I knew how to start a business, how to market it, and how to expand it. But I knew squat about basketball operations.

So I made a promise, first to myself and then to Philadelphia fans, that I would not under any circumstances interfere or meddle with the basketball side of the business. One of the most basic rules of business, after all, is that first you surround yourself with able, knowledgeable people, and then you get out of their way and you stay out of their way.

Another basic rule is to do what successful people do. So I asked around for recommendations.

In all, I interviewed six different candidates. The biggest of those names was Chuck Daly and John Gabriel. Gabe's contract as General Manager of the Orlando Magic was running out, but he would eventually renew . . . using my offer as leverage. Chuck had said he was content as a television commentator and wasn't interested in getting back in the game as a coach or GM.

 PAT CROCE POINTER
First you surround yourself with able, knowledgeable people, and then you get out of their way and you stay out of their way.

One of the strongest recommendations was given me by two men who had been general managers of the Sixers before—John Nash and Jimmy Lynam—who knew the franchise and the city. They suggested a low-profile name:

Brad Greenberg.

He had been the director of player personnel for the Portland Trail Blazers. He made a strong impression in person. He was really prepared and articulate. His presentation was striking. He was very detail-oriented, and that particularly appealed to me. He had a huge sheaf of computer printouts that gave a meticulous scouting report of every player and potential draft pick.

I hired him. My mistake.

I was inexperienced as an owner, and then I compounded that by hiring a general manager who had had no experience at all in that position.

This assessment is made with the benefit of hindsight, which, as we all know, is always a perfect 20/20. At the time, though, I thought our enthusiasm would be sufficient. And I never held anything against a person for being inexperienced. You have to start somewhere, right?

So I had good intentions. But bad results.

The next move was to hire a coach. That's the general manager's job. We made a run at John Calipari, the boy-genius head coach of the

University of Massachusetts. But he ended up signing with the New Jersey Nets, and for a king's ransom at the time.

Brad decided on someone he knew very well and felt comfortable with, someone he felt needed only the opportunity to prove himself:

Johnny Davis.

Johnny was an assistant coach at Portland. Brad felt he was ready to be a head coach. All he needed was someone willing to risk that position with him. Johnny's interviews were great, too. He was very professional. He looked you square in the eye. He told me he'd reach in his chest and tear out his heart if that's what it would take to win. I thought I detected the soul of a warrior.

How did I know that it would require more experience to motivate the warriors on the court?

When you own a team, you're on your own. There is no textbook to read. There is no audio cassette to listen to. There is no videotape to watch. There are no seminars to attend. There is no guest lecturer to advise you.

There is no owner's manual!

But of course there are legions of people—that is, the fans and the media—to tell you exactly when you've done something wrong.

Unfortunately, it's almost always *after* you've already done it.

So an inexperienced owner allowed an inexperienced general manager to hire an inexperienced head coach. The result was predictable. Again, in hindsight.

Mea culpa, mea culpa, mea maxima culpa . . .

But what is worse than making a mistake is not admitting it and correcting it. I would live with mine for a year, and then go about rectifying it as soon as possible.

Luckily, there were a lot of good things that did happen my first year. We didn't win a lot of games, but we did win the lottery . . . .

❧ ❧ ❧

I've always found it curious that a multi-billion-dollar entertainment industry like the NBA allows its weakest members to replenish themselves by the very same method that has been a staple of the Catholic Church for years and years:

Bingo.

This is how the NBA version works: Numbered ping pong balls—with numbers corresponding to the thirteen worst teams that season—are dropped into a hopper. The hopper is given a vigorous whirl. Then balls are drawn out at random. And voilà! That determines what teams will choose in which order during the first three selections of the college draft! The remaining ten lottery teams (as well as the rest of the teams in the league) are then awarded a selection in inverse order of their record, with the next-worst team at Position #4, and so on. This all takes place during an elaborate television spectacle known as the NBA Draft Lottery, which is aired during halftime of a playoff game in May on NBC, one month before the draft itself.

The worse your team's record, the more ping pong balls you get in the hopper. In other words, an attempt is made to favor the most destitute franchises so that the team at the bottom of the standings has the best chance to win the top pick. Once you have the pick, it's your ability to assess talent and rate potential that will determine how good your draft will be. But before you get a chance to prove your skill and expertise as basketball scholars, you need simple luck.

Which was just fine with me.

I have always considered myself as having been born with a four-leaf clover tattooed on my ass. I knew—*I just knew*—that we were going to win my first lottery and with it the opportunity to make the very first pick in the draft, or to trade that pick for other opportunities. Holding the first pick in the draft is like having the only Get-Out-Of-Jail-Free card in a game of Monopoly. Everyone's your friend. Everyone's got a proposition for you.

Still, it couldn't hurt to try for an extra edge, maybe a little luck of the Irish. So we had a Waterford crystal basketball flown in from Ireland, my mother's homeland, just for the occasion. That was Dave Coskey's idea. Dave had been my first hire (as Senior Vice President) as soon as the sale of the Sixers was complete. I knew him from his days as the public relations director for the 76ers back in the 1980s. Then Donald Trump stole him away. And I stole him back again. With me, the creative Dave knew that he'd get the green light for all of his marketing antics.

We had a big pre-lottery press party to drum up interest. It was held amid the impressive construction of our still incomplete arena. A

Mummers band played and strutted. We unveiled the good-luck crystal basketball. I danced an Irish jig with Philadelphia icon Ben Franklin (or, at least, an actor dressed as Franklin who is always spotted around town). We tried to instill a sense of expectancy in the Sixers fans. They had been beaten down by so many seasons of relentless losing. Now we wanted them to start *anticipating* what was to come, instead of dreading what they'd become accustomed to expect.

My first lottery was on May 19, 1996. It was held in the NBA Entertainment Studios complex in Secaucus, New Jersey, I had the crystal, and I had my father's holy medal dangling on my key chain. Bator rode with me. We went in a black limo, driven by my driver and all-around handyman, Big John. John Parkinson is his name. There are high-rise condominiums that are smaller than Big John.

It was a sunny day in May, bright with promise, and there was no doubt in my mind about which team was going to wind up with the first pick. I'm not sure why I was so certain about that, but I was. Sometimes you can feel that way—feel that you know exactly what your fate will be—and still there will be the occasional twinge of doubt that makes you shoot straight up in bed at 3 o'clock in the morning. But I never felt such a twinge. We were winning the lottery. Period.

Before TV ever comes on, the ping pong balls already have been drawn. That's done out of sight of everyone, in a closed, sealed, locked room. Each team has one representative in the room to observe, bear witness, and make sure that everything is on the up-and-up. Dave was in the room for us. So he knew that we had won. But there was no way for him to get word out of that room. There are restricted access places in the Pentagon that are easier to get into and out of than that room.

As for us—the thirteen franchise representatives who would appear during the televised portion of the lottery—we were dutifully marched on stage. Then we were assigned seats. And then we went through a full-blown rehearsal, where we were even told how *to act*. I couldn't believe that. I thought for a moment that I had wandered into the wrong studio, and into the warmups for the Miss America pageant.

The instructions were delivered sternly. Fold your hands neatly in front of you. Control yourself. Show no overt emotion. If you are the winner, remain seated and we will send an escort over for you, and you will be taken to Bob Costas for interviewing on national television.

I had a flashback to grade school. I could hear the nuns. Sit up straight. Fold your hands. Don't pick your nose. Don't bite your nails. Be prim. Be proper. *Ouch!* Undoubtably, I would get smacked for something unproper.

The red light came on. I smiled. It grew into a grin. It swelled until it split my face. I couldn't help myself. We hadn't even started and I was already the happy winner.

Russ Granik received oversized envelopes, one at a time, from the NBA's director of security, Horace Balmer. Each envelope was opened and a card extracted. The card bore the name of an NBA team.

The first card, signifying which team would get draft pick Number 13, wasn't the 76ers.

Neither was Number 12.

Or Number 11 or Number 10 or Number 9 or Number 8 or Number 7 or Number 6 or Number 5.

Wasn't Number 4, either.

And when Number 3 was revealed and it wasn't the 76ers, then I knew we really had won. There was only Toronto and Philadelphia left, and Toronto, as an expansion team, was prohibited from drafting any higher than Number 2 that year.

My feet began to thump like a kangaroo on speed. But my fingers were still interlocked as instructed—barely.

Electric eels nibbled on my knees. That quivering feeling worked its way up my legs and into my torso. Mr. Yang was like King Kong about to break loose from his chains and shackles.

Sproing! Sproing! Sproinggggggg!

He was loose!

I couldn't hold back. I bolted up out of my chair. I made sounds—strange, unrecognizable, guttural gibberish. My grin went all the way 'round to the back of my head, and came out on the other side.

And I started slapping high-fives with all the other team representatives on stage.

Mr. Yang had just slam-dunked decorum.

People were startled at first. Here was this solemn occasion, with strict rules of conduct, and the new kid on the block was hopping around like an asylum escapee.

My view was that this wasn't a funeral, it was a *lottery*. It wasn't a time for mourning, it was a time for celebrating. The winner is supposed to go nuts. And by the end, as I was working my way around the stage, everyone had gotten into the spirit of it and palms were being offered to me for the slapping from every direction. Everyone was laughing and smiling. Even the losers.

The fact is, everyone can relate to sincere joy and spontaneous celebration. It's infectious, and it makes people feel good about themselves. And that's a powerful and positive influence.

As part of the ceremony, there was an elaborate photo-op, with David Stern presenting me with the 76ers Number 1 envelope. I grinned like a lunatic, of course. Stern managed a brave smile, but he looked the least bit wary, not sure what I was liable to do next.

And his apprehension was justified. I leaned over, grabbed his head in my hands, and planted a big wet one on his startled cheek. It was one of those hearty, exuberant busses that you deliver in the sheer spontaneous joy of the moment. He's lucky I didn't do the Mummer's strut with him!

The commissioner blushed and smiled. He wasn't quite sure what to make of this. First, his newest owner burgles his office in front of his face, then he kisses him in front of millions of people!

 PAT CROCE POINTER
The fact is, everyone can relate to sincere joy and spontaneous celebration. It's infectious, and it makes people feel good about themselves. And that's a powerful and positive influence.

While he was trying to make up his mind what to think, I made it up for him by shouting to him what had become the signature slogan of his sport:

"I l-o-v-e this game!"

When all the interviews were done, Bator and I walked to the car, and Big John took one look at me and grinned and asked:

"You wanna just run alongside for the first 30 miles?"

❧ ❧ ❧

That summer, I felt like I had changed my name. I was no longer Pat Croce; I had become Pat "Iverson."

The dynamite, spring-loaded guard from Georgetown University, Allen Iverson, was the people's choice, and they were very vocal about it. They wanted the 76ers to make him the first pick. I'd be out for a run on the Ocean City boardwalk and people would scream after me:

"Iverson, Pat." "Yo, Pat, you gotta take Iverson." "Pat, Iverson."

We considered Stephon Marbury, the quicksilver point guard from Georgia Tech. And Marcus Camby, the elastic Spiderman from UMass. And Ray Allen, the marvelous jump shooter from UConn. But we always kept coming back to Iverson.

It was impossible not to. He was quick as a hiccup. His talent was incandescent. We knew he would just light up our new arena, which would open for the 1996–97 season. And he would sell tickets. The shoe companies were falling all over each other trying to land his endorsement. The money they were offering him was almost twice what an entire franchise had cost only a decade before. They recognized his appeal.

There may have been some disagreement over whether he was suited to play point guard or not, but there wasn't a basketball mind in the country that didn't see in him the ability to make an entire arena forget to exhale.

On the other hand, he would also be high maintenance. Very high maintenance.

That was part of the price. You draft the player, you get the person as well. They're inseparable. You weigh potential risk against potential performance, and then you make your decision. So we interviewed him. We interviewed John Thompson, his coach at Georgetown University. And we considered his history.

Allen had one run-in with the law, and that was back in high school. But he had been cleared. And I believe in second chances, especially for someone as young as Allen (he entered the draft after his sophomore year). We should all be allowed to grow and develop and mature. I like to think that all of us, no matter what age, are forever works in progress. Just look at me.

I had no idea what to expect from my first season. I wanted to win, of course. But that part wasn't up to me. I wanted every fan in our building to leave feeling that he or she had been entertained. And there was no doubt that Allen Iverson would be entertaining.

So we took him.

To celebrate the occasion, to continue to try to reverse Philadelphia's low expectations, we threw a draft party for 76ers season ticket holders and fans. It was on the floor of the Spectrum. Eight thousand showed up. When Allen Iverson was announced as our pick, they all roared their approval.

Unfortunately, it was the last time that we would be hearing that sound for a long, long time . . . .

♢ ♢ ♢

That '96–'97 season was a horror.

It started favorably enough. We actually won seven times in November, the first month of the season, but only fiften more in the four and a half months that followed. A record of 22–60 actually was an improvement over the previous season, but that was meaningless consolation.

Master Kwon's hissing bamboo whacks across my posterior didn't carry nearly the sting that losing did.

The worst part about being an owner, you see, is that you are utterly powerless. You have no control over the outcome. You can only sit there and suffer.

PAT CROCE POINTER
I already knew that success was contagious. Now I was learning that failure was catching, too. And soon I could understand that. But that didn't mean I had to like it. Or accept it. Or not change it.

I was accustomed to bending people and circumstances to my will. I was used to chipping away at problems day after day, gnawing on that elephant until only a pile of bones, picked clean, was left. But this, *this* was agony. I'd sit there and watch someone miss a pair of free throws with two seconds left and know there wasn't a single thing I could do about it.

Except suffer.

When the losing sets in, then everything else begins to deteriorate, too. I already knew that success was contagious. Now I was learning that failure was catching, too. And soon I could understand that. But that didn't mean I had to like it. Or accept it. Or not change it.

I fought all season long with Mr. Yang. He wanted to decapitate people. But I felt that I owed Brad and Johnny the one full season. So I kept my word. No interference, no meddling, no forced trades.

And I concentrated on that part of the business that I could control. Essentially, that involves everything except the actual playing of the game. We made the arena a fan-friendly environment, à la Disney World. We got the 76ers involved in the community, by sponsoring intercity leagues, visiting kids in hospitals at Halloween and Christmas, engaging in charity work (especially our Sixers Slam Dunk Diabetes program), initiating Playground Rebound (our public courts' backboard restoration program), and kicking off the Sixers Summer Hoops Tour (where we provided a free two-hour clinic in thirty towns surrounding Philadelphia).

I'm a big believer in being a giver and not a taker. Ironically, an amazing thing usually happens when you give: You receive! Happiness. Peace of mind. Wins!

My aim was to serve up pure entertainment. I wanted every home game to be like the old "I Feel Great Show." We unveiled a house band. We brought in celebrities to sing the National Anthem, like Grover Washington Jr., Teddy Pendergrass, and Boyz II Men. We introduced a new, energized dance team. And other stars came on their own to our big games, like Philly's own Bill Cosby and Will Smith. We created a wild acrobatic mascot—a slam-dunking rabbit named Hip-Hop. We booked live, exciting halftime acts. And I worked the room at every home game. I still do. I roam the concourse for half an hour, greeting people and being visible. I don't want to be one of those reclusive owners who whisks in and out, shielded by a bodyguard, hiding in his suite. I think the people should have access to you, like they do in Double-A baseball parks.

That's the other part of the job. The goldfish-bowl part. You're visible whether you want to be or not. Everything is very public. It's in print, it's on TV, it's on the radio. Secrets are virtually impossible to make or to keep. Like everything else involved in ownership of a professional sports franchise, you learn all this as you go along.

There are no warning signs. You don't look up and see: "Falling Rocks Ahead." No, the first hint of trouble is when that first bouncing boulder catches you squarely between the eyes.

Every day becomes an improvisation.

I'm not complaining. It all goes with the territory. The point is, it was all unexplored territory for me. But I'm a sponge. I was listening, watching, and learning.

What I came to learn in a hurry was that you can control every single aspect of the entire production, *except* the last act. The game. And if that's a flop, then all the other parts of it are rarely remembered by the customer. On the nights we lose, I always feel sorry for our people who have put so much effort into the entertainment and environment portions of the game presentation.

You can be creative, you can assemble all sorts of characters for your production, but in the end the characters on the court are the ones who matter most. Fans want to be entertained, sure. But they want a winner. Forced to choose between the two, they'll take the winner every time.

Which is why the day after the regular season ground to a merciful halt, I fired my general manager and my coach.

It was a new and disconcerting experience. I'd had 525 employees in my previous business, and I never had to fire one of them. This was more than uncomfortable. But it had to be done. We had been a success off the court, but a disaster on it.

The losing was eating away at everyone. But more importantly, the low level of discipline, lack of intensity, and broken lines of communication were polluting the very atmosphere that we had been trying to cleanse. I was hearing far too many "can'ts" and "won'ts" and "don'ts." And those words all have one thing in common—they're all dreambreakers. I couldn't afford to let this negativity take over. It was a virus that needed to be reversed before it grew into a plague. And the cure had to be found immediately.

So I followed the Tenth Commandment of Customer Service: Do It *Now!*

So on the day after my first season ended, I stood in front of a room filled with Philadelphia's top sports reporters and told them (and now the world) that I had made a mistake, I was confessing it in public, and I was apologizing. I don't think I've ever done anything that was quite as demeaning or humiliating. But it needed to be done.

Sonny Hill (the godfather of Philly basketball whose advice I always appreciate), Fran, and Dave were the only non-press there for encouragement. There were a couple of potted palm plants besides, and I remember thinking that they gave the whole room a sort of funeral parlor touch.

But in a way that was appropriate. I was burying a mistake.

And in my mind I was already at work on a resurrection.

Chapter 14

The Bend in the Road

❧❧❧

"**I**f it's to be, then it's up to me."

I love that saying. It puts responsibility squarely where it cannot be ignored.

I had spent my first season as an owner dependent upon other people and on circumstances that were totally, frustratingly beyond my control—on a general manager to get players, on a coach to get them to perform, on an inflated pebble-grained ball that was just as apt to bounce off the heel of the rim as it was to splash through the net. That season had been abysmal. So if there was to be a reversal of fortune, then it truly was up to me.

 PAT CROCE POINTER
"If it's to be, then it's up to me." I love that saying.
It puts responsibility squarely where it cannot be ignored.

I knew it would be ruinous to continue along the road we were traveling, and that a big change was necessary. I also knew that the only time a bend in the road is the end of the road is when you fail to turn.

So even before my first season ended I was pursuing a new coach. But not just any coach. The fans of Philadelphia wouldn't stand for me recycling some tired old retread, and they'd had their fill of unproven, inexperienced beginners. No, I wanted—*I needed*—a neon name right off the marquee. A hired gun with a reputation. With experience. With a winning history.

Three struck me: Rick Pitino, Larry Brown, and Phil Jackson.

The latter two were under contract to NBA teams and their availability was uncertain. Pitino, who had started in college coaching as something of a child prodigy and then had gone to the NBA's New York

Knicks, was back in the college ranks. He had already won one national championship with the Kentucky Wildcats and was a top contender for the title every year. But there were tremors along the grapevine that he could be lured away from college and back to the pros. The speculation was that the Boston Celtics were lusting after him. Like the 76ers, they were a proud team that had fallen on hard times and was in desperate need of a savior.

If Pitino was leaning just the least bit toward returning to the NBA, I wanted to be the one to give him the final nudge. So I went after him like I had pursued Harold Katz. It was March of '97. The University of Kentucky was in the NCAA tournament—March Madness—defending its national championship.

As a coach, Pitino loves to attack the opposing team with pressure—unrelenting, baseline to baseline pressure. His teams are merciless; they simply run other teams into defeat. They take your lungs, then your legs, then your heart.

So I hit him with *my* full court press.

No matter where his Wildcats were in the United States, I had something waiting for him. Every time he walked into a new hotel room, there would be a mint on his pillow and a little reminder from the 76ers:

A unique motivational book when he was in Salt Lake City.

A fancy box of basketball chocolates when he was in San Jose.

An enormous "Taste of Philly" basket when he was in Indianapolis for the finals.

And then Diane and I flew to Lexington. We went to Rick's home and had lunch with him and his wife, Joanne. I wanted him to see me face-to-face, to know the depth of my determination, to realize that this wasn't some lark by an owner who was only looking for an excuse to jet around the country. Plus, I figured that since he was a proponent of man-to-man basketball he could relate to my eyeball-to-eyeball style of business.

He couldn't get away from me. Like the boxer said, he could run but he couldn't hide. One night, he went on the QVC home-shopping network (located outside Philadelphia) at 1 o'clock in the morning to hawk his book *Success Is a Choice*, and when he came off the set I was there waiting in ambush for him, along with Ed Snider and Brian Roberts. He admitted that he sure did admire our persistence.

All of this intense courting was complicated by the fact that it had to be done on the sly. We didn't dare leave messages or use real names, because in about twenty minutes one clandestine meeting that gets found out becomes instant headlines. A bellboy tells a desk clerk, a waiter tells a diner, a diner tells a bartender . . . by whatever chain, the time that it takes for an initial contact between an owner and a prospective coach to become an item on ESPN SportsCenter is roughly the length of a sneeze.

I told Rick Pitino that the Frank Sinatra song "New York, New York" had it wrong.

"If you can make it *here*, you can make it anywhere," I told him.

He smiled. He appreciated the appeal to his competitive nature.

I told him this story about how we had applied to be the host team for the 1999 NBA All-Star Game and that as part of the process, Philadelphia was scrutinized by a group of league officials. I had ushered them around the city, selling it, selling us . . . .

We started this tour of Philly at our brand-new arena, a true pleasure palace. Everyone ooohhhed and aaahhhed. Except for one. A New Yorker with an "atty-tood" and a chip on his shoulder the size of a log. At one point, he asked:

"How long did it take to build this?"

"Two years," I replied, proudly.

"In New York," he said, all but sneering, "we could do it in a year from ground-breaking."

I looked at him incredulously. I could feel Mr. Yang stirring. Then we went to center city to see the imposing new Pennsylvania Convention Center, which would house the NBA's interactive Jam Session. Mr. New York had a familiar question:

"How long to build it?"

"Three years, I believe," I replied.

"In New York, we do it in two," he said, smiling in self-satisfaction at the others.

Now Mr. Yang was beginning to growl. Driving back to the arena, we passed the stately and historic Academy of Music.

"What's that building?" asked Mr. New York.

I knew how to play the game now.

"I don't know," I replied. "It wasn't there last week."

Mr. Yang snickered.

So, I told Rick Pitino, I tell people to get out of my face with that negative attitude. Again, he smiled.

I pushed him for a decision. I already knew that I was going to fire our coach, and I wanted to have a replacement in place. He was torn. Part of him wanted to stay in Kentucky. But his roots were in Boston. That tug was powerful. And in the end, it was irresistible.

He was going to the Celtics. And I was going back to the drawing board.

I called the attorney for Jerry Reinsdorf, the owner of the Chicago Bulls, for permission to talk with his coach, Phil Jackson. Of course before I could get to Phil directly, I would have to go through *his* agent, Todd Musburger. There is a protocol to be followed, and at times it feels like you're hacking your way through a thicket of bureaucracy, layer after layer of attorneys and agents and accountants.

What I had also come to understand was that in the NBA there is an inner circle within which no one gives anyone else a bad recommendation. It's a self-perpetuating society of mutual backscratchers. I needed someone whose advice and counsel I could trust, someone who knew the league and the sport and wouldn't sell me the usual dump truck full of crap. Also, as the new kid on the block, everyone would try to take advantage of me. You need some help, Pat? Be glad to. Bend over . . . .

I turned to Billy Cunningham for help. He was invaluable. The Kangaroo Kid's ties to the 76ers went back more than thirty years. He had played for them—a ferocious competitor—and for a while he was the best sixth man in the game. He was their coach when they won the NBA championship in 1983, and he coached as passionately as he had played. One time, he leapt out of his seat with such force that he split the seat in his suit pants. And even though he had become part of the Miami Heat organization when that expansion franchise was launched, his allegiance to the Sixers remained staunch. We must have talked two or three times a day during that frantic period that I was looking for a new coach.

Billy C. contacted Roy Williams, the outstanding coach at the University of Kansas. They share that North Carolina alumni connection. Roy wanted to remain in college coaching, at least for another year. Then Billy found out that Larry Brown was unhappy and feeling unfulfilled as coach of the Indiana Pacers—rumor had it that he was going to leave the team at the end of the season. Or in other words, *next week.*

My head lit up like a pinball machine.

Larry Brown might be available? Larry Brown was Rick Pitino before Rick Pitino was Rick Pitino! That is, a boy genius, a wizard, the Merlin of round ball. Twenty-five years in the business and brimming with a busload of winning experience—exactly what I craved. And his was a huge name in the business, besides. He had box office appeal and an incredible amount of expertise. It was like the Playmate of the Year also had a Ph.D. in biochemistry.

  PAT CROCE POINTER
I realized that, to get your man (or your goal), you had to
first listen in order to understand who you're dealing with,
then figure out what they need to hear, and then say it.
Honestly.

To get to Larry, you have to go through Joe Glass. And I mean *go through*, literally. Joe is straight out of Central Casting: "Hello? I need a Damon Runyon character." Joe is in his seventies, an inveterate cigar smoker who looks like he could be a Wise Guy, or at least a guy you'd find at the $50 window at the race track. Joe is more than Larry's agent; he is a father figure. He is very protective. And very suspicious.

I realized that, to get your man (or your goal), you had to first listen in order to understand who you're dealing with, then figure out what they need to hear, and then say it. Honestly.

I talked frantically. I told Joe that Allen Iverson was actually an angel. I told Joe that a statue of Larry Brown would replace the statue of William Penn atop City Hall when he coached the 76ers to the championship. Seriously, I told him what I believed he wanted to hear . . . that Larry Brown would have complete control over all basketball decisions—hiring assistant coaches, selecting draft picks and free agents, and making player trades. Finally, I wheedled a phone number out of him.

It was a California area code.

I was dialing it as soon as the last digit was out of Joe's mouth.

Larry answered. It sounded like he was in a gym. There was a lot of heavy breathing and guttural sounds.

But it wasn't a gym, it was a hospital! His wife, Shelly, was in labor at that very moment.

Yet he sounded as calm as a man who had spent a lifetime in a huddle with only 1.7 seconds left in the game and his team trailing by a point.

I apologized. And I wondered: *What, exactly, were the appropriate words for calling in the middle of a birth, anyway?*

Larry, on the other hand, seemed not only remarkably composed but more than willing to chat.

"No, no, enjoy the moment," I told him. "We'll talk later."

I started to hang up.

"Oh, wait . . . Larry . . . Larry?"

"Yeah?"

"Larry . . . is it a boy or girl?"

"A girl."

Instantly I was dialing another number. Ann Catania—a florist and a wild woman. I told her I wanted the hospital room of Mrs. Larry Brown to look like a Mafia funeral parlor in pink. She had experience and I knew she'd deliver—literally and figuratively.

If it was pretty and if it smelled good, then I wanted it and a few thousand of its closest greenhouse relatives in the room of the new parents. With heartiest congratulations and warmest regards and good wishes from the Philadelphia 76ers.

(On the day that Larry would be formally introduced as the Sixers new head coach, he would say that what had clinched his decision was his wife, who was impressed by the sixty-two pounds of flowers that Pat Croce had sent her while she was in the hospital. See, that floral industry slogan really does have it right: Say it with flowers.)

While the thought of landing Larry Brown was intoxicating, I couldn't afford not to have back-ups and alternatives. I hacked through the bureaucratic thicket and got permission to talk to Phil Jackson. It turns out he had a caveat in his contract that allowed him to talk to other NBA teams about future employment as long as those teams weren't in the playoffs. So we had a good ninety-minute conversation. Phil was interested but he was caught in a strange limbo. His situation was in flux. No one knew whether he would be rehired by the Bulls. No one knew whether Michael Jordan would be offered a new contract. And Michael was saying that he and Phil were a package deal, that if Phil didn't come back to coach the Bulls, he wouldn't be playing, either.

No one was quite sure what Jerry Reinsdorf was going to do, and he seemed to be in no hurry at all to make a decision. Why not? He was the lead domino, and nothing else could fall into place until he moved. I made some more inquiries, but Reinsdorf wasn't feeling pressured and wasn't going to allow himself to *be* pressured. I realized that there was a very real possibility that I could end up with my pants flapping down around my ankles.

If I waited until the Bulls were out of the playoffs, or until they won it all (which would probably assure Jackson's return to the Bulls), it would be late-June and I'd be without a coach. And Larry Brown would have been snapped up by then. There were between eight and ten teams that were going to need new coaches. I had the distinctly uncomfortable feeling that I was going to end up as the last kid standing in a very expensive game of musical chairs.

Larry Brown was still my preference. We continued the cloak-and-dagger courtship. I was careful to wipe my fingerprints off everything. Another meeting was set with Larry, and I had everything secretly planned.

I turned on the TV, and ESPN was announcing that Larry Brown had just resigned as coach of the Pacers.

No shit! I thought happily, since I already knew.

Then there was a live shot of Larry, and a reporter was asking him what he planned to do now.

"Wouldn't you like to know!" I said to myself. And then I thought, *I wonder what Larry's going to tell this guy . . . .*

Larry is very candid and has this wonderful openness about him. He looked right into the camera and said:

"Why, I'm going to Philadelphia to meet with Pat Croce."

I don't remember which part of me hit the floor first.

So much for secrecy. I was trying to *Do It Now!* before the other hopeful owners did it later.

I had a jet waiting for him in Indy. And a limo at the Philadelphia Airport. And a hotel room. We were sequestered for five hours. Ed Snider came in for the last three.

Larry Brown was my prisoner. There wouldn't be any ransom note. I wasn't letting him out of that room until we had at least a handshake deal. Already there were five other teams in the NBA in the market for a coach—Orlando, Boston, Golden State, Portland, and Denver. And

Larry would last about as long as ground chuck in a kennel.

He had a hell of a reputation. He won wherever he coached. And he had coached all over, in the old American Basketball Association, at elite colleges like UCLA and Kansas (where he had won a national championship), and in the NBA. He had a teacher's mentality. In fact, the part of the game he still enjoys the most comes after practice—when the gym is deserted, the stands are empty, and the thump of the ball is a long, repeating echo. It's then that Larry can work one-on-one tutoring a player.

He was a point guard himself. He understands the geometry of the game—who should get the ball, when, and where on the court.

But for all that he had done in his career, there wasn't a whiff of arrogance about him. His M.O. was that he always had an immediate impact and effected instant improvement whenever he took over a program, and we sure needed a jump start.

The more I talked to him, the more I respected him. And I kept coming back to his record. Yes, he had come to be known as The Travelin' Man because he had hopscotched around the country, moving from job to job. But that is pretty typical of the coaching profession. Most of them are nomads. Very few coaches in any professional sport last longer than three or four years in one city. Hardly any stay in the same place for five years. This is a very cyclical business. It seems always to be in flux.

For me, the most reassuring aspect of Larry Brown was all his experience. My first year as owner had taught me that experience was worth its weight not only in gold, but in wins.

We did a deal.

He got a lot of money. Mega millions. And a five-year contract. That was done purposely. He needed clout to be effective.

The way it works in professional sports these days, and especially in the NBA—which is a player's league—is that status and standing and respect are measured by money. The attitude has always been that it's easier, and certainly cheaper, to get rid of the coach when the team is losing than it is to fire all the players.

Well, by making a hefty financial commitment to Larry, we were sending the unmistakable message that *he* was *the* man. He most definitely was our man, and no one would be running him off.

The fact that we were negotiating was hardly a secret. Since his statement on national television about where he was going (he made "I'm going to Philadelphia to see Pat Croce" sound like "I'm going to Disney World!"), of course word was all around that he was in town. But no one really expected us to be able to land him. Years of failure, years of 50 and 60-loss seasons, years of continued coaching turnover and roster-purging had beaten down 76ers fans. They had come to expect the worst, and some of them seemed almost disappointed when they didn't get it.

So when we formally introduced Larry Brown as our new head coach, it was like we had put electric paddles on Philadelphia's heart.

  PAT CROCE POINTER
No one ever stays the same—you're either getting better or you're getting worse. But simply knowing and accepting this gives you the opportunity to make your changes positive ones.

The town jumped back to life. Interest in the Sixers was rekindled. We hadn't wasted any time in correcting our biggest mistakes.

But I knew that I was only one dribble ahead of the posse. And I knew that in Philadelphia you don't get a second chance.

But, it was pointed out to me, I *was* getting one.

"All that means," I said, "is that I'm living on borrowed time."

❧ ❧ ❧

If you're not changing, you're stagnating.

No one ever stays the same—you're either getting better or you're getting worse. But simply knowing and accepting this gives you the opportunity to make your changes positive ones.

We had definitely gotten better by acquiring Larry Brown. I wanted to capitalize on that excitement and also reinforce the perception that the 76ers were changing, that they were discarding the days of defeat.

New coach, new staff, and a new de facto general manager. Larry had recommended Billy King—a smart, sharp guy who had been on the bench with him for several years—to oversee basketball operations. Following a year of observing Billy's leadership and organizational skills, I formally promoted him to general manager. So he, our director of player personnel Tony DiLeo, and their scouting staff, rounded out the basketball brains behind the talent selection.

We also introduced a sleek new logo and jazzy new uniforms. Both emphasized the color black. It is my favorite color for backgrounds. Like the pirate flag. Like the Ninja uniform. It conveys a certain ominous edge. It says: *Uh-oh, trouble this way comes.*

Before we had opened the new CoreStates Center arena, this flamboyant NBA color-design guru who we'd hired strutted over to me to unveil the design that was supposed to be painted at center court. His face dropped when I took one look at his pride and joy and said:

"Oh no. This won't do."

He pouted. "What's wrong with it?"

"The colors," I said. "I want black."

He rolled his eyes and gave me one of those pitying, some-people-are-so-clueless looks, and imperiously informed me:

"Black is not one of your colors."

Mr. Yang answered for me:

"Well, *now* it is!"

Everyone agrees the black border around the court and the other black markings are quite handsome.

We had an unveiling of the new logo and the new uniforms at a big gala blowout in a shopping mall. Several thousand came.

No one said they didn't like black.

❧ ❧ ❧

The off-season had been a rousing success. Larry Brown was on board. Billy King was on board. We had released unproductive players and their burdensome, almost devastating long-term contracts. We had a new logo and a new wardrobe. We had moved on every front to put failure deep into our rear-view mirror.

And for one extra jolt, we had the rookie of the year:

Allen Iverson.

He had been sensational. The team may have been a bad mix in his first year, but he not only survived, he thrived.

On the court, at least.

Off it, well, he and I both ended up in a different court in the summer.

His car was pulled over by the police for speeding. He was a passenger. There was a gun. And a couple of marijuana joints.

I exploded when I found out, and went on public record as saying that neither I nor the franchise condoned what he had done. But I also said I would stand by him, and I did. I was there in the Virginia courtroom, hoping my presence would demonstrate to him my support. But I also took him aside and told him:

"Bubba, I can watch the front door for you, but you gotta take care of the back door."

He said he understood. Even if you aren't the one behind the wheel, you are the one who will pay. He was 21 years old. Sometimes we lose sight of that.

His 1993 felony conviction and brief imprisonment for his involvement in a bowling alley brawl had been overturned by the Governor of Virginia. For this incident involving his car, he received three years probation. We were all hoping that he had been scared straight.

The main lesson was accountability. There are consequences for everything that you do. We are answerable, all of us, for our actions.

My first year as owner had been a series of loop-de-loops. The pendulum seemed to swing wildly from one extreme to the other. Failure would be followed by triumph, then failure again, then resurrection.

It was all a helpful reminder: Every time you get to thinking that you're sitting on top of the world, just remember that every 24 hours the world turns over.

Chapter 15
The Genie

❦ ❦ ❦

Now it's the second year of my tenure as president, and here I am back in the owner's suite of the First Union Center, counting my blessings. Our pleasure palace is packed, and down on the floor Michael Jordan is once again trying to beat my brains in.

The Jakester and Bator are down on the floor, working the crowd. So are Fran and Dave. My vice president of communications, Lara White, has her headset on and is calling attention to our special attractions throughout the game. The Sixers Dance Team. The Mascot. The House Band. Giveaways galore.

Every game is more than a game, it's a performance. A show. And the people behind the scenes are every bit as important to me as the multi-multi-millionaire players. The Disney people have it right when, instead of the conventional label of "Employees Only," they use this designation on their doors: "Cast Members."

I hope that every one of them, each night, keeps in mind the story I told them about the rude salesman:

There was a rude, careless salesman who was late for his appointment, arrived unprepared, and left in a huff when he had failed to make a sale. On his way out, his client called to him: "Wait, you're leaving something behind."

"What?" the salesman asked, checking his briefcase.

"A bad impression," the client said.

A bad first impression is like a dented fender—it takes a lot of hammering to straighten it out. And *last* impressions tend to be, well, lasting. Every impression you make in between counts, as well. So the best way to operate any business, or to conduct your life, is to assume that every chance you get to make an impression is your first . . . and will last.

This is something that many people instinctively understand yet never take to heart. They experience the ill effects of leaving a bad or lukewarm impression, but the next time around they're apt to go and do the same thing.

One of my favorite sayings is that if you're still thinking and acting the same way at the age of 50 as you were when you were 20, then you've basically wasted 30 years.

PAT CROCE POINTER
The best way to operate any business, or to conduct your life, is to assume that every chance you get to make an impression is your first . . . and will last.

Michael Jordan hasn't left many—if *any*—bad impressions in his career, and it is sounding like this season will be his Last Hurrah. The game will be poorer for his departure, but his impression will stand unblemished for a long time to come—the impression of a winner.

But I have to tell you that while the wins and losses matter a great deal—and I still haven't learned to choke down the bitter bile of defeat—more and more I find myself preoccupied with what owning a professional sports franchise enables you to do off the court.

I've always been enamored with magic; I started doing magic tricks at a very young age. Over the years I've gotten fairly proficient at it, graduating from basic parlor tricks and sleights of hand with cards, coins, and rope, to the real heavy-duty kind of stuff. I guess magic appeals to The Artful Dodger in me. I like to figure things out and I thrive on doing things that other people can't and I mostly enjoy making people smile and go: "Holy Shit!"

Unfortunately, no matter how many wands I wave I can't conjure up an athletic all-star seven-footer, or merely by the snap of my fingers produce a winning basketball team. But there's another kind of magic that I can try to weave, a very special magic that doesn't involve shooting free throws or throwing alley-oop passes.

The most fulfilling part of being an owner has nothing to do with the pick-and-roll or with offensive rebounding or with being able to sit in a plush Nero box.

It has everything to do with being able to play The Genie.

I get to magically grant wishes—to help people's dreams come true.

And to quote one of the great philosophers, the honorable Jiminy Cricket: A dream is a wish your heart makes when you're fast asleep.

You know that glow you get when you've done a good deed? You know how your heart warms up when you're able to do something for someone that no one else is in the position to do? Well, *that* is the best part about being a sports-team owner and having some money and influence.

Wish-granter. Dream-maker. It's powerful medicine.

Don't get me wrong, I still want a parade for Philadelphia, I still want to trade in that basketball clock I shoplifted from the commissioner's office for that golden championship basketball trophy he presents to the winner every June. But being The Genie, in its own right, is like having a parade every day.

Being The Genie means you get to give basketball uniforms and T-shirts to 10,000 inner-city kids. You get to play Santa in the middle of the summer.

Being The Genie means you get to recognize the extraordinary skills of wheelchair athletes. We have a team of wheelchair stars called the "Sixers Spokesmen," and each player has their name on an authentic Sixers jersey. They even play an exhibition game right on our court in the First Union Center before a Sixers game. They will astonish you.

Being The Genie means you get to take a full team of NBA stars to Children's Hospital of Philadelphia at Christmastime to pass out presents and see children's eyes shine like tinsel when a real live basketball giant sits and talks to them. As is always the case, the ones doing the visiting and the giving turn out to be the real recipients. First, there is that special feeling that comes from doing good. Second, the little ones you're supposed to be inspiring end up inspiring you, with their bravery and their simple dignity. Invariably you walk away wondering: *What have I done to deserve such blessings?*

Being The Genie means that when you hear of a family's house burning down and the son is devastated because his treasured Sixers autographs are now in ashes, you can bring him and his parents to a game and have his favorite player personally present the son with his autographed jersey.

Being The Genie means that you get to hook up a Roderick Green with his hero . . . .

Roderick Green is a basketball player. A most special basketball player. A one-legged basketball player.

Roderick was born without a functional foot and without a fibula and a tibia. Amputation just below the knee was necessary. Roderick, who lives in Monroe, Louisiana, was fitted with his first prosthesis when he was three years old. With the encouragement of his family, he was treated exactly the same as his eleven brothers and sisters. A wise decision. He developed an inner strength and came to regard himself as special only in the way that everyone, in his or her own way, is special.

Asked what he would change about his life now that he is 18 and six-three, 200 pounds, Roderick replied: "If you're asking me if I wish I weren't an amputee, the answer is 'No!' I love who I am. In fact, I probably wouldn't be the athlete I am today if I weren't an amputee. It's made me strive to be a winner."

In the early days, before prostheses were improved, Roderick Green would play basketball until his stump bled. He ended up rated one of the top ten prep players in the state. In the fall of 1997, he enrolled at Oklahoma Christian University, with a full scholarship. Roderick's hero was Allen Iverson. Because Roderick has been a patient of NovaCare, Ray Man heard about him, and heard about who his hero was, and called Dave Coskey. Two marketing madmen working miracles.

And at the start of the 1997–98 NBA season, Roderick flew to Philadelphia for a 76ers game. And after the game he got to meet Allen Iverson.

And show Allen and the rest of us how he can *dunk!*

Roderick Green is my hero. Just like Dr. Seuss, who kept knocking on all those doors. Roderick told Allen that because he was now going to have to play against tougher competition that he was taking 1,000 jump shots a day. Every day.

Even Allen's eyes got big.

"A thousand?"

I said, "See, Allen, you can learn from him."

And maybe that's the most important point in this book. That learning should extend from cradle to grave—that you should learn and do with a positive attitude, and that no matter your age or your status or your station in life, you should always be aware. Be aware of wonder.

Be aware of possibilities.

Be aware that what we presume to be boundaries often turn out to be merely our own presumptions.

Be aware that quite often what we assume to be an unbreakable limit, an unassailable record, turns out not to be a limit at all but merely an assumption.

The unassailable *is* assailable. The unthinkable *is* possible.

I can buy the 76ers. We can beat Michael Jordan, Scottie Pippen, and the Chicago Bulls. That's not fantasy any more, by the way. It's fact. We did it!

When people tell you a thing cannot be done, they don't know for sure that it can't. They only know that it hasn't been done. So far.

If I had listened to everyone who used the word *can't*, if I had allowed the first slammed door to send me home in surrender, then today I would just be another dreamer making wishes—making them instead of being able to grant them.

I'm no genius. I'm just like you. Hank of hair, bit of bone. Filled with dreams and schemes. Believe me, if I can do it, anyone can. This is not false modesty, nor is it the blowing of smoke rings. It's an honest assessment of myself, and an honest testimony of the power everyone possesses to reach their dreams.

We're all, every one of us, bound by one common thread—that we're more important than we realize. And I believe that if we do our best, God will take care of the rest.

There is a folk tale of which I am especially fond. There once was a man, an ordinary man, who was granted one wish by God. It's a fantasy we've all had, right? But think about the awesome responsibility that accompanies such an opportunity.

The man wondered: *What can I wish for that won't make God think I'm petty or materialistic or greedy or small-minded? I don't want Him to think I'm just, well, human.*

After some thought, the man didn't ask for wealth or fame or health. None of the usual things. He said he thought maybe it would be pretty neat if he were simply allowed to go through life doing good.

But there was a catch: He wouldn't know about the good he was doing.

The wish was granted.

God watched this for a while and came to the conclusion that this was such a splendid idea that He would grant the very same wish to every human being.

It's still in effect, by the way.

Help yourself.

❧ ❧ ❧

I had no way of knowing at the time, but the day was coming when I would be wishing very hard for something for myself—that I could keep my left leg . . . .

Chapter 16

The Ecstasy
and the Agony

❦ ❦ ❦

*I*t was raining and my bones were scattered across the asphalt.

I was in the middle of the road, and I didn't know how I got there. My left leg was shattered, and fragments of it gleamed like seashells on the beach, and I was crab-crawling around, frantically trying to scoop up my parts. It was hard to tell bone bits from pebbles on the wet and dark road, so I just picked up whatever I could feel. We'll sort it all out later, I told myself.

I tried to get up. My boot flopped down and dangled against my calf. *Odd*, I thought. *I seemed to have been knocked out of my boot.*

And then I realized that my foot was still *in* the boot.

All that was keeping my foot attached to my leg was a flap of skin, a couple of tendons no thicker than strands of spaghetti, and a couple of strips of denim that were left from my jeans.

T-Bone was the first one to get to me. He went pale as chalk. "Oh, shit!" he yelped.

"Oh shit, shit, shit!"

Quite a bedside manner you've got there, T-Bone, I remember thinking. He fought the nausea roiling inside him and looked at my leg again. The big bone shone white as a full moon.

"Pat, what do you want me to do?"

Luckily, one of my biker buddies who got there next was Dr. Jack. He is the 76ers orthopedic surgeon. He is accustomed to trauma.

"Blanket!" he shouted.

"Call 911!"

He began to manipulate my leg, trying to make sense of the wreckage. The boot and my foot might as well have been a bag of rocks. He managed to restore the mess to something resembling a straight line. The pain was excruciating. I thought I might pass out and yet I was half afraid that I wouldn't.

And then a silly thought occurred to me: *Hey I'm getting wet.*

That was it . . . it was raining. It came into my pain-fogged mind how I had ended up here on the asphalt on New Jersey Route 55, picking up my bones. All I had wanted to do was get out of the rain. It seemed simple enough . . . .

We had called it our Ocean-to-Ocean Odyssey. We were to journey cross-country, Atlantic to Pacific, on our motorcycles—myself and seven biker buds. Dr. Jack, T-Bone, Meat, KO, and Fran were on choppers, while Bator and Age manned an RV that was crammed with food and support equipment. We were stocked for an Arctic expedition. We left from my house at the Jersey shore on June 17, 1999. About fifty miles into the trip, the rain began. As the lead bike, I pulled under an overpass and onto the shoulder, leaving room for the others.

There, dry and protected, we could change into waterproof and warm clothing. A summer rain may not seem like much, but at sixty miles per hour—with no roof and no walls around you—the first thing you notice is that each drop feels like a knife slash, and the next thing you notice is that June sure does feel like January; the chill is bone-deep.

I was one step into my dismount, and then . . .

I was in the middle of the road, spun like a Frisbee in a high wind, sliding on my gluteus maximus, leaving a trail of bone bits behind me.

One of the bikes had skidded out of control and clipped my leg as it passed by. There are steel rods that protrude from each side of a motorcycle called "highway pegs." You rest your feet on them while you're riding. They are about the length of the blade of a Bowie knife, and blunt as a billy club. That's what my leg was slammed into. Imagine a scythe taking down a stand of wheat with one hissing sweep. Except the scythe is surgical by comparison.

  PAT CROCE POINTER
 Sometimes, in the headiest of moments, a person's instincts kick in and take over. You can gauge someone's true character by studying their actions in these intense moments.

Basic instinct kicked in—fight or flight. This was flight. Got to get away. From what, exactly, I wasn't sure. But I had to get out of the road.

I propped up on my elbows and began to scuttle backwards toward the overpass. Meat and KO quickly grabbed me under the shoulders. Dr. Jack still had hold of my wrecked foot, squeezing it, trying to will it to somehow reunite with the rest of my leg.

I saw my bike lying on its side. There was this fleeting image of a rupture in the gas tank . . . leaking liquid bathing my body . . . a carelessly tossed match or freak strike of lightning . . . my imagination was revved and racing.

"Somebody pick up my bike!" I yelled.

I remember thinking that if I can't stand up, at least my bike can. For some reason, that seemed terribly important at the time. Defiant. Symbolic. Sometimes, in the headiest of moments, a person's instincts kick in and take over. You can gauge someone's true character by studying their actions in these intense moments.

The paramedics arrived. They put an air cast on my shattered leg and a cervical collar around my neck, and then they rummaged around my body looking for other injuries. They asked me: "What happened?"

It was a question for which I had absolutely no answer.

If I was going to end up splattering myself, you would have thought it would have happened the previous summer. That's when I went bungee jumping, after all . . . .

❦ ❦ ❦

Diane had often said how she'd really like to see the world before she got too old to enjoy it. So I made the reservations, and in the summer of '98 we boarded the Concorde and set off around the world. You know that old cliche, "It's a small world"? Don't believe that for a minute.

The lasting impact of that trip has been a complete and total sense of awe. We began to grasp just how enormous this planet really is. It was like one of those moonlight walks on the beach—you come to realize just how insignificant you are.

It was a humbling trip. It did wonders for our perspective.

We went on an African wildlife safari. We saw the Eiffel Tower and the Taj Mahal and the Forbidden City and the Great Wall. Most of the time we remembered to let our jaws drop only so far.

In Beijing, the people would be up at dawn and gathered outside, going through their tai chi movements and practicing ballroom dancing. It was eerie but mesmerizing—the sun trying to clear away the mist and all these figures, in utter silence, performing these graceful, flowing exercises. They were like living shadows.

Here was all this serenity and calm, all of this comforting yin, and into the midst of it here I come, Mr. Yang out for his morning run. They reminded me of swans gliding peacefully along in a lily pond, and I expect I reminded them of the Tazmanian Devil trying to break in a new pair of sneakers.

In New Zealand it was a different story. We were riding in a bus one day, and as we were crossing over a bridge the driver happened to mention that it was from this very span that bungee jumping originated ten years earlier.

"Anybody want to give it a go?" he asked, casually. You could tell from the tone of his voice that he didn't really expect any takers. The asylums hadn't been emptied recently.

Except some idiot shouted out: "Yo, I'll do it."

I recognized the idiot's voice—it was mine.

Diane just rolled her eyes. She knew it was coming as soon as the question was asked. She knew I had felt that familiar, irresistible tingle. Mr. Yang needed to be fed again.

What possessed me to want to try it? The old mountain-climbing answer: Because it's there.

There wasn't any fear, I do remember that, just a surge of adrenaline and anticipation. It was 150 feet down. There was a retrieval boat floating in the river below.

They trussed me up in the ankle riggings and one of them asked me: "You wanna touch the water?"

"Sure."

I doffed my 76ers cap, spread eagled into a swan dive, and did my best impersonation of a majestically soaring eagle.

And fell like a rock.

Either the guy who asked me if I wanted to touch the water should have been a bit more specific, or I should have asked him some more questions. Because I assumed I'd just tickle the surface of the water with my fingertips. Instead, I plunged in up to my chest. It was like being baptized by a waterfall.

And then about the time you think you're just going to keep on unspooling, you finally snap back up like a human slingshot.

What a rush! An all-timer.

Makes you want to stand up and beat your chest and scream: "I'm alive! I feel great!"

And yes, I'm sure a lot of people were thinking: *Yep, he sure is alive— as sure as he should be committed.*

CNN Sports showed a videotape of the jump and made it their Play of the Day.

Unfortunately, it seemed like that might be the only NBA-related jumping that we would see on television for a long time. The lockout that everyone had dreaded came to pass . . . .

❧ ❧ ❧

October came and no training camp. November came and no season opener. December passed and the All-Star Game weekend was canceled. That really stung because Philadelphia was going to be the host, for the first time since 1976, and we had campaigned hard to land it— remember that arrogant jerk I had to deal with? (We have been promised, however, that we will get it back in 2002.)

For a time, it looked as though the entire 1998–99 season would be scrubbed. The timing couldn't have been worse for us. We were just beginning to win back the city. The Sixers had endured another losing season in 1997–98, but everyone agreed we were right on the verge of a turnaround.

Certainly the people believed. We set an attendance record that season, which reinforced my theory that if you provide the people with nonstop entertainment, you can draw huge crowds even if the team isn't winning.

Well, for a while, at least.

Thankfully, a reasonable semblance of a season was salvaged. Fifty games. But they would have to be squeezed into ninety days, which meant virtually a game every other day. Tough for teams with old legs.

Ah, but we had young legs.

Sure enough, deliverance arrived at last. The Sixers achieved a winning season for the first time since 1990–91. Allen Iverson led the entire league in scoring and got some MVP votes. He was absolutely electric all season.

We also broke the attendance record that we had set the previous season. And, best of all, we were going to be in the playoffs.

The last regular season home game was Fan Appreciation Night. I wanted to observe it with something a little different, something to get the people worked up for the playoffs.

How about bungee jumping from the ceiling?

Well, a modified form of jumping. Not an all-out bungee job. I'd rappel down from the rafters, along with Hip-Hop, our acrobatic rabbit mascot, and set down on one of the free throw lines.

I tried out the idea on some people, and one of the first reactions was "Yeah, that'll be a great stunt, Pat. They got a big enough spatula to scrape you off the floor?"

I rehearsed it with a safety rescue expert. I checked the harness over and over. There were safety lines. The risk was minimal. It was a "Go."

I came down during a time-out in the first half. I was dressed in all black as I made my first move into the descent. The crowd had no idea that this was even happening, but they caught on quickly and in seconds their cheers were like an eruption. The last fifty feet or so I was upside down, descending head-first. I looked like a deranged bat.

The crowd loved it. Several people said later that they couldn't remember any owners of other sports teams ever doing such a thing. Which made me either a pioneer, or certifiable.

I ran over to Ann Iverson, Allen's mother, who is a naturally exuberant person and usually game for just about anything. I hugged her, we did a little dance step, and then we started throwing Sixers playoff T-shirts into the crowd.

Our opponent that last regular season night was the Detroit Pistons. We beat them . . . in overtime. Everyone went out into the early spring night whooping and hollering. We were pumped for the playoffs. The first game would be in Florida, against the Orlando Magic.

It was a moment we had been awaiting one day short of forever.

And I couldn't go.

❦ ❦ ❦

More than a year earlier I had made a commitment to Dr. Madeleine Adler—who is a dynamite lady and the president of West Chester

University—to be the speaker at graduation ceremonies. First of all, a promise is a promise and that's the end of that—breaking promises is the activity of traitors. And second, how often do you get banished from campus and then asked to be the commencement speaker? Not many exiles get honorary doctorate degrees. I was not only flattered, I was humbled.

And I was also dying because I couldn't be at the game.

Graduation and the start of the NBA playoffs fell on a Sunday in May. Mothers Day, to boot. By late morning, the sun was high and hot. The ceremonies were held on the football field. The gown fit just fine. The cap slid over my head like it had been buttered. Of course, there was not even a single strand of hair to impede its progress . . . .

Because a couple days earlier I had been shaved bald.

 PAT CROCE POINTER
A promise is a promise and that's the end of that—breaking promises is the activity of traitors.

It all started when I lost a bet about the Sixers making the playoffs. In fact, I hadn't made the bet; Billy King had generously made it for me. Billy was already hairless and had nothing to bet with, so he made a wager with WIP Sports Radio's popular morning show host, Angelo Cataldi, offering *my* hair as the booty. Everyone knew I was positive we'd be in the playoffs, and Billy said he was so sure I was right that he'd volunteer my head to prove it. If the Sixers made it, I would accompany Angelo to the barber's chair, where we'd both be shaved down to our skulls. The Sixers made it. And I told Billy he sure was brave with other people's hair.

So there I was on Mother's Day, in cap and gown, slick as a cue ball underneath, marching in to "Pomp and Circumstance." The crowd was large and expectant. I had made a vow to myself to *keep it simple, stupid.* I would just stand up, fire up, shut up, sit down. Preferably in that order.

The kindest, most thoughtful thing that a commencement speaker can do is stay out of the way. Graduation Day belongs to the graduates and their families. They are the ones who worked and sacrificed to arrive at this moment. And the insensitive, self-indulgent, in-love-with-the-sound-of-his-own-voice speaker who drones on and on while his captive audience melts in the heat is still remembered twenty years later . . . and not fondly.

I resolved to get in and out within ten minutes. Make it upbeat and then get to a TV set in time for our tip-off.

So this is how I started:

"Yo, West Chester! See, dreams really do come true—you're graduating from college and the Sixers are in the playoffs! Yeah!"

That established a properly festive mood and it seemed to strike a responsive chord. They whooped lustily . . . for themselves and for the Sixers.

"Now we're in a similar situation," I said. "Both you and my team have to take our game to the next level. Can we succeed? Yes! Will it be easy? No! But the power to achieve resides in your magical ability to believe. And each one of you possesses that magical power."

I told them of my fascination with magic, how I had devoted so much time and energy in trying to master sleight-of-hand and conjuring. One of my heroes is Harry Houdini, the great escapist. He was a genius at extricating himself from trouble, and since I always seemed to have a knack for getting myself into predicaments, that was probably part of his appeal to me.

I told them what an adroit locksmith Houdini was, and how he had issued a standing challenge in which he claimed there was not a jail from which he couldn't escape . . . and within sixty minutes. Jailers around the world tried all manner of containment—chains, ropes, strait jackets, handcuffs, jail cells built of the most indestructible steel—but nothing could keep him confined.

Hold Houdini? Ha! They might as well have tried to eat soup with a fork. Houdini always got away. Always.

And then came an acceptance of his challenge. A tiny European town which had just built a new jail claimed that their facility was absolutely, positively, guaranteed escape-proof. No mortal—and not even the immortal Houdini himself—had the remotest chance.

That, of course, was irresistible to Houdini. Usually, the quickest way to get to a genius is through his ego.

At the jail, Houdini was stripped of all clothes. He was led into a cell and then the locksmith closed the imposing steel door behind him and lingered secretively over the lock. Then everyone left. No spectators were ever allowed. A magician, after all, never reveals his secrets.

Alone, Houdini produced a tiny metal pick, with which he had always been able to trip even the most devious lock. Do you want to guess where he concealed this pick? You have a one-in-seven chance of being right, for there are seven openings in the human body.

Houdini took his trusty, infallible pick and set to work on the lock. After half an hour, he was stymied. After forty-five minutes, he still hadn't picked the lock, now the sweat was pouring off him. An hour went by. Then another.

Houdini was spent. His head throbbed. He had brought forth the full and mighty force of all his powers and concentration, had tried every manipulation he knew, and that damnable lock remained unsolvable. It seemed to mock him. But he wouldn't concede. He couldn't. He was The Great Houdini. He had a reputation to preserve.

So he stood up and leaned against the door to steady himself, to rest a bit before resuming the battle, and . . .

And to his astonishment, the door opened.

The jailer had never locked it! He had done so deliberately. He knew that Houdini would assume the door was locked, because that's human nature.

The door was locked only in Houdini's mind.

And then I asked the graduates: "Where will your resistance come from? Will it be a locked door or a locked mind that you allow to prevent you from achieving your goals and your dreams?

  PAT CROCE POINTER
The only place where what you want is impossible resides on top of your neck. So, unlock your mind. You have the keys. You have the magical power.

"Some of you may be fretting that your dreams are just that and nothing more—only dreams and fantasies. Maybe you are worrying that the obstacles in the real world will be too high to go over, too wide to go around, and too deep to tunnel under. Maybe you question whether your goals are really achievable at all. Well, there are three answers to all your misgivings and your doubts:

"No!

"No!

"And, NO!

"The only place where what you want is impossible resides on top of your neck.

"So, unlock your mind. You have the keys. You have the magical power. You have already demonstrated that, by coming to this moment, to graduation.

"Your parents and your teachers, and your life experiences, they all form a set of magical keys that will help you open any door . . . assuming that it really is locked. These are the things you want to carry on your own personal key chain: A positive attitude. Passion. Persistence and perseverance. Drive and discipline. An encouraging word. The power of your smile. Your capacity for love. Patience. (And, boy, do I know how hard that one is.)

"And one thing more: Party!"

This was met with an approving roar. (Hey, I knew my audience.) And I left them with these parting words:

"Celebrate. Do it *now*. Find reasons to cheer success. And look for the good in every day. Embrace each new day. Don't shrink from it, don't approach it with dread. You'll find that when you get excited about your day, then your day becomes exciting. And fun. And when a thing is fun, then it tends to get done."

Then I congratulated them the best way I knew: With a primal shout.

And then I sat down and shut up. The ovation was loud and sustained.

Now if only the Sixers could do something worth applauding . . .

❧ ❧ ❧

They could and they did.

The Sixers won one of two in Orlando and then returned home to find the city had gone bonkers over them. Philadelphia was desperate for a winner, and now even non-sportsfans were getting caught up in the positive spirit. Their civic pride perked up. They had something to feel good about. People live vicariously through sports teams, and if their team is a winner then they tend to feel like a winner themselves.

We made the home playoff games feel like block parties. We created a real carnival atmosphere. People came who didn't have tickets, just to be around the excitement. The Croce Crewcut became a popular item.

Suddenly, bald was in. They lined up outside the arena to get their skulls shaved. I lost count of the number of heads I personally sheared down to the skin.

Spring was bustin' out all over. The sun was up, everything had turned green and promising, and the Sixers were in full blossom. The city was abuzz. Inside the First Union Center, we lit up things with indoor fireworks and laser lights and waves of sound. It was Mardi Gras under a roof.

And then the home games began. We beat Orlando twice in our place to advance to the second round of the playoffs—a definite upset, but the national media began to give us genuine respect.

As the clock blinked toward all zeros in that series-clinching victory, Michael and I began to celebrate like we always do, which is to joyfully beat on each other like bongo drums. My son plays basketball, loves the sport, and usually sits next to me during Sixers games. Anyone seated near us knows to wear flak jackets and helmets. We do not conceal our exuberance. We hug, we chest bump, belly bump, high five, low five, dance in victory, agonize in defeat, and always—always—have a good time. At a very early age, I introduced Michael to my good friend Mr. Yang.

Moments after that series-clinching victory, I walked out onto a balcony just above the concourse and just stood there watching the people leaving, savoring that sea of smiles, inhaling the sweet smell of success. A couple of fans looked up and spotted me and they yelled out to me and started pumping their fists.

I pumped right back.

Pretty soon the whole joint was involved and, of course, I got caught up in all of it. I climbed up on the railing, leaned over it, and started yelling back at them. We were egging each other on, screaming at each other, gibberish mostly, but then actual words weren't important. We were all united by the same emotion.

I stood up there and I felt like I was in that scene at the end of the James Cagney movie, *Top of the World, Ma!*

Bator and my man Big Fran the security guard had death grips on my belt. Otherwise, I would have done a half gainer down into the crowd. And this time there was no rope to save me.

Down in the Sixers locker room I met up with Eric Snow, our point guard. He had played his guts out. He had scored, passed out assists, stole the ball . . . he'd played his best when it mattered the most. I hugged him and told him: "Snowman, I'm so proud of you."

And I'll never forget him standing there, a towel around him, still wet from the shower, saying: "Pat, all I needed was a chance."

For two years and part of a third, he sat on the bench in Seattle, a back-up pining for more playing time, convinced that he could produce if only he could get the opportunity. And then we acquired him and he became a starter, got his chance, and made good on it. I thought right then what a great example he was—about believing in yourself, never losing faith in your ability, and staying prepared so that when your time came you could make the most of it. His story is a wonderful lesson for all of us, in any occupation.

In the second round of the playoffs, we met up with the Indiana Pacers, a solid, veteran team that was experienced in the rigors of the post-season. Our effort wasn't lacking, but our seasoning was. We were eliminated in four straight, but there was no dishonor at all in losing to a crafty, balanced team. There were no blowouts in any of the games, and there were no excuses. Sometimes you play your best and the other guy is simply better.

So you regroup. But you don't retreat.

All in all, it had been a star-spangled season, and everyone was already anticipating the one to come. There was reason, at last, to look ahead.

In the meantime, there was a summer to enjoy, and it would start with our cross-continent motorcycle excursion. We dipped our hands into the Atlantic and climbed on our bikes and set out.

And the next thing I knew I was lying on my back on a wet road, trussed up like a mummy, being quizzed by paramedics . . . .

❧ ❧ ❧

They wanted to get me to the nearest hospital, but Dr. Jack and I agreed that the place to go for treatment of such trauma was at the Hospital of the University of Pennsylvania, back in Philadelphia, about fifteen miles away. Dr. Jack said the best in the business was Dr. William DeLong, an orthopedic surgeon in charge of trauma surgery at HUP. Somehow Bator was able to get him on a cell phone.

While they were talking, a New Jersey state trooper was interviewing people for details of the accident, and in one of those unthinking moments we all have, he looked down and asked me: "Pat, how do you feel?"

Obviously it was a reflex question, asked in a moment of brain cramp. He could see me lying there in my own blood and in the rain, my leg looking like someone had stuck a hand grenade in it and pulled the pin, and yet he wanted to know how I felt.

I couldn't resist:

I clenched my fists and slowly stuck both arms over my head and croaked my signature line: "I feel great!"

He looked like he had just bitten into an apple and found half a worm. Then he smiled and said, "You're nuts!"

An ambulance finally arrived and I was hoisted onto a spine board and loaded in. As a kid, did you ever fantasize about what it would be like to be in an ambulance rushing to the hospital? I know I did. And I imagined that it would be quite a thrill, whooshing along with the sirens blaring and the red lights flashing, weaving wildly in and out of traffic.

Well, there was nothing at all romantic or heroic about my ride in this meat wagon. It was so bumpy that I was sure we were going back and forth over railroad tracks, with occasional detours down the most pot-hole-littered streets they could find. And where was all that speed I remembered fantasizing about? This rig was s-l-o-w . . . a turtle on Valium would have left us in the dust.

At one point I yelled: "Yo! Let me off at the corner. I'll get out and hop the rest of the way."

Dr. Jack loved that.

We finally pulled up to the hospital and I thought: *All right, some relief from this pain.* I hadn't gotten anything in the ambulance, and by then all the adrenaline had long since worn off. I was in agony. All my nerve endings had been sandpapered to the nub.

But, no. First they took x-rays. Then they poked around, looking for any other damage.

Maybe just a couple of aspirin? Please? Pretty, pretty please?

Sorry.

To try to take my mind off the pain I struck up a conversation with the emergency trauma doctor who was examining me. I mentioned to him how I looked forward every summer to running on the boardwalk in Ocean City.

"Not this year, Pat," he said. He was polite and he was sympathetic. But what he was saying sounded ominous.

I mentioned that I was scheduled to take my fourth-degree black belt karate test in December. Once again, he was sympathetic. And once again he had the same grim reply: "Not this year, Pat."

They scheduled me for emergency surgery. By then, I had been pumped full of joy juice. Sweet relief from that pain, at last. In the operating room, I chattered happily away with everyone. The Charge Nurse, Susan, apologized to me.

"For what?" I asked.

"I'm afraid I'm a Dallas Cowboys fan," she said.

I smiled and told her: "You're forgiven, just as long as the 76ers are your favorite basketball team."

What she asked next had all the doctors laughing: "When are you going to bring Randall Cunningham back?"

"Just as soon as he develops a 3-point shot," I said.

And then they sent me bye-bye.

It was a deep and totally dreamless sleep, and as soon as I came back to the land of the living I asked: "Did I get a rod? Please tell me I got a rod."

I wasn't asking for the Jakester's gun. The rod I wanted was made of titanium—the stuff they use to make golf clubs and astronaut equipment—and was about a foot and a half long. And if I was lucky, it would be hammered through my tibia, and there would be screw attachments at my knee and ankle joint. The whole contraption would look like a multi-skewered medical shish kebab, but it was much preferred over the alternative procedure, which would require all the rods and pins and screws to be on the outside of my leg, then drilled into the bones.

It would look like I had an erector set attached to my limb. And for at least three months it would be impossible to shower, wear long pants, or move the leg even a centimeter without plotting out everything ahead of time.

Fortunately, when the surgeons cut everything open and assessed the damage, they decided that they could go the rod route. I was still in a morphine haze when I heard that, but in my mind at least I danced a one-legged jig of joy.

The original plan, once the rod was inserted, was that I would spend the weekend in the hospital recovering, and then go home. But that weekend would turn into two weeks. And in those two weeks I would have to undergo two more full-anesthesia surgeries.

And even with all that, I was fortunate. If this had happened to me just a few years earlier . . . well, I asked Dr. DeLong what would have been the options.

He didn't hesitate. There wouldn't have been any options. His words hung in the air like icicles:

"Automatic amputation."

Even with all of Dr. DeLong's extraordinary embroidery skills, there was still a very real possibility that I could end up losing the leg. There was a gaping hole in the lower front part of my shin that needed to be filled in—a kind of medical spackling.

Dr. DeLong recruited a renowned plastic surgeon, Dr. David Low, who planned to transplant a hunk of muscle from just below and behind my left shoulder. But if that transplant didn't take, the bones would become infected . . . and if that happened, the physicians would have no other alternative than to cut off the leg. All of this, for better or for worse, was made perfectly clear to me.

The day before, I had been out running, doing my six miles. Now there was this horrible image of me hobbling along on one leg.

So while I pondered that terrifying prospect, another less important but no less immediate problem arose . . . .

I had to pee.

I mean, I *wanted* to. And the nurses and the resident physician wanted me to.

But I couldn't.

If you don't go, they warned me, *we'll have to do it for you.* What this meant, in effect, was that they would drain me by way of a catheter. Guess where that gets inserted. Guess where it ends up. Just picturing that made me want to curl into the fetal position . . . if my leg would have permitted it.

At 5:30 in the morning, a very nice night nurse named Julie woke me to say I had one hour to "go." For the next fifty minutes I tried to fight off the sleep that the morphine was inducing. I concentrated and I strained. I tried to visualize waterfalls and rain storms and open faucets. I pretended I'd just inhaled three beers, washed down with three cold glasses of water. Anything to entice my bladder.

But nothing. Couldn't go. And now I was really on the clock. I struggled up into a sitting position and leaned forward as far as I could and pushed my right fist into my bladder. If my hand was going to have to come out the other side, I was going to go. I prayed. I pushed and pressed and drove my arm down—up to about my elbow—trying to squeeze something out of that Saharan bladder.

Just as the clock ran out, there was a drop. Then another. Like the promise of morning dew.

There wasn't a lot, but it was enough to earn me a reprieve from that artificial plumbing. In truth, Julie probably gave me a free pass out of sympathy.

I fell back onto the pillows and it struck me—the irony, how life works. Only a couple of weeks before, I had been wishing and praying for the 76ers to win that final playoff game against Orlando . . . and now here I was praying to do nothing more than pee. It's sad but true, that all the things we take for granted in our lives, we never appreciate until they're suddenly gone. Then, ironically, we finally understand their value.

When I awoke, there was Fast Eddie smiling down at me.

"Guess this means I'm not in heaven," I said, managing a weak grin.

"Everyone knows where you are," he said. "It's been on TV and radio and it's in the papers."

Dr. DeLong had held a press conference the night before. So as word spread, visitors began arriving. There is supposed to be a limit on the number of people who can see you. Preferably, fewer than ten. Diane prepared a list. The receptionist looked at it and asked: "Where's the other half of the phone book?"

  PAT CROCE POINTER
It's sad but true, that all the things we take for granted in our lives, we never appreciate until they're suddenly gone. Then, ironically, we finally understand their value.

My friends from the street corner are nothing if not inventive. They all found ways to get in. At one count, I had fifty-seven brothers.

I was wishing each of them had brought a fire extinguisher because my left knee felt like it was in flames. Dr. DeLong explained that part of the surgical procedure had involved stapling across the top of the knee, where the rod was inserted.

"How many staples, Doc?"

"As I recall, twenty-two."

He said if the injury had been only one centimeter lower, he wouldn't have been able to insert the rod. So in many respects I was very lucky to have the staples. And I needed my luck to hold because he said I was looking at one more surgery at least, probably two, before I would leave the hospital. There would be arterial grafting, skin grafting, and the transplant of muscle tissue.

Basically, my leg looked like a jigsaw puzzle that had been turned over and all the pieces scattered on the floor. Dr. DeLong, assisted by Dr. Low, would put the puzzle back together. But they would have to use parts from other puzzles to do so.

So on the third day, it was back under the anesthesia—that deep, sweet sleep—and when I came out of this one I couldn't move. I panicked. *My God, I've been paralyzed!* I couldn't distinguish between reality and my motorcycle nightmare. I tried to speak but no sound came out.

They gave me a shot to calm me. I realized I couldn't move my head because the nurse was holding it, trying to keep me from thrashing around.

"Am I paralyzed?" I asked her, fearing what the answer would be.

"No, no," she said. "You were under restraint so you wouldn't damage your leg. You're going to be fine."

It was one more valuable piece of perspective. For all that had gone so terribly wrong, more had gone good—I had kept my leg and I hadn't become paralyzed. I had a lot to be thankful for, including medical procedures and surgical skills that hadn't even existed a few years earlier. Timing really is everything.

The third surgical procedure took four hours, but I was ready. My spirits soared. I knew a positive attitude would help the healing process. For as grim as my condition was, it could have been much, much worse. All things are relative.

I was in the hospital for ten more days after that final operation. The room looked like a greenhouse. Flowers and plants arrived on the hour. There were clusters of balloons and deli trays, fruit baskets, candy, and thousands of cards and letters. It was, quite literally, overwhelming. Each night my mother, Aunt Corinne, and Diane would take turns reading from that day's mail. People sent poems, get-well cards, and letters. Many of them wrote about how they had dealt with adversity.

Once again, it was great stimulation for my perspective. One night I lay there complaining about the pain in my ankle, where the screws had been inserted into the bone, and I opened this letter:

Dear Pat:
Sorry to hear about your accident. You never know what God has in store, but if you're involved we all know that it's positive. I know about tragic accidents—mine left me a quadriplegic. God bless you and your family. I know you'll be fine. My prayers are with you.
—Toby.

First I felt shame.
Then guilt.
There I was, whining about feeling the pain in my ankle, and there were people out there who had no feeling at all. One more time, some perspective. One more time, a reminder of how lucky I really was. One more time, inspiration and strength from someone else's brave example.

The next evening my room resembled an airport during Thanksgiving week. Tons of friends. Fortunately for me, one of the visitors was Dr. Brad Fenton. He is the 76ers team internist and my personal doctor. He observed that my left arm seemed to be swollen. In fact, it was beginning to look more like a thigh than an arm. We called the attending nurse.

My veins had collapsed. And with nowhere to go, the fluids that were seeping into me through the IV drip were being absorbed by the tissues in my arm. So they removed all the wrappings and dressings, and the arm was revealed in all its hideousness, plump as grilled bratwurst and about ready to burst.

The solution turned out to be laughingly simple: Pat, raise your arm over your head and keep it there . . . for the next couple of days.

I did as instructed, and then I watched, fascinated, as the liquid started to pour out of these tiny puncture holes that ran up and down my arm like some freakish maze. I could have hired myself out as a lawn sprinkler.

The next day, for the first time in my life, I succumbed to depression. I woke up and there it was . . . .

Dr. DeLong had warned me that post-traumatic depression was commonplace in such situations. Many people, he said, go into a funk that lasts for months. The emotional and psychological damage can be every bit as devastating as the physical.

I had listened to him, respectfully, but to myself I was thinking: *Not me. Not Mr. Positive Attitude. Not the Count of Carpe Diem. No sir. I would will myself to avoid that.*

Wrong. As I laid there I took stock of my body—my pride and joy— and I could feel this sense of bleakness falling over me like a shroud. In my soul, it felt like the dead of winter.

I had dedicated my life to keeping my body honed. And now it seemed to be betraying me. My left leg was all but gone. My left shoulder was useless. My left arm had turned into a sieve. My right arm now had to serve as the pin cushion for all the needles and IVs, which in turn meant that I had no way to reposition my body and so relieve the stiffness and the numbness in my bed-sore backside.

 PAT CROCE POINTER
 The most powerful force in the human body is the imagination, and it is very much a two-edged sword. It permits us to dream glorious and soaring possibilities. And it can lead us down the path of despair.

To top it off, they were having a difficult time finding a workable vein in my right arm. I felt like I was hosting an international darts tournament (or had just lost a mean game of "darts chicken"). When they finally did get all the lines hooked up, I looked like I had been wired for cable.

And it was then that I permitted something to creep into my mind that I had always resisted: self-pity.

Lying there virtually unable to move, I was sure that I could feel the strength ebbing from my body. I knew my aerobic conditioning had deteriorated. If you're in bed for a day or two, when you get up you're wobbly as a new-born colt, and even taking one flight of stairs leaves you winded. And I was looking at a couple of weeks, not a couple of days.

I began to shotgun myself with grim questions.

What if the graft doesn't take? What if I lose the leg? What if I can never run again? If you allow it to, your mind can begin to race madly toward all sorts of conclusions and can undermine all your best intentions. The most powerful force in the human body is the imagination, and it is very much a two-edged sword. It permits us to dream glorious and soaring possibilities. And it can lead us down the path of despair.

Melancholy is an insidious thing. It can suck the life right out of you. Before, there wasn't anything I couldn't achieve. I really believed that. Now I felt powerless. I couldn't believe I was allowing myself to wallow in all of this negativity, and, worse, that I wasn't doing anything about it. I had reached what was possibly the lowest point of my life.

But then, like a serendipitous shot of adrenaline, relief arrived that very evening. Dr. Low stopped by to examine the graft site. He listened to the flow of the blood and probed at the area like a landscaper inspecting a newly seeded patch of lawn. And then he spoke three of the sweetest words my ears had ever inhaled:

"It looks great!"

I swear at that moment I heard Beethoven's "Ode to Joy" and "America the Beautiful" and the roar of a thousand motorcycles being kick-started to life, all at the same time.

Mr. Yang measured all that negativity that had enveloped me and then drew back and kicked it squarely in the nuts.

I took a vow then and there—made a private pledge to myself—that I would never again let my positivism and my optimism be subverted. I was going to make a full recovery. No, check that. I wouldn't just recover, I'd come back fitter and finer than before.

The first step was to get my sorry butt out of that bed. A week later, permission was granted.

That first step wasn't so much an actual step as it was a hop and a lunge and a wheeze. But I got to a chair and I was able to sit upright, and that did wonders for my attitude. They can't hit a moving target, right?

The next feeling that overtook me was an old, familiar friend—restlessness. It was a feeling that I embraced. It meant that I wanted to get moving again. Yang wanted to be walked.

First, I got up and stood on one leg, leaning on a walker. Pretty soon I was into locomotion, hopping a lap at a time around the hospital floor with T-Bone and Meat as my unlikely escorts. They were more interested in the nurses than my stability. It was slow going and I'd collapse into the chair afterwards. But, damn, it felt good to hear blood surging in my ears again, to feel my heart thump-thump-thumping, an engine anxious to get back in top racing form. The exercise would also help revive my appetite—no matter how anxious the engine was to get revved again, it needed fuel.

It was time to concentrate on those parts of my body that hadn't been injured. If not used, they would succumb to atrophy. I asked for ankle weights and dumbbells from HUP's physical therapy department. And Cochise, who by now was the physical conditioning coach for the Philadelphia Flyers, brought in elastic power bands and arranged them around my bed so I could work out whenever I had the urge.

And then Jakester, the king of the midnight requisition, triumphantly showed up with a getaway car. Actually, it was a wheelchair that he had managed to "borrow." It meant I could get out and see something of the outside world, shed that feeling of confinement and imprisonment. I am social by nature and hate being cooped up. Just being able to explore a little would do wonders for my attitude.

Bator devised a protective rigging for my bad leg, and we were ready to go. Bator did the driving; Jakester was the scout. We wheeled into the hospital's cafeteria. There were shouts of recognition, get-well wishes, and a whole bunch of requests for Sixers tickets. I scarfed down food. Thanks to the nourishment and the company of the liberating excursion, I almost felt normal. But fatigue soon overtook me, and my left leg began to throb painfully.

On the way back, we got lost. Jakester and Bator were not exactly Lewis and Clark.

They were having so much fun verbally busting on each other and celebrating my progress that they took a wrong turn. And a couple more after that. We tried three different elevators—zipping up and down like a trio of yo-yos—before we ended up at the right one. And when we finally got off on the correct floor, two nurses were waiting. Uh-oh. Busted. I had a flashback to grade school—were those nurses or nuns?

Ah, but we had prepared a bribe for just such an eventuality. Lunches for them. Jakester kept the chair moving and I handed them the food on the way past. Kind of like a drive-through in reverse. We got away clean, and even received some smiles as a tip.

So by now I was having no problem ingesting or digesting. But, uh, *evacuation* was another matter altogether. Between the morphine and being virtually immobilized for so long, my intestinal tract had cemented shut. It was like I had swallowed Crazy Glue.

Dutifully, I drank an ocean of water and ate an orchard of fruit and choked down the prescribed stool softener and every other foul-tasting inducement they offered.

But ten days had passed and I hadn't gone.

I would hobble to the bathroom and spend long, painful minutes trying to get balanced on my right leg while taking precautions to safely position my left leg. It was a hassle, but it was either put up with that or face the ultimate hassle—a bed pan. When success was achieved at last, it felt like I had passed a basketful of razor blades, barbed wire, and broken mirrors.

While waiting for that moment, I had an unsettling vision. And through the bathroom door I yelled to Diane, pleadingly: "If I die in here, please, please, pull me on the floor over to the bed. I don't want to go like Elvis did!"

Strange how the mind works.

  PAT CROCE POINTER
I was four to five months ahead of what they normally see in such trauma. There's no doubt that *wanting* to get better and *believing* and *expecting* I would get better was responsible for much of that progress.

As the tissue graft in my shin began to take, the impatient Mr. Yang urged me to help the healing process along. A large scab had formed and I began picking at the edges, reasoning that the more fresh air that could get in there the better.

Dr. DeLong would come in at about 7 o'clock each morning to check on me, and we would have a conversation that went something like this:

Dr. DeLong, accusingly: "You've been picking at that scab again, haven't you?"

Me, sheepishly: "Only a little. Just trying to help it heal faster."

Dr. DeLong, sternly, like a kindergarten teacher warning a 6 year old that if you touch fire you will get burned: "Pat, don't pick at that. A scab is nature's Band-Aid."

Me, in exasperation: "Well, you know what, Doc? Nature's awful slow!"

He'd smile. He is a gentle man. And a gentleman. Very soft-spoken, very deliberate. Intensely dedicated. And the absolute tops in his field.

He couldn't get mad at a patient who was so desperate to heal.

We talked about the importance of a patient's attitude, about what effect a positive approach could have on the healing process. We're both convinced that it is vital. Later, he estimated that six weeks into my rehab I was four to five months ahead of what they normally see in such trauma. There's no doubt that *wanting* to get better and *believing* and *expecting* I would get better was responsible for much of that progress.

Two weeks after the first surgery, I got sprung from the hospital. No, not in a midnight escape with Bator and Jakester and a stolen ambulance. My release was fully sanctioned by the doctors, and was highly anticipated by many others . . . .

I went through a gauntlet of high-fives. The TV cameras were waiting. I thanked the staff and the nurses—angels of mercy in every way— and tried to emphasize how lucky I was, humbly noting that on the floor where I had stayed were transplant patients who needed prayers and smiles far more than I did.

And then Diane and I went to our Ocean City home, where the aborted Ocean-to-Ocean trip had begun.

We'd had such glorious plans. We were going to bike to San Diego and touch the Pacific. Along the way we were going to stop at Graceland, the Grand Canyon, the Hoover Dam, and Las Vegas, and end up at Croce's Top Hat Bar and Grille in San Diego where we'd be greeted by proprietor Ingrid Croce, the widow of singer/songwriter Jim Croce (Jim was a distant cousin of mine).

It was a detailed plan, but I distinctly remember that nowhere in it did it say that I'd end up in a hospital, in several pieces. Ah, but as my friend Ron Rubin said when he came to visit me in the hospital: "Pat, we have an old Yiddish saying: 'Man plans and God laughs.'"

Well, I had a new plan now. I would rehabilitate like a madman all summer and into the autumn. And on the day the 76ers opened our 1999–2000 season, I would take my first step, unassisted.

No more forearm crutches. No cane. No leaning on anything or anyone. Yes sir, that was the plan.

Now if only God wasn't preparing a belly laugh . . .

Chapter 17
Parades

❧ ❧ ❧

Oh, but He was.

He was.

The road back wasn't going to be—you'll pardon the expression—a walk in the park. Walk? I couldn't even crawl. But I was determined to win my leg back, and even more importantly that I was going to win back my active lifestyle.

Either that or . . . well, I wouldn't let myself even consider the implications of what the word "or" might have in store.

The first two things I did when I hit Ocean City were to recruit Doug Dannehower ("Dougger") as my personal physical therapist, and instruct Bator to convert my two-car garage into a makeshift gym. Within 24 hours it was done. Besides the few pieces of equipment that were already there, Bator and Marky Mark had moved in free weights, exercise machines, rehab gizmos, floor mats, a treatment table, and a three-wheeled arm-powered racing bike. I asked, "Where did all this other stuff come from?" Marky Mark laughed, and Bator replied, "Don't ask."

It was a first-class training facility, and there I would do my twice-daily rehabilitation and workout sessions. And sweat rivers.

It was the middle of summer and there was no air conditioning. The temperature in the garage swelled to three degrees above Hades. After ten repetitions of any exercise you would look like you'd been hosed down.

And that was just perfect. Sweating is purging and cleansing, and I had toxins to lose in my mind and body. And sweating reminded me of my fitter days, a condition I was determined to reclaim. Sweating is psychologically beneficial. Every drop was proof of progress. Every drop represented one more step forward on the road back.

I needed companion sweaters, of course. People to work out with me, keep me company, and urge me on. Someone to yell at, someone to yell at me, someone to celebrate small successes with, someone to crank out endorphins with, and someone to exult in the glory of fitness with.

Every morning at 6:30, Dougger would conduct a two-hour physical therapy session on my leg and shoulder. He had managed one of my South Jersey SPT centers in our earlier lives. So he knew I prescribed to the philosophy of "no pain, no gain." I often thought of the endless list of former patients and athletes who would have loved to watch Dougger inflict pain on me.

They wouldn't have been disappointed.

After a breakfast break, the next couple of hours inside the Hades Garage were dedicated to the rest of my body. In addition to my regular workout partners—Marky Mark and Stevie Ang, an Ocean City police sergeant—an array of well-intentioned and unsuspecting visitors would drop by from time to time. I think they would come with the single intention of paying their respects, but once they got in, they couldn't get out. Not without sweating.

My brothers, V and Johnny, were regular weekend warriors. Rick Tocchet of the Phoenix Coyotes hockey team (who recently returned to the Flyers) and Mutzi received three-week memberships. What was a vacation without a little pain and suffering? And sweating.

Did I mention the flies?

Green heads. They've got a bite that can cut through a chain link fence. And they have an insatiable appetite for sweat-salted human flesh. And every day, as soon as we'd begin working out, they would come streaming in as though someone had shouted down the beach to them: "Lunchtime!"

The trick was to complete each exercise set while enduring their bites, and then capture the SOBs. It turned into a contest—whoever caught the most green heads by the end of the workout could name an additional exercise for the losers to endure.

One of my best workout partners, who loved to push me as hard as anyone else, was Kelly. My daughter had an intuitive understanding that this place was like a cocoon for me—a retreat and a refuge. Here, she knew I could isolate myself, insulate myself, and intensely concentrate on healing—on willing my leg to get well and my body to get better. Plus, Kelly was willing and able to jest with the best of my buddies.

Bator was the best of best friends. We were like high school buddies again. If I left home, he was my bodyguard and chauffeur. Talk about tempting fate! Every time I rode shotgun with my shattered leg elevated on his dashboard, I thought of our hangin'-at-the-high days and his idea of defensive driving . . . "Ooops!" There goes another fender bender.

Less than two weeks after I got out of the hospital Bator had to drive me to New York. Several NBA players and team owners were meeting to discuss player/management relations. I was honored to have been chosen by David Stern and the deputy commissioner, Russ Granik, to attend the meeting, and I was going to be there, one-legged or not. Luckily, there was a bonus to the trip—I saw Chuck Barris for the first time in a long time.

So I got to introduce two wild and crazy guys to each other, over dinner.

"Still scribbling creative ideas on napkins, Chuck?" I asked.

To answer my question, he held up a fistful of them.

"Still putting religious medals as good luck charms on the backs of watches, Chuck?"

"Oh yeah, and I gotta give you guys these . . . they really work," he replied. And he handed Bator and me one each of what he called "The Little Blue Lady." They were tiny blue Virgin Mary pins that he picked up in Rome. Bator and I laughed out loud at the thought of two Catholic boys receiving blessed medals from my wild-haired, *Jewish* mentor.

The New York trip, short as it was, still wore me down to the bone. It made me realize just how far I had to go in my rehabilitation to reclaim the physical conditioning that I had enjoyed most of my life. At first, that thought depressed me, but I reminded myself: *Turn a negative into a positive.* Use that depression as a motivation.

As part of my aerobic conditioning, Stevie A and Marky Mark, and sometimes Diane, would escort me on bicycles as I'd go for a spin on my three-wheeled "chariot" on the Ocean City Boardwalk. I still had drainage tubes running out of my rib cage and bandages running the length of my leg. People must have thought there was an escapee from the asylum on the loose, but at least I was out and about, getting sun and air, trying to remind my body of all the glorious things we could get back to doing when—not *if*—my leg cooperates.

People would gape and stare, and then when recognition set in, they would shout and wave, and many of them would yell: "Pat, how you feeling?" I would raise my fist in the air and shout back my customary reply: "I feel great!" Their encouragement was a welcome dose of medicine. When you offer encouragement to someone, you may not know it but you are drawing the best out of them—often more than they even know they have to give.

For eight straight weeks in the summer of '99, I would rise each day and rejoice in another sunrise, and then train in the Hades Garage until noon. By then, I would be spent. But I welcomed the exhaustion because I was having trouble sleeping through the night in one position. My leg was stuck in neutral but my mind was racing—and the rest of my body was screaming for more activity as well.

In the afternoons, I might as well have been behind bars because I was confined like a prisoner. My traumatized leg demanded that I lie on the floor and elevate it higher than my heart. Again, I tried to turn a negative into a positive. I used that time to try and respond to all the cards and letters I'd received from well-wishers. I formed what I called the "Broken Bones Club"—I'd write or call all those people who were patients themselves who'd sent me prayers and encouragement. They would be receiving tickets to future Sixers games.

  PAT CROCE POINTER
When you offer encouragement to someone, you may not know it but you are drawing the best out of them—often more than they even know they have to give.

I can't emphasize enough the powerful generosity of spirit that radiated from those people who, despite suffering from trauma—in many cases far more serious than mine—could reach out to someone else. That is rare courage.

And on the subject of courage, I have to cite one special name: Lance Edward Armstrong.

In many ways, he saved my summer.

I'd lie there with my leg propped up and watch him on TV, winning the Tour de France, and I would be inspired and moved to cheers. And at the same time that I was feeling awe, I was also feeling very humble. Here I was riding one-legged for forty minutes at a time on my stationary bike, and this man had overcome cancer and was winning the oldest, longest, hardest cycling race on earth.

He was riding 140 miles in a single day, then doing it again the next day. And the day after that. And the day after that. And so on . . .

A couple years before, when he was only in his mid-20s, Lance Armstrong had been diagnosed with testicular cancer. By the time they got to it, the disease had practically enveloped his body. They took off his right testicle. They took out lethal lesions in his brain. They took out tumors—some the size of golf balls—from his lungs and abdomen.

It would be quicker to tell you what part of him didn't have cancer than what did. And then when they had cut out all that they could find, they said he had maybe a fifty-fifty chance to live. But certainly no chance to ever ride again, much less compete in the Tour de France, much less actually win it.

Here comes the best part: Lance Armstrong listened patiently to the grim odds and the bleak prognosis, nodded politely, and said to himself: *I don't think so.*

He arose from his deathbed and began to pedal. He pedaled his way right into the Tour de France. And once there, he pedaled for more than 2,300 miles.

In three weeks.

He pedaled across two mountain ranges. He pedaled in scalding heat and in shivering cold and in lashing rain. He pedaled around hairpin curves and down steaming straightaways.

He pedaled like a man who has been given that rarest of chances—a second one.

He pedaled against the very best cyclists in all the world, and he not only beat them, but he did it faster than anyone before.

And each afternoon I'd lie there and watch him, and this geyser of pride would surge within me. My God, look at what he's doing!

Every sports banquet banality, every trite locker room saying, had come roaring to life: You should never ever yield, because no cause is too hopeless, too lost.

Each time after he had undergone chemotherapy, which is extremely debilitating, Lance Armstrong would get on his bike and ride—30, 40, 50 miles. It was a glorious display of spit-in-the-wind defiance. Those rides were his way of saying: "There's no way I surrender."

When I heard that Lance had reacted to his chemo in that way, for some reason I was reminded of the great racehorse, Secretariat. No one was quite sure how that magnificent beast could run so fast, so far. He was tireless and his spirit was unbreakable. And then after he died they found that his heart was much larger than average. That seemed to explain it all.

Big Red, meet Lance.

Lance, this here is Secretariat.

You two have a lot in common.

So at a time in my life when I needed any encouragement I could find, along came a man on a bicycle. He made a lie of the odds. And he gave hope.

And most of all, he was a reminder. A reminder of a simple, powerful truth: that all things really are possible.

❧ ❧ ❧

I was in such a frenzy to start working out in the Hades Garage that, motivated by my favorite Jimmy Buffett music, I probably tried to do too much too soon. What else is new?

I put only 70 pounds on the weight rack and started doing lat pull-downs, an exercise that works your shoulder and back muscles, specifically your lats (latismus dorsi). Of course, that's the very same area where Drs. DeLong and Low had removed some lean muscle mass and transplanted it to my leg (leaving me with a neat zipper under my armpit).

I probably shouldn't be bleeding while I'm doing this exercise, I thought to myself in one of those particularly blazing moments of insightful perception.

Saint Diane was not only my nurse, but also my warden. Medical monitoring was minimal, but physical monitoring was another animal all together. She would ask a familiar question whenever she visited the Hades Garage: "Did the doctor say it was okay for you to be doing that?"

And I always had the same answer: "Well, he didn't say I *couldn't.*"

Of course, he didn't say that I couldn't go bungee jumping, either. He assumed that I would know better; he assumed that his patient would be smart enough to figure out for himself that you shouldn't be trying to do lat pulldowns when you don't have a lat. Or at least not a whole lat.

Fortunately, Dr. DeLong has a home in Ocean City. It meant that I had a doctor who made house calls. In truth, I think he made a habit of dropping by every week because he was afraid of what I might do if he wasn't monitoring me, along with Diane.

At the beginning of my rehab, he would prescribe certain exercises and activities for daily living, and follow up with the instructions: "Do them to tolerance."

In other words, when there is the first sign of pain, this is what you do: STOP!

Of course, saying "to tolerance" to me was like telling a teenager who is standing in front of an open refrigerator: " . . . until you're full."

But I kept trying to push the envelope. Dr. DeLong couldn't be very mad at all at my impatience. In that Hades Garage I could focus completely; I could channel all of my intensity and pent-up energy into overcoming mental and physical obstacles. I could force the issue. I could help myself heal. Though I knew the consequences of overexertion, I also understood—and committed to—the benefit of attacking the healing process with therapy.

It worked.

At the end of the summer, Dr. DeLong took a picture of my leg as a rare example of the healing powers of intensive exercise. He said the physical appearance of my leg was similar to that of patients who were into their sixth month of recovery.

Being an incurable optimist, I was certain this had all happened for a reason. I just hadn't been able to puzzle it out yet. Maybe I would understand by the time we began a new Sixers season.

And I took my first step . . . .

❧ ❧ ❧

Opening Night, 1999, was close to a disaster.

The 76ers' home opener was on November 8 against the Seattle Supersonics. This was the date I had set for my triumphant entrance, and the whole city knew it.

I would rip off the hospital ID bracelet that I had worn around my wrist as a reminder, and I would walk again. Crutchless. Painless.

I had locomotion all right. I could propel myself. But it was only with the aid of two forearm crutches. The leg was still stubbornly resisting. It was refusing to grow new bone.

But at least I could be there for Opening Night, and what a blowout we had planned!

Which was exactly what we got: a blowout. The jumbo video scoreboard blew out! We had a sentimental video tribute planned for Sixers' great, Wilt Chamberlain (who had passed away during the off-season), and it went up in smoke. We kicked off the game with indoor fireworks, but they were a bit too, uh, ambitious, and one of the championship banners that hangs from the rafters got singed. The smoke and fog were so heavy and thick, and lingered for so long, that the start of the game had to be delayed.

Yes, I know: Man plans and God laughs.

But there was one salvation: We won the game!

Even with the things that went wrong, the crowd was upbeat and excited. The city itself was on fire with 76ers fever. After our great play-off appearance last season, the expectations now were off the charts.

 PAT CROCE POINTER
Work as if it all depends on you. Pray as if it all depends on God.

Meanwhile, my medical charts revealed that I would need to undergo more surgery. Two weeks after the first game of the season, I had operation number four. It was an outpatient operation—I was scheduled to go in in the morning and go home in the evening . . . but when it was over and I stood up to leave the hospital on my crutches, I noticed that my foot hurt worse than my leg. A lot worse. There turned out to be a very good explanation.

They had broken my foot!

During surgery, which was to remove a couple of the screws and inject bone marrow from my hip, some forceful manipulation was required to get the fragments of my shinbone to align closer together. Some hammering, too. As Dr. Bator might say: "Ooops."

The worst consequence of this accident was that I had to walk on this newly broken bone if the broken leg was ever going to heal properly. This was truly adding insult to injury.

But I thought none of this would matter in the grand scheme of things, especially if the bone marrow transplant worked and stimulated my leg to start manufacturing its own bone.

Leave it to my mom to send me a card with this message inscribed on the inside:

"Work as if it all depends on you. Pray as if it all depends on God."

And then she wrote: "Pat, I guess He didn't want to make it too easy."

Guess not, because six weeks later I was scheduled for a fifth surgery.

I had another doctor's office appointment, on a Monday, so Dr. DeLong could check to see if my leg had finally relented and was manufacturing some new bone. I was so convinced that they would find nothing that I told them to go ahead and get me on the operating room schedule for the next morning.

For the first time since my rehabilitation process began, I had allowed negativity to creep into my gray matter. I was despondent. I guess I had finally reached my limit. "This is like trying to get a dead tree stump to sprout leaves. He won't find anything," I said to myself, glumly.

But he did! Dr. DeLong held up the new X-rays to the light and there it was. Some calcification. Some new bone. I had to take his word for it, because in all honesty, no matter how hard I squinted, I couldn't discover anything connecting the shish kebob of bone fragments.

"It's not much," he cautioned, "but it's there and it's a very positive sign. It looks like the healing process has started. So tomorrow's surgery is postponed . . . for now."

The scream that I made next . . . well, dogs that were ten miles away pricked up their ears and cocked their heads. And the patients who were lying ten feet away probably shit themselves.

I wanted to dance on the ceiling.

A few days later, though, I would feel like the ceiling was falling on me . . . .

❀ ❀ ❀

It is the Sunday before Christmas. The sun is out. I am in my robe, on my crutches, with a song in my heart, gimping down the driveway to get the morning paper, certain that I can feel, really *feel*, my leg healing.

Surely walking without any aid is now only a short step away.

I inhale the bracing air and exhale sheer joy. I feel great! I bend, pick up the paper, turn around to start back up the driveway, and open to the sports section for a preview peek.

And this headline leaps at me like a tiger springing from ambush: "IVERSON WANTS TO BE TRADED"

Now I'm tearing at the paper and pages are scattering everywhere. I'm propped up on my crutches and ripping away sections to get to the sports. And right there on the front page of the sports section is an article that takes the air right out of me. During the game the previous night, Allen Iverson was benched by coach Larry Brown. Allen's attitude in the article strongly implied that maybe we should just go ahead and get rid of him since it was obvious the coach didn't respect him.

And then, as the disheartening article went on, Coach Larry Brown would kick in with the opinion that he had been thinking how maybe it might be best if *he* just stepped aside.

So, in one glorious swoop, our coach and our star are feuding in public, and the season—the season that's supposed to be one more huge stride back—isn't even two months old.

I get back to the house and wake up Diane and say: "We've got to get to church. Now! I need help!"

Later, as we were sitting at the kitchen table, I opened to the employment classifieds section of the paper and said to Diane: "Think there might be something in here for me?"

But that wouldn't work. This was the time to draw on some of my commandments—and there was no commandment about jumping ship. I'd have to listen very carefully to both sides, to understand each view point. But most of all, there could be no delay. Do It Now! This wouldn't resolve itself.

I spent most of the day on the phone with Larry and Allen. I told them we'd have a meeting first thing Monday. I didn't ask them if they wanted to meet, I told them we were going to meet.

There was, after all, no option. The future of the franchise hung in the balance.

The next day I felt like a referee at recess. I mediated and manipulated and negotiated and intimidated and legislated and levitated. It went on for hours.

And all my words kept coming back to two major points. There was so much talent between them. And there was so much temperament and passion between them. They both acknowledged that. At least, it was a start.

After countless words and several heartfelt appeals and entreaties and invocations, we finally reached a resolution—an understanding. And then, that very night, we played one of those games that you look back on and realize was both pivotal and magical. Two days of sheer turmoil vanished in two spectacular moments of epiphany . . . when the 76ers tied the Detroit Pistons on a buzzer-beater in regulation, and then won the game in overtime on yet another buzzer-beater.

There was a Hoover Dam's worth of electricity in the building. And the players were leaping into each other's arms like they'd just won a playoff series. Such a marvelous punctuation to what had been such a tense time.

We took it as an omen of good things to come.

And so it was . . . .

On the night of the third day of the year 2000, I walked into the First Union Center with Diane, Kelly, and Michael.

On my own. No crutches, no cane, no helping hand. I was starting off the new millennium on the right foot. Literally.

A little later than I had planned, yes. Fifty-six days after the season-opener, which had been my original target date. My goal.

But measured against the alternative—losing the leg—the delay was of no real consequence. All that mattered was this: I could stand upright on my own two legs and howl at the moon again!

Did I throw away the crutches too soon? Of course! Mr. Yang took care of them. But what good is an envelope if you can't keep pushing at the edge of it?

 PAT CROCE POINTER
 Every day I work toward the completion of my goals. Little by little. Chip away here, bang away there, with my goals and dreams always in sight.

So there was discomfort at first, but it became a little less constricting each day. And each day I was getting a little stronger, a little steadier, a little surer. Come to think of it, that's not a bad way to get through every day.

Every day I work toward the completion of my goals. Little by little. Chip away here, bang away there, with my goals and dreams always in sight.

That night, January 3, we played the Milwaukee Bucks in a close game, and we won. So it felt like a double victory. I know it felt that way for my family and friends as well.

A couple of hours prior to the start of the game, I sat on the apron of the court laughing with Bator and Jakester. Reliving great memories. Then I made my rounds, escorted by Big Fran.

His name is Fran Czyzewski. Just sneeze and you've pronounced his last name. Big Fran is large and imposing and he's my one-man security force. He follows me all over the arena, watching my back, taking pictures of me with fans who ask, handing me stuff to autograph, and recording notes onto my little to-do list that will help us enhance the fans' game experience.

While I was on crutches, Big Fran would drive me around the arena in a golf cart. Bator volunteered, but I nixed that idea. ("Ooops" . . . . Sorry, Bator.) Armed with a walkie-talkie, some serious brawn, and good old horse sense, Fran would make sure my leg didn't get crushed or that I wouldn't topple down a flight of stairs.

Big Fran, Bator, Jakester, the press, and thousands of Sixers fans may have been even happier than I was when I showed up without crutches. As for me, it was a reminder: There's nothing wrong with leaning on someone—friend or family—but there's no feeling quite like being able to stand on your own.

Literally.

It's also a reminder that I can't achieve my goals without help. We all need help.

I need the help of God to manufacture new bone. And I need the help of a great coach and team to manufacture the wins necessary for a championship parade. But that doesn't stop me from doing my best to make it happen.

❧ ❧ ❧

There's a saying I've carried around for quite a time, and it became especially meaningful when I was going through the ordeal with the shattered leg:

There's a choice you have to make
In everything you do.
And you must always keep in mind,
The choice you make, makes you.

In other words, you have two options to choose from: "I'll let whatever happens, happen." Or: "I will resolve to wring from this day something good, something a little special."

I choose to pursue my passion. And that, in turn, helps ensure that I will realize it.

Me? I haven't had my parade. Yet! But I think we're on the right track. Besides, a parade is only one moment in one day. The memories you make along the way are what endure.

And in the end, that's what matters the most—the journey itself, not the destination. It's the getting there that you will carry with you always. The people, places, and pursuits that define the memories.

So maybe the best thing about a parade is, you can make your own. Every day.